Embo

MARK JOHNSON

Embodied Mind, Meaning, and Reason

HOW OUR BODIES GIVE RISE
TO UNDERSTANDING

The University of Chicago Press   Chicago & London

The University of Chicago Press, Chicago 60637
The University of Chicago Press, Ltd., London
© 2017 by The University of Chicago
Published 2017

26 25 24 23 22 21 20 19 18 17   1 2 3 4 5

ISBN-13: 978-0-226-50011-9 (cloth)
ISBN-13: 978-0-226-50025-6 (paper)
ISBN-13: 978-0-226-50039-3 (e-book)
DOI: 10.7208/chicago/9780226500393.001.0001

Library of Congress Cataloging-in-Publication Data
Names: Johnson, Mark, 1949– author.
Title: Embodied mind, meaning, and reason : how our bodies give rise
to understanding / Mark Johnson.
Description: Chicago : The University of Chicago Press, 2017. | Includes
bibliographical references and index.
Identifiers: LCCN 2017018048 | ISBN 9780226500119 (cloth : alk. paper) |
ISBN 9780226500256 (pbk. : alk. paper) | ISBN 9780226500393 (e-book)
Subjects: LCSH: Mind and body. | Philosophy of mind. | Human body
(Philosophy) | Meaning (Philosophy) | Consciousness. | Cognition.
Classification: LCC BF161 .J64 2017 | DDC 128—dc23
LC record available at https://lccn.loc.gov/2017018048

CONTENTS

Bringing the Body to Mind

This book develops an argument for the central importance of our bodies in everything we experience, mean, think, say, value, and do. It proposes an embodied conception of mind and then shows how meaning and thought are profoundly shaped and constituted by the nature of our bodily perception, action, and feeling. In short, it argues that we will not understand any of the issues that are so dear to philosophy until we have a deep and detailed understanding of how our embodiment gives rise to experience, meaning, and thought.

The view of mind, meaning, thought, and language that I elaborate here was anticipated, in part, in the writings of the American pragmatist philosopher John Dewey, and to a lesser extent in the works of William James and C. S. Peirce. However, I am not just serving up a heaping portion of warmed-over Dewey. Since Dewey's day we have had the privilege of important scientific and philosophical developments that supply crucial details about the processes of meaning and understanding that take us beyond what Dewey could provide. This research from the sciences of mind helps give flesh and blood to some of Dewey's more skeletal remarks about how organism-environment interactions generate meaningful experience. I do, nonetheless, remain a fan of Dewey's insistence on the key role of experience as the starting and ending point of any useful philosophical inquiry. Consequently, I take issue along the way with the orientation known as "linguistic" or "analytic" pragmatism, which grew mostly under the inspiration and influence of Richard Rorty, who saw philosophy as focused on language and what he called "vocabularies," while rejecting any appeal to experience in the sense that Dewey understood that term.

My other important targets of criticism are traditional Anglo-American analytic philosophy of mind and language, along with what George Lakoff and I (1999) have called first-generation (disembodied) cognitive science. However, my focus is not primarily on the criticism of existing views, but rather on constructing a positive account of human meaning-making and understanding that draws on the cognitive science of the embodied mind. As I work up the details of that positive account, it will become clear how the cognitive science research on which I rely calls into question many key tenets of the analytic tradition in philosophy. The account of embodied mind, meaning, thought, and language developed in these essays runs directly counter to some of the fundamental assumptions in analytic philosophy and early cognitive science of the last seventy-five years. It behooves us, therefore, to begin with an explanation of why the body has mostly been ignored in mainstream analytic philosophy and its correlative conception of cognitive science.

The Invasion of the Body-Snatchers: Philosophy without the Body

When I was a graduate student in philosophy back in the mid-1970s, people did not have bodies. Well, perhaps I exaggerate a bit. What I mean is that a good deal of mainstream philosophy, both in Anglo-American and European traditions, acted as if our bodies aren't really that important for the structure of mind, and that our bodies don't play any significant role in anything that mattered to philosophers. What mattered to them, especially in so-called analytic philosophy that dominated the last three-quarters of the twentieth century in the Anglophone philosophical world, was language, concepts, logic, reason, knowledge, and truth. In all the massive literature that was generated on these topics from this analytic perspective, there is hardly any mention of the body, beyond the fact that one needs a body to secure perceptual inputs into our conceptual systems and knowledge structures, plus occasional recognition that we have feelings and emotions.

In this tradition, philosophy was defined by what Richard Rorty, borrowing a term from Gustav Bergmann, called the "linguistic turn." Bergmann described this turn as "the shared belief that the relation between language and philosophy is closer than, as well as essentially different from, that between language and any other discipline" (1967, 64–65).

He went on to emphasize the exclusively linguistic focus of philosophy when he said, "Generally, no philosophical question is ever settled by experimental or, for that matter, experiential evidence. Things are what they are. In some sense philosophy is, therefore, verbal or linguistic" (ibid., 65). In three short sentences, Bergmann has drastically restricted philosophy to linguistic analysis, and he denies any significant role for either experimental scientific research or experiential evidence! Here we have a vision of philosophy as an autonomous armchair discipline, entirely independent from science, and consisting of rational analysis of linguistic structures, terms, speech act conditions, and knowledge claims.

Rorty appropriately titles his highly influential anthology *The Linguistic Turn: Recent Essays in Philosophical Method* (1967), in which he collects many of the defining documents of what came to be known as "analytic" philosophy. In the introduction to that book, Rorty explains that "the purpose of the present volume is to provide materials for reflection on the most recent philosophical revolution, that of linguistic philosophy. I shall mean by 'linguistic philosophy' the view that philosophical problems are problems which may be solved (or dissolved) either by reforming language, or by understanding more about the language we presently use" (1967, 3).

The two methodological orientations that Rorty is describing came to be known as the "ideal language" and "ordinary language" perspectives. Those who lament the messiness, ambiguity, and incompleteness of everyday language argue that we need a clarified, precise "ideal language," if we ever hope to see how words have meanings and how genuine knowledge and truth are possible. Those who, like J. L. Austin (1970), see everyday speech as manifesting the accumulated insights and values of speech communities, argue that philosophical analysis should always start from distinctions embedded in ordinary language, even it if turns out that some of those distinctions are misleading and ought to be abandoned. In Austin's words, "Certainly, then, ordinary language is *not* the last word: in principle it can everywhere be supplemented and improved upon and superseded. Only remember, it *is* the *first* word" (1970, 185).

Consequently, linguistic philosophy went off in two different directions, one in search of a reconstructed ideal language of thought capable of expressing knowledge claims, and the other in search of an expansive mining of the conceptual resources embedded in ordinary language. Both movements, however, thought that linguistic analysis would eventually help us either to solve certain perennial questions about mind, meaning, thought, and knowledge, or else to show them up as pseudo-problems that have needlessly perplexed us and ought to be jettisoned.

Now, the question I want to address concerning linguistic philosophy in either its "ideal language" or "ordinary language" versions is this: What is it about the character of this language-oriented philosophy that led it to almost completely ignore the body? The answer, I shall argue, is that (1) its exclusive focus on language as the object of philosophical analysis turned attention away from anything that was not linguaform, and (2) it operated with a remarkably impoverished, and scientifically unsound, view of language as entirely conceptual and propositional.

This seriously inadequate view of language resulted in large measure from the influence—on both the ideal language and ordinary language schools—of Gottlob Frege's celebrated conception of meaning and thought developed in a number of essays collected by Peter Geach and Max Black as *Translations from the Philosophical Writings of Gottlob Frege* (1966). In his classic 1892 essay, "Uber Sinn und Bedeutung" ("On Sense and Reference"), Frege hoped to validate the universal and objective stature of mathematical, logical, and scientific claims. In order to explain the alleged objectivity possible within these disciplines, Frege distinguished sharply between (1) the sign (the word or expression), (2) its reference (the object or state of affairs referred to), (3) its sense (the objective understanding, or the mode of presentation, of the reference), and (4) any subjective "associated ideas" that might be triggered in an individual's mind by a given sign. The *sense* was supposedly the public, shared meaning or understanding of the referred-to object or state of affairs, whereas the *associated idea* was merely an image or idea called up by a sign in the subjective mind of a particular individual. Frege claimed that it was the objective sense of a thought or proposition, not any associated ideas, that made shared understanding and knowledge possible. He summarized the relations between sign, sense, reference, and associated idea as follows:

> The reference and sense of a sign are to be distinguished from the associated idea. If the reference of a sign is an object perceivable by the senses, my idea of it is an internal image, arising from memories of sense impressions which I have had and acts, both internal and external, which I have performed. . . . The same sense is not always connected, even in the same man, with the same idea. The idea is subjective: one man's idea is not that of another. . . . This constitutes the essential distinction between the

idea and the sign's sense, which may be the common property of many and therefore is not part or a mode of the individual mind. (Frege [1892] 1966, 59)

Notice that, in this famous passage, there is no mention of the body in relation to the sense of a sign. As presumably objective, senses supposedly cannot depend on the peculiarities of particular minds, let alone of particular bodies. They are universal and objective, in sharp contrast to associated "ideas," which depend on the body and experiences of those who have the ideas. Thus, Frege said, "One need have no scruples in speaking simply of *the* sense, whereas in the case of an idea one must, strictly speaking, add to whom it belongs and at what time" ([1892] 1966, 60). For example, the sense of the English word *mother* would allegedly be an abstract meaning or understanding "grasped" (to use Frege's term) by all who understand English. In addition, each of those individuals would have their own associated (and highly subjective) ideas that come to mind when he or she thinks about mothers, but none of this is held to be part of the objective sense of the term. Consequently, Frege claimed that senses are not dependent on the particulars of the bodies and brains that grasp them, so they constitute universal meanings, whereas associated ideas and images lay no claim to universality, precisely because they depend on our embodiment and experiences: "The reference of a proper name is the object itself which we designate by its means; the idea, which we have in that case, is wholly subjective; in between lies the sense, which is indeed no longer subjective like the idea, but is yet not the object itself" ([1892] 1966, 60).

Frege went on to argue that the *proposition*, not the word or concept, was the basic unit of meaning. Propositions have a subject-predicate structure. When the subject is specified and a concept is predicated of it, only then does the whole expression (i.e., the proposition) have a truth value (i.e., true or false). As a mathematician and logician, Frege was especially concerned with explaining how there could be shared, public meaning that provides a basis for objective knowledge and truth. His answer was that to understand the thought (i.e., proposition) expressed in a sentence is to grasp its public, universal sense, which is "not the subjective performance of thinking but its objective content, which is capable of being the common property of several thinkers" (Frege [1892] 1966, 62n.).

In order to explain the objectivity of the senses of terms, Frege proposed what many consider to be a somewhat odd ontology consisting of three independent realms: the physical, the mental, and a third realm (to which he gave no name) that consists of abstract quasi-entities including senses, concepts, propositions, numbers, functions, and the strange objects "the True" and "the False." Because Frege believed that both physical (bodily) events and mental (psychological) processes are incapable of guaranteeing the objective and universal character of publicly shareable meaning and thought, he posited the third realm to house the objective contents of thought. Consequently, in this view, a theory of language need not pay any special attention to our embodiment, other than to notice how perception might be shaped by our bodily capacities.

With Frege, the die were fatefully cast. Few philosophers could fully embrace Frege's unusual ontological picture (especially his third realm), but the vast majority of so-called "analytic" philosophers agreed with his basic assumption that thought is propositional and relies on the objective senses of the component concepts of the proposition. They shared his view that thought is linguaform—that is, sentential, propositional, and conceptual in nature. Not surprisingly, one can find no serious account in Frege of the body's contributions to meaning and thought. This neglect of the body carried over into most of the major figures in the analytic tradition, such as Bertrand Russell, Rudolf Carnap, Carl Hempel, Gustav Bergmann, J. L. Austin, W. V. O. Quine, Donald Davidson, and a host of other philosophers, *none of whom had anything deep or extensive to say about the body's role in meaning and thought.* Even Hilary Putnam—who is much celebrated for his brain-in-a-vat thought experiments (1981), in which he emphasized that meaning requires a body interacting with a world—never supplied any detailed account of how the body shapes our thought and communicative practices. This is not to deny that there may be some insightful comments on embodiment scattered throughout their writings (especially in Wittgenstein and in Putnam); but their perspective remains mostly disembodied in its accounts of meaning, language, and thought. The overwhelming tendency in mainstream analytic philosophy of language is to begin with concepts more or less well formed, and then to analyze their relations to one another in propositions and to objects of reference in the world. This leads one to overlook the bodily origins of those concepts and patterns of thought that constitute our understanding of, and reasoning about, our world.

What is at stake here is not just analyses of the meaning of particular terms or sentences, but something much more important: the very nature of meaning and thought as grounded in and shaped by our human embodiment. Moreover, the na-

ture of philosophy itself is called into question, once we realize that it is inextricably tied to our embodiment! At issue here are the origins of meaning, language, and all our forms of symbolic expression and communication that define our world and our personal identity. Although most analytic philosophers are not strictly Fregean, Anglophone philosophy of language developed mostly in this "disembodied" Fregean mode, in the sense that a theory of meaning, thought, and language is given without any serious study of the workings of the body and brain in how we make and communicate meaning or how we think. In the seventy or so years since the emergence of the field of philosophy of language, there has been remarkably—and depressingly—little variance from these early ideas that (1) language is conceptual and propositional, and (2) other than noting that we need a body to have perceptual inputs, it is asserted that concepts, propositions, and thoughts are not profoundly shaped by the nature of our bodily capacities and modes of engagement with our material environments.

The first-generation cognitive science that developed within this linguistic framework was therefore a blending of analytic philosophy of language, Chomskyan generative linguistics, information-processing psychology, computer science, and budding artificial intelligence research—all of which were relatively disembodied perspectives. Moreover, in line with Bergmann's dismissal of empirical scientific research and experiential evidence (as supposedly being irrelevant to the primary analytic tasks of philosophy), early cognitive "science" seemed often to be driven more by armchair philosophical assumptions than by empirical research on cognition. Consequently, little of the vast scientific research on how our bodies and brains underlie cognition found its way into the philosophy of mind and language during most of the twentieth century.[1]

Although Rorty's particular version of the linguistic turn obviously does not adequately represent all the methods and perspectives that make up so-called "analytic" philosophy, I suggest that his view of language and philosophy captures several of the deepest assumptions and motivations of the larger movement of linguistic philosophy. Consequently, a brief account of his argument about the priority of language gives us a good understanding of why the body played little or no role in large parts of analytic philosophy for most of the previous century. Fifteen years after *The Linguistic Turn*, Rorty collected several of his essays into another influential volume, entitled *Consequences of Pragmatism* (1982). In this book, Rorty articulates his particular interpretation of what some of his followers would later call linguistic (or analytic) pragmatism. He correctly praises pragmatism for its antidualism and its antifoundationalist view of knowledge and truth. However, he then goes on to claim, mistakenly, that antidualism and antifoundationalism require a concomitant rejection of any metaphysical commitments whatsoever. In particular, Rorty argues that when Dewey claimed that philosophy must start from "experience" in all its fullness, and then develop an "empirical metaphysics" that identifies recurrent structures and characteristics of all experience, Dewey was inconsistently falling right back into the very foundationalist metaphysics he had earlier so deftly criticized. Rorty sums up this critique as follows: "Dewey's mistake—and it was a trivial and unimportant mistake, even though I have devoted most of this essay to it—was the notion that criticism of culture had to take the form of a redescription of 'nature' or 'experience' or both" (ibid., 85).

Rorty liked Dewey's insightful criticism of deeply rooted epistemic and metaphysical assumptions that underlie different cultural systems, but he could not abide the idea that such a criticism might need to be based on a metaphysics of "experience" or "nature." Contrary to what he says in the previous quotation, Rorty's large corpus of later writings makes it quite clear that he did not think Dewey's "mistake" was trivial, insofar as Rorty saw such a project as leading us to an illegitimate foundationalist metaphysical program. Rorty conceives of philosophy as linguistic analysis and, where appropriate, criticism of our language games and linguistic practices. However, he also insists that we cannot carry out such analysis or criticism by claiming to "ground" it in some allegedly mind-independent "experience" or "world." According to Rorty, language communities operate with what he calls "vocabularies" that carry with them norms for what can be said and how any claim can be validated or criticized. We inhabit these vocabularies, but we cannot step outside any one of them to compare it to the world beyond language that it pretends to describe:

> This Davidsonian way of looking at language . . . lets us see language not as a *tertium quid* between Subject and Object, nor as a medium in which we try to form pictures of reality, but as part of the behavior of human beings. On this view, the activity of uttering sentences is one of the things people do in order to cope with their environment. The Deweyan notion of language as tool rather than picture is right as far as it goes. But we must be careful *not* to phrase this analogy so as to suggest that one can separate the tool, Language, from its users and inquire as to its "adequacy" to achieve

our purposes. The latter suggestion presupposes that there is some way of breaking out of language in order to compare it with something else. But there is no way to think about either the world or our purposes except by using our language. One can use language to criticize and enlarge itself, as one can exercise one's body to develop and strengthen and enlarge it, but one cannot see language-as-a-whole in relation to something else to which it applies, or for which it is a means to an end. (Rorty 1982, xviii–xix)

From Rorty's perspective, we dwell in our vocabularies and language games, and we cannot extricate ourselves from some particular vocabulary to see how it—or any other vocabulary, for that matter—might or might not map onto a mind- and language-independent reality that we call either "experience" or "the world." Moreover, since Rorty defines metaphysics as precisely such attempts to see how language could be foundationally grounded in "reality" or "the world," he rejects all metaphysics out of hand. That is why he denigrates Dewey's "empirical metaphysics," and *any* metaphysics, for that matter. For Rorty, there can be *no* good metaphysics.

Here's where embodiment gets discarded, insofar as Rorty thinks that any talk of "embodied" or "body-based" cognition, thought, meaning, experience, or language could be nothing but one more misguided attempt to find absolute foundations for our preferred vocabularies. In other words, Rorty is led to regard reference to "the body" as nothing but one more deluded metaphysical grounding or founding device, which throws us right back into illegitimate and unachievable foundationalist metaphysical and epistemological projects. Therefore, it should not be surprising that Rorty has little or nothing to say about embodiment, the body, and experience, and that he has almost nothing significant to say about aesthetics, insofar as aesthetics focuses on the embodied patterns, images, schemas, feelings, emotions, and qualities through which we experience things and events in our world. Nor should it be surprising that Rorty eschews utilization of any privileged scientific accounts of mind, cognition, meaning, language, and values, since he thought of them as just one more vocabulary among the many we might employ to order our lives. In short, for Rorty, "the body" and "experience" are linguistic and textual notions that only have meaning in the context of some particular vocabulary, and so they have no special status for grounding philosophy.[2]

As I said earlier, Rorty does not speak for all linguistic philosophy, but he perceptively understands the deepest motives and implications of the linguistic turn. He accepts the defining idea of linguistic philosophy as exclusively focusing on language. He regards thought as linguaform. And he thinks that any attempt to talk about "experience" or "the body" as the ground of meaning and thought is a reversion to misleading and counterproductive foundationalist metaphysical systematizing. It comes as no surprise, then, that there is little or no talk in linguistic philosophy about the body and its role in meaning and thought.

Incidentally, it was not just analytic philosophy that overlooked our embodiment. There were parallel dismissals in certain strands of European philosophy. Although phenomenology — especially the variety developed in the later Husserl, in Heidegger, and in Merleau-Ponty — did most certainly acknowledge the fundamental role of embodiment in our experience, the more deconstructivist developments in the 1960s and '70s had no place for the body as a locus of meaning and thought. Among those who recognized the importance of our bodies, Edmund Husserl made remarks on the body that are fairly general; and, in my opinion, he never overcame his reliance on a transcendent ego as the ultimate unifying agent of thought and action (Stawarska 2009). Martin Heidegger's key notions of "earth" and "world" also evoke bodily experiences, but his criticism of science and technology left most Heideggerians uninterested in scientific treatments of embodied cognition. Following Husserl and Heidegger, Maurice Merleau-Ponty uncovered the central role of the "lived body" in how our world opens up to us, but, unfortunately, Merleau-Ponty's philosophy of the body came to be eclipsed by Jacques Derrida's attack on what he called the "metaphysics of presence." Derrida argued that words have meanings, not by indicating nonlinguistic realities, but only through a network of relations and differences with other terms in one's language. There is no way to specify "the" meaning of a term by connecting it up with some underlying reality. Instead, each term takes its place in a web of other terms, all of which are mutually interdefined. Consequently, most deconstructionists (whether faithful to Derrida's original insights or not) reject any attempt to ground language in experience or bodily processes. Indeed, they rejected any notion of grounding whatsoever. "The body" then gets discarded along with every other "metaphysics of presence," just as Rorty dismisses any reference to embodiment as reversion to foundationalist metaphysical speculation. And it goes almost without saying that people disposed toward this deflationary view of meaning had no interest in, or even tolerance for, scientific claims about how bodies and brains generate meaning, thought, and language. In short, just as classical pragmatism's recognition of the body was buried by the upsurge of analytic philosophy, likewise the appreciation of the body's role in meaning and thought developed within phenomenology and hermeneutics was criticized and marginalized by the popular deconstructionist games of the late twentieth century.

Consequently, when I found myself immersed in linguistic philosophy as a graduate student in the 1970s, I did not even realize that I had been plunked down in a landscape that had been invaded by the body snatchers, who had systematically scoured the philosophical landscape to remove bodies from the scene. Although I did not then understand why, I found myself increasingly alienated from the rigorous linguistic analysis that most of my peers regarded as the very heart and soul of philosophy. I appreciated the rigor and thoroughness of those analyses, but they too often failed to engage me at an existential level that was meaningful and ethically motivating. I felt unmoored and adrift in conceptual analyses of the logic and structure of scientific laws and knowledge claims, analyses of the emotive use of value terms, inquiries into referential opacity and indeterminacy of translation within and across conceptual systems, and accounts of logic as conventional relations among arbitrary symbols. As an undergraduate in the late 1960s, I had fallen in love with philosophy because I thought it could help me understand who I was, whether (and if so, how) my life might be meaningful, and how I ought to live. But there I was, instead, in a top-tier graduate program, trying to answer W. V. O. Quine's question about whether there was any way for someone who does not speak the language of an alien group to learn what *gavagai* means in their language (Quine 1960). There I was, asking whether, in the presence of the animal I call a "rabbit" my alien interlocutor utters "*gavagai*," she *really* means "rabbit," "undetached rabbit part," "rabbit stuff," or none of the above! There I was, trying to figure out where Frege's third realm existed, since I had been assured that it was what made objective knowledge and truth possible. There I was, trying to give arguments for C. L. Stevenson's emotivist view that moral expressions like "X is good" really mean "I approve of X; do so as well." I found that I could not shake off the nagging suspicion that none of this had much to do with the lives of ordinary folks like me.

And so I quit philosophy. Not forever, but for two years. The questions about meaning, purpose, values, and knowledge that had enticed me into philosophy as an undergraduate at the University of Kansas in the late 1960s were not the questions being asked in the world of professional analytic philosophy. When I returned to graduate school, I did so because I found teachers who were talking about things that might actually relate to the quality and direction of my life. At the time, I didn't understand what this really had to do with embodiment; but that would come later.

Retrieving the Body from the Body Snatchers

It was not until I took courses from Paul Ricoeur—one on metaphor, a second on hermeneutics, and a third on imagination—that I began to see that there was an experience of meaning and value that went deeper than language. I learned to see the entire hermeneutic (interpretive) process of understanding not merely as an intellectual and linguistic act, but rather as constituting our whole embodied way of being in, and making sense of, our world. Ricoeur taught me that understanding is not just a conceptual achievement, but rather a whole-body, visceral engagement with our world that defines who we are and how we comport ourselves. Ricoeur had little interest in the scientific study of meaning and thought, but as a brilliant phenomenologist and hermeneutic thinker, he understood the body's role in meaning, reasoning, imagining, and communicating a sense of the world.

At the same time, I came under the humane influence of Ted Cohen, who was not explicitly interested in embodiment, but whose courses on J. L. Austin and on the philosophy of art led me to probe beneath language proper into the very conditions that make it possible for us to experience meaning and to communicate with one another. These dimensions of meaning and value are manifest partly in language, but also in nonlinguistic events in painting, sculpture, music, dance, architecture, film, ritual practices, spontaneous gesture, theater performance, and so on. And so I came to see aesthetics as involving more than just a theoretical investigation into art and aesthetic judgment. I came to conceive of aesthetics more broadly as a general exploration of how humans make and experience meaning at many different levels of our engagement with our world. Both Ricoeur and Cohen, although coming from very different philosophical traditions, helped me begin to see some of the embodied and imaginative dimensions of human cognition and understanding.

Eventually, I had the good fortune to write my doctoral dissertation on metaphor with Cohen and Ricoeur on my committee. It was there that I got my first glimpse of how metaphor is not just a matter of words, not merely a linguistic device, but instead a basic irreducible imaginative process by which humans are able to recruit body-based meaning for abstract conceptualization and reasoning. I also had a vague suspicion that the constitutive role of metaphor in thought called into question large parts of the linguistic philosophy framework that dominated the philosophical scene at that time, and so I began to realize that the assumptions and methods of analytic philosophy were not up to the task of giving an adequate account of the richness and visceral depths of human meaning.

For me, a fuller appreciation of the bodily dimensions of meaning would not come until later, after I went out to Berkeley as a young visiting assistant professor for the winter and spring of 1979 and met the linguist George Lakoff. In our intense and far-ranging conversations about metaphor, meaning, and thought, Lakoff and I saw immediately that abstract conceptualization and reasoning depend on conventionalized conceptual metaphors that could not be adequately accounted for by the reigning philosophical and linguistic traditions of the day. Those traditions were objectivist and literalist. They assumed the objectivist theory that a language is a formal system consisting of a set of meaningless symbols embedded within innately grounded syntactic frameworks and ordered by means of logical relations, which are themselves simply possible orderings of symbols. Ordinary language was modeled as a formal language system of this sort, and the meaningless symbols were supposedly given meaning by being placed in referential relations to objects, properties, and relations in the mind-independent world, usually by means of some idealized model of the world. According to this objectivist view, the meaning of any cognitively significant expression has to be literal, insofar as the sentence has to map directly onto states of affairs in the world (see Searle 1979, 117f). It followed from this objectivist orientation that a metaphor, which was taken to be merely a condensed statement of similarities between two different domains, has its meaning (if, indeed, it has any distinct meaning at all) only as a set of proper literal concepts and propositions to which it can be reduced. The other alternative theory popular at that time claimed that there is no distinctive metaphorical meaning, beyond the literal meaning of the words used in the utterance, and so metaphor is merely a pragmatic, not a semantic, device (Davidson 1978; Rorty 1989).

Those who regarded metaphor as a semantic phenomenon typically preferred the twenty-five-centuries-old comparison (or similarity) theory, according to which the meaning of a metaphor consisted merely in a set of literal similarity statements, so that a metaphor "*A* is *B*" was supposedly reducible to "*A* is like *B*, in respects *X, Y, Z*" (where *X, Y,* and

Z are literal similarities (either properties or relations) between objects *A* and *B*). Lakoff and I realized that if *that* was all a metaphor was, then it was no surprise that it was regarded as a linguistically and philosophically unimportant figure of speech that could, and should, ultimately be replaced by a string of statements about literal similarities existing between two domains of experience.

Once we came to see that virtually all our abstract concepts are defined by multiple metaphors that could not be reduced to literal similarity statements, Lakoff and I realized that something was rotten in the state of analytic philosophy of language. *Metaphors We Live By* (1980) was our first attempt to explore the implications of the central role of metaphor in our everyday—as well as our theoretically sophisticated—conceptualization and reasoning. Those implications were far reaching and stunning. Metaphor would need to be moved from the distant periphery to the very center of the study of thought and language. To understand how metaphors work, it was necessary to set out the cross-domain mapping structure that constituted the conceptual metaphor being studied, and then to show how each part of the mapping gives rise to polysemous terms and phrases and also to inferences within the source domain that get carried over into the target domain. For example, the UNDERSTANDING IS SEEING metaphor maps the entities, properties, and relations of the source domain (vision) onto the target domain (understanding) as follows:

- An object seen maps onto an idea or concept understood.
- Shedding light maps onto "illuminating" an idea.
- Seeing an object clearly maps onto understanding an idea.
- Visual acuity maps onto intellectual "vision" or "insight."
- An object blocking our view maps onto something that obstructs understanding.

A cross-domain mapping of this sort (here, from vision to understanding) is a conceptual metaphor that gives rise, via each of the submappings within the metaphor, to the use of terms with multiple related meanings (polysemy). In this manner, terms relating to vision (such as *see, light, illuminate, obscure, brilliant, blind*) have related meanings appropriate both for visual experience and also for the processes of intellectual understanding (e.g., "I *see* what you mean now"; "Could you *shed a little more light* on the last part of your theory?"; "That was a terribly *illuminating* explanation"; "What she said was very *enlightening*"; "I've been so *blind* to what she was up to"). Moreover, beside the polysemous use of terms based on the metaphor mapping, we also *think* and *draw inferences* via the metaphor.

Many linguists and psychologists began to study how inferences from the source domain are used to make target-domain inferences (Gibbs 1994; Kovecses 2010; Dancygier and Sweetser 2014). For instance, if something is obscuring or blocking your line of sight, then you cannot see whatever is behind it fully or clearly (visual domain inference); correspondingly, if some idea or thought is dominating your understanding, you will not fully discern some competing or alternative idea (target domain inference). To sum up, the cross-domain mappings are conceptual and support both systems of meaning and patterns of inference and reasoning.

And where is the *body* in all of this? Well, as we investigated how metaphors work, we discovered that the source domains of common cross-cultural metaphor systems are typically based on our sensory, motor, affective, and interpersonal experiences and cognitive capacities, all of which involve our embodiment. In other words, metaphors are shaped by the nature of our bodies and brains as we engage our physical and social environments. Metaphors thus "recruit" sensory and motor experience and inferential patterns to perform abstract conceptualization and reasoning. It is in this sense that they are body based. We saw that, contrary to the reigning comparison theory, metaphors are not typically based on perceived literal similarities between two different domains (e.g., vision and understanding aren't significantly similar), but rather are based on *experienced correlations* between the source and target domains. A few years later, Joseph Grady (1997), a student of Lakoff who was investigating why we have the metaphors we do, developed a theory of how these cross-domain experiential correlations are learned unreflectively, simply by growing up with a body of the sort we have, interacting with environments of the sort we inhabit. Grady called these basic metaphors "primary" because they emerge naturally in our embodied experience, through the coactivation of sensory-motor experiences and "higher level" thought processes that establish reentrant neural connections between the source and target domains that make up the metaphor. These primary metaphors could then be combined to generate more complex metaphor systems. Although these body-based metaphors (e.g., UNDERSTANDING IS SEEING, MORE IS UP, CAUSES ARE PHYSICAL FORCES, THINKING IS MOVING, TEMPORAL CHANGE IS RELATIVE MOTION) are good candidates for metaphorical universals tied to our shared embodiment, it is also the case that different cultures tend to elaborate the primary metaphors in different ways, giving rise to cultural variations in their meaning and use.

The fact that these conceptual metaphors are based on experiential correlations between aspects of the source and target domains revealed the crucial role of our embodied interactions with our environment in our ability to experience and make meaning. Consequently, the whole illusion of disembodied meaning went out the window! Also discarded were any dualistic and disembodied views of mind and cognition. In short, taking metaphor seriously required a massive rethinking of some of our most deeply rooted views about meaning, thought, and symbolic expression that had defined objectivist, literalist, and disembodied views. What was needed, then, was a philosophical and scientific perspective rich enough to explain these aspects of embodied meaning and thought.

The Embodied Cognitive Science of Meaning and Thought

In the emerging cognitive sciences, up through the mid-1970s, the dominant orientation, which Lakoff and I dubbed "first-generation cognitive science," was a blend of generative linguistics, information-processing psychology, analytic philosophy of language, and artificial intelligence (Lakoff and Johnson 1999). It got its conception of grammar from Chomsky's claims about innate formal structures. It got its view of natural languages as formal languages from logic and computer science. It got its conceptual and propositional focus from linguistic philosophy and generative linguistics, and it got its functionalist conception of mind from artificial intelligence and computer science. It got its view of mental operations from the cognitive psychology of the day, which parsed thought into a series of discrete mental operations on perceptual inputs, carried out sequentially, and eventually issuing in behavioral outputs. Mind was taken to be a capacity for formal operations and functions that was not dependent on any one particular form of embodiment. The MIND IS A COMPUTATIONAL PROGRAM metaphor captured people's imaginations so thoroughly that they seemed not to notice how our bodies play a crucial role in what is meaningful to us, how we think about it, and how we communicate our insights.

Fortunately, by the mid-1970s there was a mushrooming interdisciplinary body of empirical work on cognition that began to challenge the most basic assumptions of the dominant first-generation paradigm

(Patricia Churchland 1986; Lakoff 1987; Varela, Thompson, and Rosch 1991). Studies of human conceptual systems changed our understanding of how our categories and concepts are structured. Research in cognitive neuroscience challenged mind/body dualism and revealed the importance of feeling and emotion in all thought processes (Damasio 1994, 1999, 2003, 2010). New research on how humans actually reason challenged our inherited Enlightenment faculty psychology and its conception of a pure, nonemotional rationality. The new orientation known as cognitive linguistics challenged Chomsky's innatist views about language by drawing on empirical studies of the syntax, semantics, and pragmatics of natural languages (Lakoff 1987; Langacker 1987–91; Talmy 2000). In this new view, language was seen to be mostly a development of cognitive capacities for perception, bodily motions, and action. The result was an emerging vision of embodied mind, meaning, and thought that Lakoff and I (1999) later named "second-generation (or embodied) cognitive science." This was not a completely unified and monolithic perspective, but at first a somewhat disparate collection of empirical research programs that began to provide converging evidence for the central role of our brains and bodies in everything we experience, think, and do.

One of the central tasks of this second-generation orientation was to determine how—precisely and in detail—our bodies give rise to the meaning we can experience, the reasoning we do, and the ways we communicate with others, not just through language proper, but also through all our many forms of symbolic action in the arts and associated practices. Where was one to look for evidence of embodied cognition? Since cognitive neuroscience was a new and relatively immature field in the late 1970s, it took a while for it to establish a more unified identity.

At the same time, however, in addition to the psychological research and linguistic theory mentioned above, there were philosophical resources for developing a broad theoretical explanation of embodied mind, meaning, and thought. One of those was pragmatist philosophy, to which I was introduced in the early 1980s by my colleague Tom Alexander in a seminar he was teaching on John Dewey's classic *Experience and Nature* (1925).[3] I began to see the pragmatism of C. S. Peirce, William James, and John Dewey as the most appropriate nondualistic and scientifically responsible framework for understanding human experience and cognition. I got a glimpse of the central role of our bodies in the habits of action and thought that define who we are, and in the patterns and qualities that make meaning possible for us.

The other useful philosophical perspective was phenomenology. A year or two earlier I had sat in on a seminar taught by another colleague, Glenn Erickson, on Maurice Merleau-Ponty's *Phenomenology of Perception* (1962), where I had come away with a similar aha moment about what a truly nondualistic, experientially based philosophy would look like — one that placed the *lived body* at the center of human reality. In spite of their very different philosophical styles and temperaments, I came to see that Dewey and Merleau-Ponty were exploring the same deep dimensions of embodied meaning and thought, in ways that were being mostly ignored in the mainstream philosophical traditions of the day.[4]

It was this philosophical background — along with a general familiarity with speech-act theory, phenomenology, and hermeneutics — that I brought into my ongoing discussions with George Lakoff about what a new embodied view of mind, thought, and language would involve. It was Lakoff, though, who convinced me that I had to pay attention to the burgeoning cognitive sciences and could no longer rely solely on my philosophical training, precisely because some of that training was profoundly at odds with the scientific research on mind. We couldn't keep doing philosophical business-as-usual. Though it sounds arrogant to say so, what was needed was a new philosophical perspective, and not merely some tinkering with existing methods and orientations. This new emerging, second-generation cognitive science perspective might be essentially pragmatist in character, but it would have to incorporate the half century of cognitive science that had emerged since the heyday of classical pragmatism. In doing so, it would give important new details of embodied cognition not available to Dewey in his day. What was needed was what Patricia Churchland (1986) called a "co-evolution" of philosophy and science to generate an empirically responsible philosophical theory of mind, thought, and language.

What follows are some of the key components of this emerging embodied, interdisciplinary framework that is giving rise to a new understanding of mind, meaning, thought, and language.

Meaning Arises from Organism-Environment Interactions

What we call "mind" is an emergent character of an ongoing series of interactions among certain kinds of organisms and their environments (Dewey [1925] 1981). Mind is not a metaphysical entity or fixed structure, and it cannot possibly exist independent of bodily processes, activities, and engagements with other people. Instead, mind has reality only as an emergent process of meaning-making, acting, and communicating among creatures capable of certain kinds of complex functions and communicative interactions (Merleau-Ponty 1962; Varela, Thompson, and Rosch 1991). In order to see this, one has to start where all animals start: with a bounded, embodied organism as it engages its various environments in ways that allow it to maintain the basic conditions for life and growth. The more complex the organism is, the more ways it has by which it can meaningfully interact with the energy structures that make up its environments. Depending on the specific bodily makeup of the organism, particular situations will provide for the organism what James Gibson (1979) called "affordances"—patterns for meaningful perception and action relative to the nature of the organism, its needs, and its purposive activity in the world that it inhabits. For example, for human animals of our size, makeup, and interests, certain caves afford relations of containment (here, as space for habitation) and they may afford, for certain animals, protection from the elements and predators. Small caves do not afford access for large mammals, such as elephants, and so such enclosures do not have the same meaning to elephants as they do to humans. The world of an animal is demarcated by a large number of affordances provided by various objects, spaces, and structures within that animal's environment. What we call "objects" are affordances relative to the kinds of creatures we are.

Notice that, already at this basic level of animal-environment affordances and transactions, I have spoken of the "meaning" of specific environmental structures for a certain type of creature. I use "meaning" here for any experiences enacted or suggested by various affordances in our surroundings (M. Johnson 2007). Any aspect or quality of a situation means (for a specific type of creature) what it calls forth by way of experience. That includes past experiences, present experiences, and projected future experiences perceived to be possibilities developing out of one's current situation.

There are at least two very important consequences of this conception of meaning. (1) It acknowledges our evolutionary continuity with many other species, and therefore allows that certain nonhuman animals might be capable of various sorts of meaning-making. However, species lacking capacities for abstraction and symbolic interaction will have available to them a very attenuated range of meanings, relative to the richness of meaning available to humans; but it will be meaning nonetheless. (2) Conceiving of meaning in this embodied, experiential manner enables us to go beyond the narrower confines of language-based meaning to embrace the full range of human meaning-making in such practices as painting, sculpture, music, architecture, dance, spontaneous gesture, and ritual practices, in a way that no merely linguistically centered account of meaning can. No traditional understanding of signs as having meaning only through some conceptual/propositional content grounded in reference to states of affairs in the world could even begin to capture the richness of body-based meaning that is experienced in all these varied forms of human meaning-making and communicative activity.

Body-Part Projections

One important way that the body undergirds languages and systems of meaning the world over is the use of *body-part projections* for understanding objects, events, and scenes (Lakoff and Johnson 1999, chap. 3; Talmy 2000). We use our own body-part relations to make sense of objects and spatial relations in our surroundings. A good example of this is the way we experience our own bodies as having *fronts* and *backs*, and so it seems natural for us to project these *front/back* relations onto other objects, such as trees, rocks, houses, and lines of people, none of which have inherent fronts or backs. We experience computer screens as *facing* us, when we sit *in front of* them. We tend to project fronts onto moving objects (cars, buses, airplanes, ships), with the front defined relative to the canonical direction of motion for the object. Cars, buses, airplanes, and ships mostly move forward, and so their "front" is specified by that direction of motion. If they reverse direction, they are then said to "back up." We extend this *front/back* orientation even onto simple physical objects like bottles, balls, and rocks. For instance, if I rotate a plastic water bottle into a horizontal orientation, and then move the bottle in a line through space, you will project a front onto the bottle based on the direction of its motion.

The relation *in front of* is defined in most languages relative to the space between a viewer and some object in their field of vision. So, a dog that is located between me and a tree is experienced by me as in front of that tree, as if the tree faces me. Some languages, such as Hausa, reverse this, projecting the front of the tree as facing away from the viewer. Therefore, in Hausa, a dog who is located between the viewer and the tree would be "behind" or "in back of" that tree; and if the tree is between me and the dog, then the dog is described as "in front of" the tree. However, despite such orientation reversals between English and Hausa, in both cases the *in front of* relation is the result of a body-part or body-orientation projection, and so the meaning of spatial relations phrases is body relative. It is also common to experience objects such as mountains, trees, towers, poles, and people as being oriented *up* and *down*, as having *tops* and *bottoms*, and often as having *heads* and *feet* (as in the *foot of* a mountain, tree, or tower). Moreover, as will be discussed below, we use body-part terms imagistically and metaphorically when we conceive of rivers as having *arms*, and when we attribute body parts like *eyes* and *hearts* to objects and events, such as the *eye* of a needle or a storm, or the *heart* of an artichoke or a problem.

Image-Schematic Affordances

Body-part projections are meaningful because they enact aspects of our fundamental ways of relating to, and acting within, our environment. The way our perceptual and motor systems get characteristically wired up (neuronally) as we grow and develop—through ongoing relations with energy patterns in our environment—establishes a large number of recurring, intrinsically meaningful patterns that George Lakoff (1987) and I (M. Johnson 1987) dubbed "image schemas." The basic idea was that, given the nature of our bodies (how and what we perceive, how we move, what we value) and the general dimensions of our surroundings (stable structures in our environment), we will experience regular recurring patterns (such as up/down, left/right, front/back, containment, iteration, balance, loss of balance, source–path–goal, forced motion, locomotion, center/periphery, straight, curved) that afford us possibilities for meaningful interaction with our surroundings, both physical and social. For example, the fact that humans exist and operate within earth's gravitational field generates recurring experiences of *up/down* (i.e., *verticality*) relations. We understand objects as rising *up* and falling *down*, as upright or lying *down*, as *on top of* or *below* (or *under*), relative to our own bodily orientation and our physical surroundings. The fact that we routinely, and crucially, experience *balance* or *lack of balance* gives rise to a BALANCE schema that applies literally to balancing physical objects and metaphorically to our internal bodily states, to mathematical equations, and to notions of political fairness and justice (M. Johnson 1987; 1993). Through our numerous daily experiences with containers and contained spaces we develop a CONTAINER schema that consists of a boundary that defines an interior and an exterior (Lakoff 1987; M. Johnson 1987). Our thousands of daily encounters with moving objects and with moving our own bodies gives rise to a LOCOMOTION schema (Dodge and Lakoff 2005). Importantly, such schemas are typically multimodal, and so are not tied to any single sensory or motor area of the brain. This multimodality is evident when we experience containment both through vision and touch, or when we see something far off and also hear it as far away.

A list of common image schemas might run into the scores or even hundreds (Cienki 1997; Hampe 2005). Cross-cultural analysis cannot yet verify any definite list of universal image schemas, but schemas such as CONTAINER, SOURCE-PATH-GOAL, VERTICALITY, and COMPELLING FORCE would appear to be excellent candidates, insofar as people the world over routinely have experiences that manifest such patterns. Ellen Dodge and George Lakoff conclude that, although all languages do not have the same spatial-relations concepts, nevertheless, they appear to build their particular spatial relations from "a limited inventory of basic primitive image schemas and frames of reference" (2005, 71).

Image schemas are meaningful to us both *before* and *beneath* linguistic meaning. They are intrinsically meaningful embodied structures. Focusing on image-schematic structure was my first attempt to figure out how the body might give rise to meaning. Lakoff and I realized that image schemas perform an important role in structuring the source domains of primary metaphors, and this was partly what it meant to say that conceptual metaphors are "embodied," "grounded in our bodies," and "experientially based." In *The Body in the Mind* (1987) I therefore gave numerous examples of how conceptual metaphors appropriate the image-schematic structure (relations and logic) of the source domain for abstract conceptualization and reasoning. Consider the SOURCE-PATH-GOAL schema that is present in all our experiences of seeing an object move along a path or moving ourselves from an initial location to a (temporary) terminal location. The SOURCE-PATH-GOAL schema manifests a recurring pattern for moving objects in our experience, and it has its own distinctive corporeal or spatial logic. So, if two objects start out at the same source location, moving along the same path, at the same speed, then they will both reach the same location at the same time. This is an inference grounded in our experience of moving objects. If one moves faster than the other, then the faster-moving object will arrive at the goal destination sooner. If I have moved halfway along a path from *A* to *B*, then I have "covered" all the points on the path up through the halfway point.

Such knowledge of source-path-goal movements may seem quite banal and mundane, but it is nonetheless the basis for spatial and temporal inferences we make about moving objects and the path on which they move. Moreover, if we later come to understand the path of motion metaphorically as the "path" or "course" of a temporal process, then we can appropriate the logic of spatial motion, plus our knowledge about moving objects, to draw appropriate inferences in some abstract domain, such as the domain of state change. For example, if we understand a causative change-of-state process metaphorically as motion along a path, from one state-location to another, then we can use the logic of moving objects to understand processes such as change of state. Thus, we speak of water on the stove as *going* from cold to hot in minutes. And if the water is getting hotter, then it is progressively getting less cold, and at some time in the process, it will cease to be cold, or even cool. Change of state is understood metaphorically as change of location. In this way, image schemas provide much of the embodied meaning—and correlative logic—that makes it possible to conceptualize and reason abstractly via metaphor.

Perceptual Concepts

Lawrence Barsalou (1999, 2003) argues that our perceptual symbols for various concrete objects (e.g., cars, glasses, houses) are grounded in the sensory and motor experiences afforded us by those objects. The key idea is that the same sensory, motor, and affective neural processes involved in our bodily engagement with such objects are activated when we conceptualize, reason, and talk about those objects. There are not two different and independent systems, one for perception and another for conception; instead, to conceive some object is a matter of engaging in a simulation process that activates selective sensory and motor aspects of that object and our typical physical and cultural interactions with it. For example, understanding a concept like *chair* involves a sensory, motor, and affective simulation of possible experiences with chairs of all sorts. Such simulations will involve multiple modalities (such as vision, touch, audition, and proprioception), insofar as our interactions with chairs are multimodal. We see chairs from various points of view as we walk around them, we know what it feels like to sit on and touch various types of chairs made from different materials, and we know the types of motor programs required for sitting in and standing up from chairs. We also learn the different roles various types of chairs can play in different social and cultural situations. To know the meaning of *chair*, to understand what a chair is in a certain context, is to simulate experiences with chairs using all the sensory, motor, and affective modalities available to us.

The key idea here is that understanding a concept does not consist in accessing a list of abstract essential features or properties that define a thing. Rather, to have a concept of a particular object is to be able to simulate the kinds of perceptual, motor, and affective interactions you typically have with that kind of object. This simulation is not run in some abstract conceptual domain, but instead is enacted in the very bodily processes (employing the same functional neural clusters) involved in physically engaging that object.

Barsalou summarizes the six basic dimensions of his theory of body-based perceptual symbols as follows:

> Perceptual symbols are neural representations in sensory-motor areas of the brain; they represent schematic components of perceptual experience, not entire holistic experiences; they are multimodal, arising across the sensory modalities, proprioception, and introspection. Related perceptual symbols become integrated into a simulator that produces limitless simulations of a perceptual component (e.g., *red*, *lift*, *hungry*). Frames organize the perceptual symbols within a simulator, and words associated with simulators provide linguistic control over the construction of the simulation. (1999, 582)

Barsalou's use of the term *representation* might seem to support what is known as a representational theory of mind, in which thought proceeds via operations on internal mental representations that are somehow supposedly relatable to external, mind-independent realities. However, Barsalou's view could be made compatible with a nonrepresentational theory of mind, where having or entertaining a concept is merely running a neural simulation in which sensory, motor, and affective areas of the brain are activated not as representations mediating between an inner and outer world, but rather as *the very understanding of the concept*. In other words, the neural activations involved in the sensory, motor, and affective simulations within a specific context (including the social and cultural dimensions) *just are* what it is to grasp the meaning of the concept in question.

Simulation Semantics: Language Understanding as Embodied Simulation

In several articles (e.g., Gallese 2003, 2007, 2008; Gallese and Lakoff 2005; Glenberg and Gallese 2012; Gallese and Cuccio 2015), the neuroscientist Vittorio Gallese and colleagues have provided evidence of embodied simulation in our processing of action verbs. Gallese summarizes the results of those studies as follows: "Language, when it refers to the body in action, brings into play the neural resources normally used to move that very same body. Seeing someone performing an action, like grabbing an object, and listening to or reading the linguistic description of that action lead to a similar motor simulation that activates some of the same regions of our cortical motor system, including those with mirror properties, normally activated when we actually perform that action" (Gallese and Cuccio 2015, 13).

The notion of understanding and conceptualization as on-line neural simulation has now been expanded to a general theory of language understanding. Ben Bergen (2012) has surveyed a large number of recent neuroimaging studies of how such simulations work as we read or hear sentences. He proposes an "embodied simulation hypothesis"; namely, that "we understand language by simulating in our minds what it would be like to experience the things that the language describes" (Bergen 2012, 13). For example, one group of studies reveals that "the motor system is often used when people are understanding language about action, and that this is more likely when the language uses progressive rather than perfect aspect. We know that interfering with the perceptual system—by having people look at lines or spirals moving in one direction or another—affects how long it takes them to determine that a(n) (action) sentence makes sense, and so on" (ibid., 249). In other words, research suggests that sentences with the progressive aspect, in which the action is currently ongoing, are more likely to activate motor and premotor cortical areas used in that specific kind of action than in a sentence in which the action is already completed (i.e., perfect aspect). Moreover, if we interfere with the normal direction or motor processes for the action specified in the sentence, it takes longer to understand the sentence.

It is too early to make any sweeping claims about the scope and adequacy of the embodied simulation hypothesis, but there is growing evidence that many parts of language understand work in this fashion (Feldman 2006; Lakoff and Narayanan 2017). It is an elegant and parsimonious hypothesis that meshes well with many neuroimaging studies that are revealing how our understanding of sentences is an ongoing temporal process in which sensory, motor, and affective areas of the brain are progressively activated as we read or hear parts of sentences. Moreover, it is a highly testable hypothesis, especially as we are developing more fine-grained and time-sensitive techniques for neuroimaging.

The Embodiment of Abstract Concepts

Disembodied theories of language often cite abstract concepts as evidence that thought and language cannot be accounted for solely in terms of bodily processes. Chairs and cars may be good candidates for an embodied simulation treatment, but what about abstract concepts like mind, freedom, love, knowledge, and property? The most well-researched and detailed accounts of such concepts to date, from an embodied perspective, come from the orientation known as conceptual metaphor theory, which gives evidence that body-based metaphor is our principal means of abstract conceptualization and reasoning. As mentioned earlier, George Lakoff and I first put this idea forward in a detailed fashion in *Metaphors We Live By* (1980). We observed that our abstract concepts are typically defined by multiple metaphors, by which we map entities, patterns, and relations from a physical or social domain to structure our understanding of a more abstract domain of experience. For example, English and most known languages have a basic metaphor by which acts of thought are understood metaphorically as acts of perception. A much-studied example would be the previously mentioned UNDERSTANDING IS SEEING metaphor, in which thinking is conceptualized as seeing something, which gives rise to expressions such as "I *see* what you mean," "Could you *shed* more *light* on that idea," "What she said was incredibly *illuminating*," and "His concept of time is too *obscure*." Over the past three decades, hundreds of cross-linguistic studies have revealed scores of conceptual metaphors shared across disparate cultures (Gibbs 2008).

A crucial claim of Conceptual Metaphor Theory is that the vast majority of metaphors are not based on similarities, but rather emerge from common experiential correlations occurring between the source and target domains. So, for example, it is not that vision and thought are "similar" or share literal similarities as the basis for metaphorical mapping; instead we have certain vision metaphors in cultures the world over because people routinely experience the correlation between seeing something and thereby gaining an understanding of it. As stated above, Joseph Grady (1997) called these basic correlational phenomena "primary metaphors," and he showed how we could learn scores of them simply by having the kinds of bodies we have and interacting with the kinds of environments that we routinely inhabit. In this way, primary metaphors would arise without any conscious awareness, simply from the neural coactivations of the source and target domains. In this fashion, we would acquire the neural basis of primary metaphors like MORE IS UP, AFFECTION IS WARMTH, INTIMACY IS CLOSENESS, SIMILARITY IS CLOSENESS, IMPORTANT IS BIG, PURPOSES ARE DESTINATIONS, ACTIVITIES ARE MOTIONS, ORGANIZATION IS PHYSICAL STRUCTURE, and CAUSES ARE FORCES.

Combinations of two or more primary metaphors can give rise to more complex metaphor systems that constitute our abstract conceptual systems. The LIFE IS A JOURNEY metaphor, for example, is built from a number of primary metaphors that constitute the submappings of the metaphor. Conceptualizing life metaphorically as a journey involves primary metaphors like ACTIONS ARE MOTIONS, DIFFICULTIES ARE IMPEDIMENTS TO MOTION, CAUSES ARE PHYSICAL FORCES, RESPONSIBILITIES ARE BURDENS, PURPOSES ARE DESTINATIONS, and so on (Lakoff and Johnson 1999). The submappings of complex metaphors give rise to specific inferential patterns by which we are able to reason about the target domain given our knowledge of the source domain. For instance, in the source domain of physical motion, we experience the way a physical obstacle or impediment can temporarily or permanently stop our forward motion. Via the DIFFICULTIES ARE IMPEDIMENTS TO MOTION submapping, we draw the target-domain inference that difficulties can temporarily or permanently impact our ability to realize some purpose we are pursuing.

Embodied Construction Grammar

Embodiment is not just the source of semantic content that would then somehow be ordered by a pure, disembodied system of formal relations, manifested either as syntax or logical patterns of thought. Instead, even syntax is shaped and given meaning by the contours of our bodily experience.

Noam Chomsky famously argued that syntactic deep structures are innate universals, in no way dependent on our particular embodiment (Chomsky 1965). According to this generative linguistics view, syntax is a matter of purely formal relations—that is, of our innate ability to recognize and produce linguistic expressions according to specific structural patterns. As such, syntactic form was believed to operate separately from our capacities to process meaning (construed as semantic content of sentences), and it was supposedly not dependent on the uses (pragmatics) to which linguistic utterances are put.

As far back as the late 1960s, however, there was growing evidence for the interdependence of syntax, semantics, and pragmatics and for the importance of the body for defining the syntax of natural languages. On this view, linguistic forms are meaningful (hence, tied to semantics and pragmatics), and they are meaningful because they encode the structures of events, actions, agents, purposes, objects, and so on, that we experience as embodied creatures in a world. Instead of being born with all the syntactic knowledge we need, we learn the syntax of specific languages by exposure to conceptual and linguistic constructions that capture important aspects of our daily experiences and actions. We are exposed to grammatical constructions, which are "pairings of form with semantic or discourse function" (Goldberg 2003, 219). Grammatical patterns are thus the product of cognitive mechanisms of perception, bodily movement, and action that come to shape our conceptualization and reasoning.

Over the past forty years, a number of these grammatical and other cognitive structures have been studied as they operate in our conceptual systems and determine all the ways we have of making sense of a situation. These structures include body-part relations (Brugman 1983), image schemas (M. Johnson 1987; Lakoff 1987; Hampe 2005), semantic frames (Fillmore 1982), action schemas (Narayanan 1997), prototype effects (Rosch 1975), radial category structure (Lakoff 1987), force dynamics (Talmy 2000), conceptual metaphors (Lakoff and Johnson 1980, 1999), and blends (Fauconnier and Turner 2002).

A good example of this type of research is the grammar of actions. Charles Fillmore (1982) showed how individual words get their meanings through their relations to other terms within a larger conceptual frame. One important example of this semantic framing is the way prototypical actions are understood via a conceptual frame with slots of the following sort: action, actor, object acted with or on, goal of action, manner of action, and so on. Srini Narayanan (1997), in developing neurocomputational models of schemas for certain kinds of bodily actions, discovered a general control structure for actions, which he dubbed an "executing schema," with the following temporal dimensions: preparatory state (getting into a state of readiness), starting the process for the event, main process (either instantaneous or prolonged), an option to stop, an option to resume, an option to continue or to reiterate the main process, a check to see if the goal has been met, the finishing process, and the final state. Narayanan was able to create neurocomputational models that could both recognize and carry out (via appropriate robotics) action events.

According to *embodied construction grammar*, people learn, in addition to action frames and executing schemas, a range of schemas for other dimensions of experience, simply by perceiving and having bodily experiences in the world. These embodied conceptual structures underlie grammatical constructions. We would thus expect any natural language to have some way of coding each of these general dimensions and parameters of actions, events, and objects, although different languages will often vary in the details of how they grammatically code these recurring dimensions of human experience. The relevant frames and schemas will depend on the nature of our bodies, our brain architecture, and the recurring dimensions of the environments we inhabit. Embodied construction grammar extrapolates from cases of this sort to propose that we learn *all* our basic grammatical patterns in this experiential manner (Goldberg 2003), based on our shared sensory and motor capacities, other shared general cognitive mechanisms, and our exposure to natural languages.

The Neural Theory of Language

In 1999 Lakoff and I published *Philosophy in the Flesh: The Embodied Mind and Its Challenge to Western Thought*, in which we tried to summarize the main types of evidence then existing for the embodiment of meaning, thought, and language. The first third of the book surveyed some of the most important empirical research on embodied cognition. The second part gave analyses of key philosophical concepts (such as causation, time, mind, thought, identity, morality), using the tools of second-generation embodied cognitive science. The third section turned those tools on the very nature of philosophy itself, showing how philosophies are built up from the resources of embodied meaning and thought that make us who we are. We also summarized some of the supporting evidence for embodied cognition coming out of the new field of cognitive neuroscience. At that time, we relied mostly on research into the neural basis of image schemas, category structure, conceptual metaphor, action schemas, and grammatical constructions.

Prior to that time, in the 1980s, when cognitive linguists and embodied cognition theorists gave evidence for things like image schemas, action frames, and conceptual metaphors, they relied heavily on phenomenological descriptions of patterns of our experience, coupled with empirical linguistic studies of the types of structures that show up in meaning, grammatical forms, logical inferences, and a host of linguistic acts that exhibit distinctive constraints.

With the meteoric development of cognitive neuroscience, it next became necessary to bring the brain into the story—to ask how brains and bodies like ours develop to process meaning and to order thoughts as we do. It was no longer enough to provide polysemy evidence for the existence of conceptual metaphor, by showing how concepts used directly to capture patterns of our mundane bodily experience are recruited for abstract reasoning. There was abundant evidence, gathered from large numbers of cross-cultural studies, that there is a directionality in metaphor, from source domain to target, in which sensory-motor-affective dimensions of the source are used to structure our understanding of the target. *Now*, however, it became necessary to see if there was any neuroscientific evidence that our brains (and bodies) actually work this way! The intuitive idea that metaphors are based on *experiential correlations* needed to be translated into an account of metaphors as *coactivations of neural clusters* that involve neural maps and cross-domain reciprocal connections within the brain. The intuitive idea of image-schematic patterns of our felt, lived experience, once supported mostly by linguistic evidence and phenomenological description, now required explanation in terms of patterns mapped within the brain and the connections among those maps and neural architectures. As we moved into the twenty-first century, cognitive linguistics and embodied cognition research had to explore vast new neuroscience horizons.

The cognitive processes and structures discussed above and in subsequent chapters—image schemas, semantic frames, action schemas, primary metaphors, complex metaphors, and grammatical constructions—are just part of the large array of cognitive mechanisms that give rise to thought and language. The approach that has come to be known as the "neural theory of language." Feldman (2006) attempts to model the neural mechanisms that give rise to the structures and processes that make language possible. George Lakoff and Srini Narayanan (2017) have emphasized that an adequate theory would need to involve multiple levels of explanation:

> Neuroscience is only one part of the answer, for a simple reason. Neuroscience does not study the detailed nature of thought and language. For that you also need the field of cognitive linguistics. . . . We also need to understand how neural circuitry functions to produce thought. For that we need neural computation to model that functioning. And we need to know how thought impacts behavior. For that you need experimental research on embodied cognition. In short, what is needed is a way to integrate all four sciences: Neuroscience, Cognitive Linguistics, Neural Computation, Experimental Embodied Cognition. (Lakoff and Narayanan 2017)

The neural theory of language is thus a vastly ambitious attempt to understand how our brains and bodies give rise to our thought, language, and other forms of symbolic interaction. It studies, from multiple perspectives, how cognition is tied to the body and its engagements with its environments to generate the marvelous resources of natural languages. It models the various neural and brain architectures that make linguistic activity possible. One key challenge is to supply bridges between the various levels of processing, starting with molecules and biological neural systems, which then need to be modeled neurocomputationally, guided by the cognitive linguistics of natural languages, which tells us precisely which constructions need to be modeled and explained. Jerome Feldman captures the challenge of this vast undertaking as follows: "This integrated, multifaceted nature of language is hard to express in traditional theories, which focus on the separate levels and sometimes view each level as autonomous. But constructions can provide a natural description of the links between form and meaning that characterize the neural circuitry underlying real human language. They offer a high-level computational description of a neural theory of language (NTL). . . . In particular, it allows the embodied and neural character of thought and language to take center stage" (2006, 9).

Emotion and Meaning

Neurocomputational theories of thought and language are typically not good at capturing the emotional and feeling dimensions of human meaning, since they often do not include the hormonal processes so crucial to emotions. Traditional philosophy of language has fared no better. In fact, it has tended to either downplay or entirely dismiss the emotional dimensions of meaning. C. K. Ogden and I. A. Richards (1923) set the stage for this when they distinguished "descriptive" from "emotive" meaning, and then concluded that only the former has significant cognitive content relevant to understanding and knowing our world. The unfortunate result of this illegitimate bifurcation of thought and feeling, reason and emotion, has been, until quite recently, the ignoring of emotions in mainstream accounts of language. William James ([1890] 1950) long ago deplored this radical separation of thought and feeling, arguing that all thought has a feeling dimension that includes both a felt sense of the horizon or fringe of meaning surrounding a particular term, and also a feeling of the direction of our thinking. Instead of "thought" or "feeling," James preferred the hyphenated "thought-feeling" to capture the true embodied, affective character of our mental processes.

In a series of books, Antonio Damasio (1994, 1999, 2003, 2010) has developed a theory of emotions that places them at the center of human thought, meaning, and value. He argues that emotions are automated neurochemical response patterns to the body-mind's ongoing assessment of how it is being affected by its environment. In order to survive and flourish, organisms must establish a semipermeable boundary within which they sustain the conditions of life by maintaining a homeostasis, or dynamic equilibrium within the organism. Jay Schulkin (2011) uses the term "allostasis" to emphasize that the process is geared not just to returning to a prior set state, but also to constructing, in an ongoing fashion, the equilibrium necessary for life and growth. This, in turn, requires that the body continually monitor changes in its body state in response to its engagement with its environment. Emotional response patterns arise, therefore, when an "emotionally competent stimulus" (Damasio 2003, 53) causes the body to recover equilibrium by adjusting its internal milieu and instigating bodily changes that often result in overt action. Emotional response patterns typically run their course automatically, without need of conscious reflection. However, on those occasions when we become aware of changes in the body as it interacts with its environment and gives rise to an emotional response pattern, we then *feel* an emotion.

The connection between emotion and meaning is that emotions are our most elementary way of taking the measure of our current situation and responding to it. As such, they can be said to indicate "how things are going for us" and "what's happening" (Damasio 1999). I have summarized this emotion/meaning connection as follows: "Our emotional responses are based on both our nonconscious and conscious assessments of the possible harm, nurturance, or enhancement that a given situation may bring to our lives. . . . Emotional responses . . . are bodily processes (with neural and chemical components) that result from our appraisal of the meaning and significance of our situation and consequent changes in our body state, often initiating actions geared to our fluid functioning within our environment" (M. Johnson 2007, 60–61). Rather than opposing emotion to reasoning, emotions and feelings lie at the heart of our ability to conceptualize and reason. They provide ongoing contact with our situation at the most primordial level where we feel ourselves in our environment. These affective dimensions are not lost when language comes onstage; rather, they are taken up into the very processes of meaning-making and come to permeate our words, phrases, and sentences (Gendlin 1997).

Don Tucker, a psychologist and neuroscientist, has also argued that all our thought is shaped by the basic motivational systems within our mammalian brains (Tucker and Luu 2012; Tucker 2017). In other words, all cognition is motivated cognition, and so there is no meaning or thought that is not connected to the (mostly unconscious) values and motive forces that arise from our need to survive and grow within our environment. We now have some of the neuroscience necessary to explain the brain architecture that keeps our thought tied to feelings, emotions, and motive forces.

The Seven E's

To sum up: Language is intimately shaped by all aspects of our bodily being in the world—from perception to movement to feeling. Empirical studies of language processing do not support a disembodied mind. On the contrary, they reveal that the body-mind emerges from our bodily engagement with our physical interactions with things and events, and from our interpersonal interactions with other human and nonhuman animals. Cognitive neuroscience is beginning to provide us an elementary understanding of the neural architectures that give rise to thought and language. Through a multilevel dialogue between neurocomputational modeling, cognitive linguistic accounts of language understanding, empirical psychological experiments on thought and language, and neurophysiology, we are beginning to understand how the body lies at the heart of our ability to make, understand, and communicate meaning and thought.

In recent years, this general orientation toward the grounding of mind in organism-environment interactions has come to be known as "4E cognition"; that is, cognition as *embodied, embedded, enactive,* and *extended.* Cognition is *embodied* in some of the ways surveyed above, it is *embedded* insofar as it arises from interactions with its environments (both physical and social), it is *enactive* in the way it creates meaning and thought in an ongoing fashion, and it is *extended* in the sense that we offload certain cognitive operations and contents onto (or into) aspects of our environment, such as books, computers, buildings, and signs.

However, the neural theory of language suggests that we should add at least three more E's to this list: *emotional, evolutionary,* and *exaptative.* I have briefly indicated the importance of emotions in our ability to grasp the meaning and significance of our situation and of what is happening at any given moment as we engage language, through reading, writing, and speaking. Second, although I have not focused explicitly on the evolutionary dimension, I hope it is clear how the organism-environment development process discussed above is evolutionary in nature, in response to changing conditions in ourselves and our environment over vast spans of time. Third, I have merely hinted at the fact that our capacities for abstract thought are largely exaptations of evolutionarily earlier structures and capacities (Tucker 2007; Tucker and Luu 2012). As Lakoff and Narayanan put it: "With the development of larger forebrains, human beings have 'repurposed' the circuitry types already present in animals. The technical term is *exaptation,* the use of evolutionarily inherited traits for new purposes. We hypothesize that this evolutionary repurposing underlies much, if not all, of human thought and language" (2017, chap. 1, sec. 1). A primary example of this is the recruitment of brain areas evolved for sensory and motor processing to perform conceptualization and reasoning about abstract, nonphysical domains, as in the case of conceptual metaphors based on mappings from a source to a target domain.

Language therefore appears to be very much a product of "E" cognition, whether we count four E's or seven. However long the list, embodiment comes first, because it is our bodily habitation of our world that gives rise to our capacity to create and use language.

The Structure of This Book

In this introductory chapter, I have used a brief account of my own intellectual journey as a way of tracking what I consider to be some of the most important discoveries over the last forty years regarding the role of the body in mind, meaning, thought, and language. The essays collected here are arranged so as to explain some of the key structures and processes of embodied meaning and thought. Together they provide one type of argument for the need to restore the body to its deserved place at the heart of human meaning-making and understanding.

I begin with three chapters that lay out the general naturalistic, nondualistic, and nonreductive view of mind and thought that I believe to be supported by second-generation (embodied) cognitive science. These essays argue that a classical pragmatist philosophy of experience provides the most promising philosophical framework for understanding the significance of embodied cognitive science. As a way of introducing my particular interpretation of pragmatism, chapter 1 focuses mostly on John Dewey's view of mind, meaning, and thought as intrinsically embodied. Chapter 2 further elaborates the pragmatist perspective by turning to William James's revolutionary account of mind and consciousness as embodied active processes, both of which depend inescapably on emotion and feeling. Chapter 3 (coauthored with Tim Rohrer) explores some of the continuities between human and nonhuman animals, especially as a way of elucidating the pragmatist claim—a claim well supported by extensive cognitive science research—that everything related to mind and thought arises always from complex, ongoing organism-environment interactions. Some of the stronger parallels between classical American pragmatism and contemporary mind science emerge from such an investigation. These three chapters, along with the overview developed in this introduction, indicate the value and significance of a perspective that places a classical pragmatist orientation into productive dialogue (both critical and constructive) with what I have been calling embodied cognitive science.

The next three chapters provide additional detailed evidence, first, for how meaning emerges from our embodied engagement with our environments, and, second, how both what we are able to think and reason about, as well as the very character and structure of that understanding and reasoning, depend on the nature of our bodies, our brains, and the affordances of our environments. This argument begins in chapter 4 with an explanation of the broad and expansive conception of meaning-as-embodied that is required by certain bodies of cognitive science research on how people make sense of and reason about their world. Chapter 5 focuses primarily on the central role of image schemas in our ability to experience and make meaning. It then shows some of the ways these body-based image schemas are appropriated for abstract conceptualization and reasoning. This is true not just in our mundane inferences in daily life, but also in our philosophical reflections, which have too often been held up as the pinnacle of pure, disembodied thought. Chapter 6 then foregrounds the central role of *action* in our ability to make sense of our world and to reason about it. This is an articulation of the pragmatist insistence that thinking is a form of action, and that even our high-level cognitive operations and acts exapt preexisting structures of perception, movement, and feeling to perform abstract understanding and reasoning. The essays in this section explore how our abstract concepts and reasoning recruit sensory-motor processes and embodied meaning (through image schemas and conceptual metaphor) to achieve our most impressive intellectual and creative accomplishments of thought, thereby obviating any need for erroneous and misleading conceptions of pure rationality or disembodied mind and thought.

In line with the crucial roles of perception and action, chapter 7 looks at knowing as an *action*, rather than a product, in which experience is transformed and redirected through the resources of embodied meaning. Chapter 8 carries this action orientation further, by regarding truth as the temporary outcome of certain incarnate modes of inquiry aimed at helping us navigate our way through life. Truth is not some static relation between mental structures (e.g., propositions) and an allegedly mind-independent and structurally complete world. Instead, truth is a term of praise we apply whenever our understanding and reasoning appear to us to increase our at-home-ness in our world.

It is my hope that these collected essays reveal why and how we need to rethink some of our deeply held notions about mind, meaning, thought, and language, and that they also open up a scientifically and philosophically sophisticated path for pursuing this fundamental reconstruction of our understanding of who we are and how we make sense of our world.

CHAPTER 1

Cognitive Science and Dewey's Theory of Mind, Thought, and Language

Over eighty years ago, half a century before the term *cognitive science* had even been coined, John Dewey developed his view of mind, thought, and language in ongoing dialogue with the biological and psychological sciences of his day. He drew on empirical research in a number of fields, including biology, neuroscience, anthropology, cognitive psychology, developmental psychology, social psychology, and linguistics. Dewey's approach thus offers a model of how philosophy and the cognitive sciences can productively work together. The sciences reveal aspects of the deepest workings of mind. Philosophy evaluates the underlying assumptions and methods of the sciences, and it places the empirical research on cognition in its broader human context, in order to determine what it means for our lives.

In a nutshell, Dewey's theory of mind is naturalistic, nonreductive, and process oriented. His view is *naturalistic* in that it employs empirical research drawn from a number of natural and social sciences. It eschews explanations that rely on supernatural notions, rejecting any idea of a nonempirical ego or pure rationality. However, even though Dewey appropriated modes of inquiry characteristic of the sciences, he took great care to avoid the reductionist tendencies that limit the explanatory scope of certain sciences. His account is thus *nonreductive* because he saw that no single scientific account, cluster of scientific perspectives, or particular philosophical orientation ever tells the whole story. Consequently, he insisted on a plurality of methods from various sciences, he recognized multiple levels of explanation for mental phenomena, and he famously used art and aesthetic experience to reveal the depths of human experience and understanding. His view is *process oriented* insofar as it always regards experience and thinking as ongoing processes of organism-environment interaction. He never hypostatizes cognitive functions into discrete faculties and never turns dynamic cognitive processes into fixed structures.

These three defining aspects of Dewey's view are manifested in his insistence that any useful philosophical account of mind, thought, and language must do justice to the depth and richness of human experience. *Experience* is Dewey's most important notion. It is meant to include *everything that happens*—both from the side of the experiencing organism and from the side of the complex environments with which that organic creature is continually interacting. Experience "includes *what* men do and suffer, *what* they strive for, love, believe and endure, and also *how* men act and are acted upon, the ways in which they do and suffer, desire and enjoy, see, believe, imagine—in short, processes of *experiencing*" (Dewey [1925] 1981, 18).

Dewey argued that we are the inheritors of seriously mistaken views of mind, thought, and language that are the unfortunate result of fragmenting experience into subjective versus objective elements, passive versus active processes, and mental versus physical components. He was especially disturbed by early empiricist views of experience as built up out of passively received atomistic sensations that must somehow then be synthesized into unified experiences.

In stark contrast to such reductive and atomistic accounts, Dewey argues that the basic unit of experience is an integrated dynamic situation that emerges through the coordination of an active organism and its complex environment. Experience thus has aspects of the organism and characteristics of the environment in dynamic relation. It is only within such a multidimensional purposive whole that we mark distinctions and recognize patterns relative to our purposes, interests, and activities as biological and social creatures. In an early important article, "The Reflex Arc Concept in Psychology" (1896), Dewey challenged the reigning stimulus-response view of experience, according to which a given, passively received, perceptual stimulus gives rise to some action (response), either immediately or via some inner mediating mental ideation. Dewey argues that experience does not come to us as discrete stimuli and responses; rather, it comes to us as unities organized relative to our ongoing engagement with (i.e., action within) our environment. Dewey's point is that "the reflex arc idea, as commonly employed, is defective in that it assumes sensory stimulus and motor response as distinct psychical existences, while in reality they are always inside a co-ordination and have their significance purely from the part played in maintaining or reconstituting the co-ordinations" ([1930] 1988, 99). Dewey's resistance to any account that trades on rigid dualisms, hypostatized functions, or one-dimensional reductive explanations is thus based on his argument that all such accounts falsify our experience.

A Nondualistic, Functional View of Mind

Dewey founds his theory of mind and thought on the assumption that a human being is a living organism, with at least a mostly functioning brain and body, engaged in continuous interaction with various environments, which are at once physical, social, and cultural. Mind has deep biological dimensions, but it is also fundamentally a social phenomenon. The critical challenge for any naturalistic view like Dewey's is to explain mind solely in terms of dimensions of experience, without "the appearance upon the scene of a totally new outside force as a cause of changes that occur" (Dewey [1938] 1991, 31). What are known as "higher" cognitive functions (e.g., conceptualizing, reasoning, language use) must be shown to emerge from "lower" (perceptual, motor, and affective) functions, without relying on nonnatural entities, causes, or principles.

Dewey's naturalism is thus defined by what he calls the "principle of continuity," according to which, "there is no breach of continuity between operations of inquiry and biological operations and physical operations. 'Continuity' . . . means that rational operations *grow out of* organic activities, without being identical with that from which they emerge" ([1938] 1991, 26). In other words, Dewey attempts to explain "mind" and all its operations and activities nondualistically, as grounded in bodily operations of living human creatures, who are themselves the result of prior evolutionary history and who have typically passed through a crucial sequence of developmental stages that have shaped their cognitive capacities and their identity.

In light of the principle of continuity, the old distinction between nonliving things (the physical), living things (the psychophysical), and creatures capable of thinking and communicating (the mental) must be reconfigured in terms of "levels of increasing complexity and intimacy of interactions among natural events" (Dewey [1925] 1981, 200), such that novel biological and cognitive functions emerge at each higher level. The psychophysical is distinguished from the merely physical by the emergence of sentience and self-movement in an organism. The mental emerges in select species through the development of the ability to conceptualize, reason, and communicate symbolically. Mind is thus embodied:

> Since mind cannot evolve except where there is an organized process in which the fulfilments of the past are conserved and employed, it is not surprising that mind when it evolves should be mindful of the past and future, and that it should use the structures which are biological adaptations of organism and environment as its own and its only organs. In ultimate analysis the mystery that mind should use a body, or that body should have a mind, is like the mystery that a man cultivating plants should use the soil; or that the soil which grows plants at all should grow those adapted to its own physico-chemical properties and relations. (Dewey [1925] 1981, 211)

Dewey coined the term "body-mind" ([1925] 1981, 217) to avoid the dualism inherent in speaking of body *and* mind. The terms *body* and *mind* are thus merely convenient abstractions from our primary experience, which is an ongoing process of feeling-saturated awareness and thinking that has physical, emotional, intellectual, social, and cultural dimensions inextricably woven together. He summarizes: "Body-mind simply designates what actually takes place when a living body is implicated in situations of discourse, communication, and participation. In the hyphenated phrase body-mind, 'body' designates the continued and conserved, the registered and cumulative operation of factors continuous with the rest of nature, inanimate as well as animate; while 'mind' designates the characters and consequences which are differential, indicative of features which emerge when 'body' is engaged in a wider, more complex and interdependent situation" (Dewey [1925] 1981, 217).

In other words, we can appropriately speak of mind whenever our engagement with our environment involves capacities for recognizing patterns, marking distinctions, and coordinating behaviors by means of symbolic interactions. Mind is an evolutionary accomplishment that cannot exist without a body in continual interaction with its world. Thus, for Dewey, mind is not an innate capacity or a distinct metaphysical entity or substance. Rather, mind emerges out of the strivings of certain highly developed organisms who have learned to inquire, communicate, and coordinate their activities through the use of symbols. Mind is the primary vehicle by which creatures like us are able to sustain our existence, pursue our various conceptions of well-being, share mean-ing, and engage in the distinctive forms of inquiry that mark our species. Dewey attributes mind only to humans, because he thinks that they alone are capable of the complex symbolic interaction and communica-tion that he regards as necessary for the mental in its fullest sense. How-ever, notwithstanding Dewey's anthropocentrism, most ethologists today would surely grant some form of mind at least to certain higher primates who appear to communicate symbolically and to coordinate their behaviors in acts of problem solving and social intercourse.

Dewey's nondualist functional approach is quite compatible with mainstream views in cognitive neuroscience today, according to which *organism* and *environment* are correlative terms, definable only in relation to their continuous interaction. There is no mind without a functioning body and brain, nor a functioning brain without cognitive activity en-gaging the world. Cognitive neuroscientist Antonio Damasio captures these organism-environment and mind-body couplings in a way that Dewey would embrace: "(1) The human brain and the rest of the body constitute an indissociable organism, integrated by means of mutually interactive biochemical and neural regulatory circuits (including endo-crine, immune, and autonomic neural components); (2) The organism interacts with the environment as an ensemble: the interaction is neither of the body alone nor of the brain alone; (3) The physiological opera-tions that we call mind are derived from the structural and functional ensemble rather than from the brain alone: mental phenomena can be fully understood only in the context of an organism's interacting in an environment" (1994, xvii).

Given his insistence on the multidimensionality and nonduality of experience, the only thing Dewey might add to this quotation is per-haps that not only are brain and body an indissociable organism, but so also body and environment constitute an indissociable organic whole. In *Experience and Nature*, Dewey emphasizes all this complex interconnect-edness in his provocative claim—a claim that would be completely at home in contemporary cognitive neuroscience—that "to see the organ-ism *in* nature, the nervous system in the organism, the brain in the ner-vous system, the cortex in the brain is the answer to the problems which haunt philosophy" ([1925] 1981, 224). However, Dewey understandably devoted more attention to the social and cultural dimensions of mind than one might expect from a neuroscientist like Damasio. For Dewey, mind emerges when symbolic interaction and sharing of meanings be-comes possible for a group of creatures. Mind represents the horizon of potentially shareable meanings available to certain highly complex organisms, whereas individual consciousness is a particular organism's actual awareness of specific meanings: "Mind denotes the whole system of meanings as they are embodied in the workings of organic life; consciousness in a being with language denotes awareness or perception of meaning; it is the perception of actual events, whether past, contemporary or future, *in* their meanings, the having of actual ideas. . . . Mind is contextual and persistent; consciousness is focal and transitive. Mind is, so to speak, structural, substantial; a constant background and foreground; perceptive consciousness is process, a series of heres and nows" (ibid., 230). This passage construes mind as an intersubjective network of meaning, and consciousness as an ongoing process by which we can be aware of meanings and the emergence of new meaning. However, I do not think it precludes our speaking, in a derivative fashion, of an individual organism (for example, a person) having a "mind." Yet, no individual alone could have a mind unless there had been other conspecific social animals to establish a shared system of meaning and to coordinate their behavior via that system. Dewey would say that certain animals develop what we call "mind" only when they acquire a specific set of interacting functional capacities within a communal context in a society. "As life is a character of events in a peculiar condition of organization, and 'feeling' is a quality of life-forms marked by complexly mobile and discriminating responses, so 'mind' is an added property assumed by a feeling creature, when it reaches that organized interaction with other living creatures which is language, communication" (ibid., 198). To say that I have a "mind" is to say that I am an organism whose potential for very complex interactions has risen to the level where I can communicate meanings with other creatures (who have "minds"); can engage in various modes of inquiry, reasoning, and creativity; and can coordinate activities with others using symbols that have shared meaning for us.

However phenomenologically rich this description of mind might be, it still leaves us with the critical problem of explaining how processes that we call "thinking" can emerge for certain types of animate creatures, yet without any breach of continuity with their basic biological functions.

Thought as Embodied Cognition

If there is no pure soul or transcendent ego to serve as the locus of thinking, then where does it come from? Once again, Dewey's answer is *experience*. All thinking arises from bodily processes of organism-environment transaction, and it takes whatever value it has from its ability to enrich and transform that experience. In his *Logic: The Theory of Inquiry* (1938), Dewey famously argues that our views of thinking and logic have been mesmerized and held captive by disembodied, ahistorical, and overly intellectualized theories of cognition. We tend to fixate on certain concepts, logical principles, and methods of thinking as though they constitute eternal, pure, universal structures of an allegedly transcendent reason. This kind of selective abstraction reinforces the illusion of a pure seat of thought in something variously called "mind," "reason," or "pure ego." Our ability to think then becomes an utterly inexplicable mystery, on a par with the alleged mystery of how mind can affect body. On this view, thought and its supposedly universal logical forms appear to be absolute givens that drop down from above into certain species of bodily creatures, as though their embodiment had no role in shaping their conceptualization and reasoning.

In sharp contrast with this disembodied view, Dewey honors his principle of continuity by arguing that thinking is a naturally evolving process of experience that occurs only for certain complex animals, under certain very specific bodily conditions. Thinking operates through the recruitment of sensory-motor and other bodily processes. Following William James and C. S. Peirce, Dewey crafts a nondualistic, body-based theory of human cognition, a view grounded in the brain science and psychology of his day, but also remarkably consonant with so-called "embodied cognition" views in contemporary cognitive neuroscience, as summarized by Don Tucker:

> Complex psychological functions must be understood to arise from bodily control networks. There is no other source for them. This is an exquisite parsimony of facts.
>
> There are no brain parts for abstract faculties of the mind—faculties like volition or insight or even conceptualization—that are separate from the brain parts that evolved to mediate between visceral and somatic processes. (2007, 202)

Dewey argues that we must stop conceiving of thinking as a disembodied, transcendent activity and instead see it only as one of several very remarkable processes of embodied experience. The experiential prompt for human thinking is our human need for inquiry to help us resolve problematic situations. Indeed, Dewey even suggests that "the

word 'thought' . . . is a synonym of 'inquiry' and its meaning is determined by what we find out about inquiry" ([1938] 1991, 29). Dewey
characterizes the experiential process of inquiry as having three phases.
In the first phase, an organism (here, a live human creature) is con-
fronted with an indeterminate, problematic situation that upsets his or
her normal habits of interaction. For example, yesterday you were feeling just fine, going about your mundane business of living, with little
or no thought—or even consciousness—of what you were doing. Your
routine habits carried you unreflectively through your day. However,
today you feel nauseous, your joints ache, and you have the chills. Your
situation is disrupted, and its entire quality has changed in a distressing
way. Your normal habits of living do not suffice to carry experience forward to some happy issue.

This prompts the second phase, in which you begin to wonder what
is wrong and how you might fix it. You want to feel better. Inquiry has
commenced. You start to discriminate aspects of your experience to
see what they mean and how you can transform them for the better.
For example, you notice what is most dominantly characteristic of your
situation—chills, fever, upset stomach, and headache. You project various hypotheses about what this particular set of symptoms might indicate. That is, you engage in a *thought* process that employs distinctions
(concepts) and looks for their implications. You make some preliminary
judgments based on your past experience. Could this be the flu? Or
maybe food poisoning? Perhaps it is a reaction to the new antibiotic you
just started taking for a chronic infection? You consult with others. You
make judgments about what to expect if one hypothesis or another is
the correct one. In short, you inquire. You speculate on how you might
cure yourself.

Already—and this is a third stage—you are beginning to take action
(by thinking and inquiring) to try to change the quality of your experience for what you perceive to be the better. Thinking itself is action, for
it transforms experience as it develops. Successful thinking is thus part
of an arc of experience that starts with your problematic situation and
eventually, if thought is effective, returns to transform your situation.
As such, thinking is value laden and purposive, insofar as it is directed
toward resolving some problem, reestablishing a flow of experience, or
discovering new ways of organizing experience that lead to growth and
enhanced meaning.

Because Dewey rejects mind/body dualism, he regards the activity of
thinking as just as much a matter of habits as any other form of human

bodily activity. Just as when a potter employs motor skills to mold clay by means of the manual eye-hand habits she has painstakingly developed, so also the ways we think are the present result of developed and still-developing habits for working through experience. Dewey boldly affirms that "ideas, thoughts of ends, are not spontaneously generated. There is no immaculate conception of meanings or purposes. Reason pure of all influence from prior habit is a fiction" ([1922] 1988, 25). The character of our thought is thus the present result of the quality of the intellectual habits we have acquired. Those habits are realized in our bodies and brains, in relation to our surroundings. They are not lodged in some mental substance or transcendent, disembodied ego.

Contemporary neuroscience would no doubt translate Dewey's talk of habits of thought into the language of neural connectivity and synaptic weights. Having an "idea" or "concept" is correlated with specific patterns of neural activation in the brain (in response to interaction with one's environment), all of which have affective dimensions. An "inference" is construed as our tendency to move from one set of neural activations to another set, as a result of weighted connections among those functional neural assemblies. Neither in Dewey's account nor in recent cognitive science is there any notion of a disembodied process, carried out in some inner theater of consciousness, in which an allegedly non-material mind or ego inspects and manipulates disembodied ideas. The ways we think are just as much bodily habits as the ways we walk, sing, or throw a ball. Consequently, Dewey's account of thinking situates thought not in "the mind," but in the world, as an ongoing process of habitual ways of engaging experience, and sometimes of reshaping it.

The previous example of trying to figure out why you feel ill is but one instance of human thinking, but it represents in its structure the most salient aspects of all thinking—from mundane practical problem solving to scientific or mathematical or logical theorizing to moral reflection, political deliberation, or artistic creativity. All thinking begins within an integrated, embodied, felt situation. Dewey notoriously claims that the start of every thought is a felt experience of a pervasive unifying quality of the entire situation that you inhabit at a given moment. Thought arises out of this qualitative experience, as we begin to discriminate objects, notice their properties, and trace out relations and connections among them. The ways we notice patterns and discriminate objects will be the result of the habits of perception, thought, and action that we have acquired through our previous experience, given our bodily and neural makeup.

Dewey's idea of a pervasive unifying quality is the key to his view of thinking, but it is perhaps the most problematic and neglected part of his theory. What makes Dewey's idea seem so strange to us today is our engrained habit of conceiving the world as populated by discrete objects that possess discrete properties, toward which we direct our thinking. Dewey doesn't deny that we experience objects; but he insists that beneath and before any experience of objects and qualities, there is always one's encounter with the whole situation, which is uniquely characterized by its pervasive distinguishing quality. In *Art As Experience* (1934), Dewey explains this key idea: "An experience has a unity that gives it its name, *that* meal, that storm, that rupture of a friendship. The existence of this unity is constituted by a single *quality* that pervades the entire experience in spite of the variation of its constituent parts. This unity is neither emotional, practical, nor intellectual, for these terms name distinctions that reflection can make within it" ([1934] 1987, 37).

Imagine that you have just entered a colleague's office. There is an all-encompassing way it feels to be in that place, and the unifying quality of that place is clearly different from your own office. Your qualitatively unified experience is a blend of perceptual, emotional, practical, and conceptual dimensions intertwined in *that* particular place. Granted, as soon as you enter the office, you have already begun to recognize objects, mark patterns, and focus on various parts of the entire setting, but Dewey argues that all this discriminating activity takes place within a unified experienced background out of which objects, people, and events emerge.

Dewey often turned to art as a way of explaining the primacy of this unifying quality that defines a given situation. Consider the experience of walking into a large room of an art museum and having your attention fall immediately on a large painting on the far opposite wall. Although you may have never seen this particular painting before, you can discern that it is a Picasso. Nobody will mistake that pervasive quality by which you identified the Picasso for what you encounter in the next room in a Matisse paper cutout or in a sunset by Emil Nolde. We cannot describe that unifying quality, because in attempting to do so we begin to identify particular lines, colors, shapes, and qualities that are already abstractions from the organic reality of the work. All thought, says Dewey, emerges within some such global grasp of a situation. It is just that we are so busy marking distinctions that we are seldom aware that our first encounter—our primary experience, as it were—was fundamentally qualitative and felt.

In line with contemporary neuroscience today, Dewey argues that what we experience as objects are actually selections of elements out of the ongoing flow of our experience, which is saturated with feeling, meaning, and interest. Dewey explains that an "object" is "some element in the complex whole that is defined in abstraction from the whole of which it is a distinction. The special point made is that the selective determination and relation of objects in thought is controlled by reference to a situation—to that which is constituted by a pervasive and internally integrating quality" ([1930] 1988, 246). The qualitative situation is primary and objects emerge within it, relative to perceiving, acting agents who have values and purposes. In other words, we do not start with properties or objects and then combine them into experiences; rather, we start with integrated scenes within which we then discriminate objects, discern properties, and explore relations. Objects and their qualities—along with our ability to think about them—emerge for us via our ability to orient ourselves within particular situations, given our perceptual and motor capacities, our past experience, our interests, and our values.

It is no accident that Dewey prefers to cite artworks as exemplary of pervasive qualities, for Dewey believed that in art we find human meaning-making in its most intensified and eminent form. Not surprisingly, he held that thinking in art is just as rigorous as thinking in any other discipline, such as science, mathematics, or philosophy. Most people will readily acknowledge that artworks are characterized by unifying qualities, but they fail to recognize that this is true for *all* types of experience, including *all* types of thinking. In Dewey's words: "All thought in every subject begins with just such an unanalyzed whole. When the subject-matter is reasonably familiar, relevant distinctions speedily offer themselves, and sheer qualitativeness may not remain long enough to be readily recalled" ([1934] 1987, 249).

There is empirical evidence from brain science suggesting that Dewey was correctly describing the process of a developing thought, which moves from the felt pervasive quality to higher-level conceptual discrimination and inference. Tucker (2007) describes the core-shell architecture of the brain (in addition to the front/back and left/right structures) that is principally responsible for our global grasp of any situation.[1] To vastly oversimplify, our brain developed through evolution by adding new structures and layers on top of more primitive parts shared with some of our animal ancestors. It also recruits (or exapts) previously evolved structures to perform so-called "higher-level" cognitive operations. The present-day result is a brain with core limbic structures (mostly responsible for body monitoring, motivation, emotions, and feelings) that are connected to the shell of "higher" neocortical layers that have more differentiated functions, such as perception, body movement, action planning, and reasoning. One striking feature of this core-shell organization is that structures in the core regions are massively interconnected and involve limbic processes responsible for emotions and feelings, whereas structures in the shell are more sparsely interconnected and are less directly tied to affect centers. An important consequence of this neural architecture is that there is more functional differentiation and more modularity of brain areas in the cortical shell than in the limbic core. Tucker summarizes:

> First, *connections stay at their own level*. With the exception of "adjacent" connections (paralimbic connects to higher-order association, higher association connects to primary association, etc.), connections from one level go primarily to other brain areas of that same level. . . .
>
> Second, *the greatest density of connectivity within a level is found at the limbic core*. There is then a progressive decrease in connectivity as you go out toward the primary sensory and motor modules. . . . In fact, the primary sensory and motor cortices can be accurately described as "modules" because each is an isolated island, connected with the diencephalic thalamus but with no other cortical areas except the adjacent unimodal association cortex of that sensory modality or motor area.
>
> The exception is that the primary motor cortex does have point-to-point connections with the primary somatosensory cortex. (2007, 80–83)

The structures and functions Tucker is describing here would make sense of Dewey's claim that our experience always begins with a pervasive unifying quality of a whole situation, within which we then discriminate objects by their properties and their relations to one another. The limbic core, with is dense interconnections and emotional valences, would present us with a holistic, feeling-rich, emotionally nuanced grasp of a situation. The more modular and highly differentiated sensory and motor regions of the shell (cortical) structure would permit the discrimination and differentiation that we call conceptualization. Tucker explains: "The meaning, or semantic function, of a network may be allowed greater complexity as its architecture becomes more differentiated" (ibid., 102). In Dewey's terms, the meaning of a situation grows as we mark more differences, similarities, changes, and relations; that is, as we are able to make finer discriminations within the ongoing flow of experience.

Cognitive processing does not occur merely in a linear direction from core to shell structures, however. There are "reentrant connections" (Edelman and Tononi 2000), so that what occurs at "higher," or more differentiated, levels can influence what happens in the limbic areas, which then affect shell regions, in a never-ending dance of self-modulating experience. But the core-to-shell movement of cognition helps explain why and how there can be pervasive felt qualities that then issue in acts of differentiation and conceptualization. Tucker summarizes the structural basis for this growing arc of experience that Dewey described as the movement from a holistic pervasive qualitative situation to conceptual meaning:

> At the core must be the most integrative representations, formed through the fusion of many elements through the dense web of interconnection. This fusion of highly processed sensory and motor information . . . together with direct motivational influences from the hypothalamus, would create a *syncretic* form of experience. Meaning is rich, deep, with elements fused in a holistic matrix of information, a matrix charged with visceral significance. Emanating outward—from this core neuropsychological lattice— are the progressive articulations of neocortical networks. Finally, at the shell, we find the most differentiated networks. . . . The most differentiated networks of the hierarchy are the most constrained by the sensory data, forming close matches with the environmental information that is in turn mirrored by the sense receptors. (2007, 179–80)

Conceptual meaning arises from our visceral, purposive engagement with our world. As Gallese and Lakoff (2005) show, our ability to formulate and reason with both concrete and abstract concepts recruits structures of sensory-motor processing and operates within an emotionally charged motivational framework that evolved to help us function successfully within our complex environments.

Embodied Meaning and Language

Dewey's notion of *meaning* is notoriously obscure, but throughout all the many definitions of the term in various parts of his writings, certain characteristic elements stand out. A word or symbol has meaning to the extent that, within a certain community of people, that symbol points beyond itself to past, present, or future possible experiences that can be had: "Meanings are rules for using and interpreting things; interpretation being always an imputation of potentiality for some consequence" (Dewey [1925] 1981, 147). Dewey anticipates the deepest insights of what later came to be known as speech-act theory when he insists that speaking a language is a matter of coordinated social action: "The heart of language is not 'expression' of something antecedent, much less expression of antecedent thought. It is communication; the establishment of cooperation in an activity in which there are partners, and in which the activity of each is modified and regulated by partnership" (ibid., 141). We use symbols that have acquired meaning through "conjoint community of functional use" (Dewey [1938] 1991, 52) to inform, question, beg, help, plan, joke, flirt, and a host of other forms of human interaction.

Dewey also anticipates some of the most significant empirical findings of recent cognitive science research on the bodily grounding of meaning (Patricia Churchland 1986; Varela, Thompson, and Rosch 1991; Lakoff and Johnson 1999; Gibbs 2006). We have seen that in Dewey's theory of mind and thought, there is no place for ideas as quasi-entities floating around in some disembodied mental space, subject to manipulation by an allegedly pure ego. On the contrary, meaning has to come from experience, and experience is at once irreducibly bodily, biological, and cultural. From an evolutionary and developmental perspective, our higher cognitive functions—including language use and abstract thinking—appropriate structures of our bodily, biological engagements with our environment. Dewey observes that

> Just as when men start to talk they must use sounds and gestures antecedent to speech, . . . so when men begin to observe and think they must use the nervous system and other organic structures which existed independently and antecedently. That the use reshapes the prior materials so as to adapt them more efficiently and freely to the uses to which they are put, . . . is an expression of the common fact that anything changes according to the interacting field it enters. . . . In a similar fashion, unless "mind" was, in its existential occurrence, an organization *of* physiological or vital affairs and unless its functions develop out of the patterns of organic behavior, it would have no pertinency to nature. ([1925] 1981, 217–18)

What Dewey hinted at some eighty years ago has today become a commonplace in cognitive neuroscience. What are known as "higher" cognitive functions (e.g., abstract conceptualization and reasoning) appropriate the embodied meaning and the cognitive structures and operations (e.g., making inferences) of our sensory-motor processes:

> The brain evolved to regulate the motivational control of actions, carried out by the motor system, guided by sensory evaluation of ongoing environmental events. There are no "faculties"—of memory, conscious perception, or music appreciation—that float in the mental ether, separate from the bodily functions. If we accept that the mind comes from the brain, then our behavior and experience must be understood to be elaborations of primordial systems for perceiving, evaluating, and acting. When we study the brain to look for the networks controlling cognition, we find that all of the networks that have been implicated in cognition are linked in one way or the other to sensory systems, to motor systems, or to motivational systems. There are no brain parts for disembodied cognition. (Tucker 2007, 59)

Tucker's claim that "mind comes from the brain" does not reduce the mind to the brain. It only claims that mental operations must be correlated with various processes in the brain and central nervous system, including all the bodily centers responsible for perception, motivation, feeling, emotion, and action. Moreover, the neural processes that underlie our cognitive functions occur only through bodily interaction with our environments—environments with tightly interwoven physical, social, and cultural dimensions.

In Dewey's theory of mind, language permits us to mark distinctions and to stabilize the meaning that makes mind and abstract thought possible. This view requires the broadest conception of *language* as involving all forms of symbolic human interaction, and not just words alone: "Language is taken in its widest sense, a sense wider than oral and written speech. It includes the latter. But it includes also not only gesture but rites, ceremonies, monuments and the products of industrial and fine arts" (Dewey [1925] 1981, 51). The possession of language allows humans to mark crucial distinctions in their experience, to refer to past and future things and events (things that are not now present to us), and especially to formulate abstractions as means of solving problems and coordinating actions. A natural language, for Dewey, would thus be a repository of symbols for all the distinctions and demarcations of aspects of experience that a culture has found it significant to identify and remember over its long history.

The acquisition of language is such a monumental achievement, according to Dewey, because it makes possible our use of objects and events as *signs*, which can have symbolic and representational value. Felt qualities of a situation have a certain unreflective meaning to us (insofar as they point toward other past, present, or future possible experiences), but language permits us to become reflectively aware of meaning and to organize our experience in terms of that meaning:

> Where communication exists, things in acquiring meaning, thereby acquire representatives, surrogates, signs and implicates, which are infinitely more amenable to management, more permanent and more accommodating, than events in their first estate.
>
> By this fashion, qualitative immediacies cease to be dumbly rapturous. . . . They become capable of survey, contemplation, and ideal or logical elaboration; when something can be said of qualities they are purveyors of instruction. (Dewey [1925] 1981, 133–34)

In light of Dewey's principle of continuity, then, the central problem for a naturalistic theory of language is to explain the syntax, semantics, and pragmatics of natural languages and symbol systems, but without employing any notion of disembodied mind, conceptualization, or reasoning. Dewey does no more than sketch the broad outlines of such a theory. Key to his view is the idea that meanings of abstract terms must somehow be based on sensory-motor processes of cognition. Structures of perception and action must be appropriated for higher-level cognition and abstract thinking.

Over the past three decades, a new field—known as cognitive linguistics—has developed, which attempts to explain the phenomena of natural languages as products of cognitive mechanisms that have their origins in perception, object manipulation, and bodily motion (Lakoff 1987; Langacker 1987–91; Talmy 2000; Feldman 2006). Although not directly influenced by Dewey, cognitive linguistics argues that our most impressive feats of abstract conceptualization and reasoning operate through the recruitment of more garden-variety cognitive processes in sensory-motor parts of the brain. The basic form of explanation is that meaning is grounded in our sensory-motor and affective experience and that these embodied meanings are then extended—via imaginative mechanisms such as images, schemas, conceptual metaphors, metonymy, radial categories, and various forms of conceptual blending—to shape abstract thinking. For example, the conceptual metaphor KNOWING IS SEEING is widespread across cultures because it is based on the experiential correlation (and neural coactivation) of visual experience with gaining knowledge of a situation.

Joseph Grady (1997) has hypothesized that any normally functioning human being will acquire hundreds of basic, shared "primary" metaphors of this sort, simply because we have the bodies we do and interact with recurrent regular features of our environment. For instance, hundreds of times each day we typically interact with containers (boxes, cups, rooms, our bodies, vehicles) and thereby automatically acquire the spatial logic of containers. If my keys are in my hand, my hand is in my pocket, my pocket is in my pants, and my pants are in my office, then my keys are in my office. This is a corporeal logic that I acquire without conscious reflection, just by interacting repeatedly with my environment (an environment populated by many types of containers that stand in various relations). This "container" logic can then be recruited, via the cross-domain mapping of a primary metaphor (here, the metaphor CATEGORIES ARE CONTAINERS), to structure our understanding of abstract conceptual "containment." Once categories (or concepts) are understood as metaphorical containers, then the logic of physical containment (e.g., If container A is in container B, and container B is within container C, then container A is in container C) carries over to relations of abstract concepts (e.g., All As are Bs; all Bs are Cs; therefore, all As are Cs).

Primary metaphors can be blended and extended to create more elaborate conceptual metaphors for all our abstract concepts, such as causation, will, justice, mind, knowledge, and love. Lakoff and I (1999) have argued that entire philosophies and scientific theories are based on elaborate developments of systematic conceptual metaphors that are shared by members of a particular culture. Our most important abstract concepts, which are absolutely crucial for our reflective thinking, are typically defined by multiple inconsistent metaphors, each of which has some source domain tied to concrete bodily experiences.

Although Dewey does not offer an explicit account of conceptual metaphor as lying in the heart of human thought and language, there are places where he appears to have glimpsed just such imaginative processes as crucial to abstract thought: "Every thought and meaning has its substratum in some organic act of absorption or elimination of seeking, or turning away from, of destroying or caring for, of signaling or responding. It roots in some definite act of biological behavior; our physical names for mental acts like seeing, grasping, searching, affirming, acquiescing, spurning, comprehending, affection, emotion are not just 'metaphors'" ([1925] 1981, 221). Were Dewey alive today, he would no doubt take an interest in the large number of cross-cultural analyses of body-based metaphors by which we frame our conceptions of mind, mental operations, and knowledge. Like Nietzsche, Dewey seems to have understood that culturally shared conceptual metaphors—of which we are hardly ever conscious—constitute the deepest habits of our conceptualization and reasoning. As a result, our scientific theories and philosophies are vast systematic developments of underlying metaphors. Such metaphors are not errors or falsifications of a pre-given reality, but are instead the very means by which we can recruit the corporeal logic of our bodies for the purpose of abstract reasoning. Formal logic and mathematics—the allegedly most pure and universal forms of thought—are actually based on metaphoric elaborations of patterns of inquiry that employ the experiential logic of our sensory-motor experience. Lakoff and Núñez (2000), for example, have shown how the spatial logic of physical containers underlies Boolean algebra, and they have extended this form of metaphor analysis into aspects of higher mathematics.

Because he recognized the metaphorical character of our abstract concepts, Dewey was highly critical of our human tendency to hypostatize concepts and meanings, as though they were eternal, fixed, disembodied essences. Dewey cites the example of Platonism in mathematics, where patterns found to be useful for inquiry are elevated to the mysterious status of absolute entities and relations: "Consider the interpretations that have been based upon such essences as four, plus, the square root of minus one. These are at once so manipulable and so fertile in consequences when conjoined with others that thinkers who are primarily interested in their performances treat them not as significant terms of discourse, but as an order of entities independent of human invention and use" ([1925] 1981, 153). Our mostly unreflective postulating of abstract entities, coupled with our desire for fixity and certainty in the face of our finite, contingent existence, leads us to hypostatize meanings, concepts, and thought processes as though they were eternal, disembodied, and pure of carnal entanglements. Dewey reminds us of the bodily roots of meaning, thought, and language, for he sees that only in this way could we explain where meaning comes from and how language can be about our world.

Language is thus a complex, systematic mode of interaction among certain types of creatures, by means of which they use symbols to coordinate their actions, establish relationships, and understand and transform their world. Dewey cannot clearly separate out mind, thought, and language, because mind signifies a reservoir of shared meaning and communication, meaning in its eminent sense requires language, language permits symbolization and abstraction, and thought is a process of inquiry that uses symbols that have meaning for the inquirers.

Dewey's Naturalism and Cognitive Science

Dewey's naturalism represents his attempt to avoid what he considered the most catastrophic errors of Western philosophy—errors caused by the model of mind as a disembodied theater of consciousness in which abstract entities (ideas) are examined and manipulated (by a pure ego) according to absolute logical rules to secure epistemic certainty and unchanging truth. What is missing in this model is the inescapable temporal and bodily character of all experience and thought. Thinking, for Dewey, is a *process* that emerges from our bodily engagement with our surroundings. Dewey learned from the dominant behaviorist psychology of his day to emphasize the importance of action and the transformation of the world, rather than internal "mental" states and operations. At the same time, however, he is no mere behaviorist, because he appreciates the critical role of the felt unifying qualities of situations and the role of feelings and emotions in meaning and thought.

It is such tendencies in Dewey's thinking that align him with so much cognitive science in the twenty-first century. The relevant cognitive science is not the disembodied sort popular during the first two-thirds of the twentieth century, which grew out of computer science, artificial intelligence, and analytic philosophy of mind and language (Varela, Thompson, and Rosch 1991; Horst 2016). Indeed, Dewey's nondualistic, nonreductive, and process-oriented account of cognition provides a critique of disembodied, functionalist theories that characterize the first-generation orientation. Dewey would have been much more at home with "second-generation" (embodied) cognitive science, which requires a radical rethinking of some of our most enduring conceptions about human thinking and communication (Lakoff and Johnson 1999). Virtually every key term (e.g., *reason, mind, self, meaning, thought, logic, knowledge, will, value*) has to be reconceived from the perspective of embodied cognition. There can be no assumption of disembodied entities, capacities, or processes. Concepts are not quasi-entities but rather "takings" from the flow of experience—a flow that is not merely mental or merely physical but both at once. There can be no single unified center of consciousness that controls perceiving, thinking, and willing. Neuroscience reveals no such center, but instead finds massive parallel processes loosely coordinated within a certain temporal window that is experienced by us as a moment of experience (Edelman and Tononi 2000; Damasio 1999, 2010).

In short, pragmatism's greatest contribution to cognitive science is to construct the appropriate general philosophical context for understanding the empirical results about mind, consciousness, meaning, thought, and values. Second, pragmatism can identify and criticize limiting or mistaken methodological assumptions that define the various sciences of mind. Finally, beyond sketching the broadest possible framework for studying mind and language, pragmatism can show us how to interpret the relevant implications of cognitive science for our everyday lives.

For example, if Dewey were alive today, one can imagine him challenging reductionist tendencies in scientific explanations, wherever he might discern them. The complexity of brain functioning understandably leads some researchers to isolate functions and then look for neural correlates for them. However unavoidable such decontextualizing moves might be in actual research, Dewey would have rightly insisted on always remembering that mind, thought, and language are grandly multidimensional, requiring not just a functioning brain, but also a functioning body it is serving, which in turn is continually interacting with complex environments that have physical, social, and cultural dimensions. Fortunately, reductionism need not be an intrinsic part of any of the cognitive sciences, which can recognize multiple irreducible levels of explanation (Bechtel 2008). This is why Dewey's theory of mind, thought, and language can be seen as loosely compatible with contemporary cognitive science of the embodied mind. However, because we are just beginning to glimpse what the discoveries of the cognitive sciences mean for our lives, pragmatism's work has only begun.

CHAPTER 2

Cowboy Bill Rides Herd on the Range of Consciousness

A mere three decades ago, no self-respecting analytic philosopher would be caught dead espousing a theory of consciousness. It just wasn't done. Talk of some mysterious nonmaterial thing called "consciousness" would cause hard-minded philosophers to cover their mouths and noses with a hankie and turn away, as though they feared contamination from meta-physical impulses and phenomenological extravaganzas of idle specu-lation. While it was all right, and even noble, to *be* conscious, one cer-tainly was not supposed to have a metaphysical theory of what made it possible to be conscious.

All that seems to have changed in a few short years. Today, you can become a philosophical celebrity just by throwing around a little cog-nitive neuroscience, talking about the "hard" problem of consciousness, and wrapping the whole subject in mystery. How are we to explain this fairly sudden and radical transition in our thinking about consciousness? What propelled us from the philosophical milieu of the 1950s, '60s, and '70s, with its characteristic avoidance of the whole idea of conscious-ness, to our current fascination with the subject? The answer seems pretty clear. It has been the rise of cognitive neuroscience. The scientific study of cognition has, once again, made it respectable for hard-minded philosophers to talk of consciousness, just so long as they can back up their theoretical speculations with at least some reference to empirical evidence of some sort.

Here's where Cowboy Bill (Willy James, that is) comes riding into view. He's one of the James boys, although his brother, Henry, wasn't much of a cowboy. A century ago he gave us what may still be the best account of consciousness ever articulated, and he based it on extensive work in biology, neuroscience, and psychology. James did this, and he did something more—something that might still serve us today as a theoretical model for much contemporary cognitive neuroscience. What he did was to give a remarkable phenomenological analysis of aspects of conscious experience, which he tied to what was known at that time about the biological basis of mind, thought, and language.

Whenever I read James on mind, I get this "Aha!" kind of feeling—a sense that what he is saying is right, or could be made right with just a little tweaking. You could back up almost everything he said on the subject with evidence from recent cognitive science, just like he would have done were he alive today. Let's see how this might work, starting first with James's account, and then measuring it against the work of Antonio Damasio, who has provided one of the more comprehensive contemporary treatments of consciousness from the perspective of cognitive neuroscience. Damasio stands almost alone when he chides neuroscientists for too quickly dismissing James and failing to appreciate his profound insights into the nature of emotions and consciousness (Damasio 1994, 1999, 2003, 2010).

The first important thing Cowboy Bill tells us is that we humans are inescapably embodied creatures. There is no disembodied "I"—no transcendent ego—that serves as the site of all my experiences and thoughts. There is no disembodied *me* that thinks my thoughts, feels my feelings, and performs my actions. There is only the continuous flow of thought, experience, and feeling all tied up together, but without any little transcendent self to do the tying up. Cowboy Bill describes our passing thoughts as cattle grazing on the vast range of potential consciousness: "And by a natural consequence, we shall assimilate them [these thoughts] to each other and to the warm and intimate self we now feel within us as we think, and separate them as a collection from whatever selves have not this mark, much as out of a herd of cattle let loose for the winter on some wide western prairie the owner picks out and sorts together when the time for the round-up comes in the spring, all the beasts on which he finds his own particular brand" (James [1890] 1950, 1:333–34). So, some of Wild Bill's thoughts have the "Lazy WJ" brand on them, which lets him identify those roaming thoughts as "his" and nobody else's. This brand isn't some objectively perceivable mark on the publicly observable roaming-mental-state cattle of the mind. No. It is the *felt sense* of "warmth and intimacy" that accompanies one par-

ticular set of experiences and thoughts, and not others. The cattle of
thought are bound together because they resemble one another and because they are somehow continuous with one another, but these two
properties are a consequence of the fact that we first *feel* our thoughts as
ours. What Cowboy Bill says about this binding process merits an extended quotation:

> For, whatever the thought we are criticising may think about its present
> self, that self comes to its acquaintance, or is actually felt, with warmth and
> intimacy. Of course this is the case with the *bodily* part of it; we feel the
> whole cubic mass of our body all the while, it gives us an unceasing sense
> of personal existence. Equally do we feel the inner "nucleus of the spiritual
> self," either in the shape of yon faint physiological adjustments, or (adopt-
> ing the universal psychological belief), in that of the pure activity of our
> thought taking place as such. Our remoter spiritual, material, and social
> selves, so far as they are realized, come also with a glow and a warmth; for
> the thought of them infallibly brings some degree of organic emotion in
> the shape of quickened heart-beats, oppressed breathing, or some other
> alteration . . . in the general bodily tone. The character of "warmth," then,
> in the present self, reduces itself to either of two things,—something in the
> feeling which we have of the thought itself, as thinking, or else the feeling
> of the body's actual existence at the moment,—or finally to both. (James
> [1890] 1950, 1:333)

But just one doggone minute here! Do you expect me to believe that
there really is no Cowboy Bill who rounds up his thought-doggies on
the range of consciousness? It's starting to look like there never was any
Cowboy Bill in the first place, nobody who could put his Lazy WJ brand
on his thought-cattle so he could recognize them as *his*, when he makes
his spring round up of the self? What's to keep some skunk of a rustler
from sneaking on in during the night and leading off those little doggies, claiming that they're *his*? If those doggies aren't *mine* just because
they graze together (continuity) or just because they look alike (resem-
blance), then why are they mine, anyway?

Now, I think that the answer is: these little thought-doggies are *mine*
just insofar as they are grazing the range of consciousness that is my embodied self. Thus, in one great sweeping hypothetical stroke, Cowboy
Bill points out that "*it would follow that our entire feeling of spiritual activity,
or what commonly passes by that name, is really a feeling of bodily activities whose
exact nature is by most men overlooked.*" (James [1890] 1950, 1:301–2, italics in

the original). Here we confront James's infamous claim that each present thought only incorporates within itself our prior thoughts, just insofar as we feel the warmth and animation that marks them as "mine." Each present thought has to take up into self only those prior thoughts and experiences that it *feels* connected to—that is, that it experiences with warmth and intimacy.

If I think of each of my present thoughts as a distinct moment of consciousness, then, to pose Hume's problem all over again, what would bind them all together? Cowboy Bill insists that what binds my thoughts together is only the felt sense of connection, when a present thought warmly recognizes a preceding thought: "A uniform feeling of 'warmth,' of bodily existence (or an equally uniform feeling of pure psychic energy?) pervades them [our past and present selves] all; and this is what gives them a *generic* unity, and makes them the same in *kind*" (James [1890] 1950, 1:335). Well, pardner, are you beginnin' to think that Cowboy Bill's been alone too long on the range of consciousness? Even on a charitable interpretation, it looks like maybe he's been eatin' too many beans and drinkin' bad whiskey. Sometimes it looks like all he's sayin' is that you sure as heck know your own doggies when ya see 'em (or maybe smell 'em).

Since I was brought up in Kansas, about fifty miles from where "Home on the Range" was written, and since I've subsequently moved to the Wild West out beyond the Rocky Mountains, I've become somewhat partial to Cowboy Bill's open-range metaphors for mind. I want to leap ahead a century or so in order to compare Cowboy Bill's view of consciousness, self, and thought with some more recent reports of scouting parties on the contemporary range of consciousness. The scouting party I'm talking about is present-day cognitive science.

The cowpoke I want to focus on most is someone who used to ride herd on the prairies of Iowa but has since journeyed out to the West Coast to make a new homestead. I'm talking about Antonio Damasio, the cognitive neuroscientist who has written so eloquently on the nature of mind, consciousness, thought, and feeling (see Damasio 1994,1999, 2003, 2010). What he tells us is that the best available evidence from neuroscience today reveals that Cowboy Bill was more or less right in many aspects of his view of consciousness and thought. What both these cowpokes tell us is this: the mind is embodied, thought is tied to feeling, and consciousness is a matter of feeling our body states.

The details of this new account form a difficult and incredibly complicated story, one that requires forays into brain anatomy, neuron functioning, neurochemical bases of emotions, brain lesion studies, philosophy, and psychology. However, a grotesquely oversimplified account would go something like this: Damasio identifies two major problems concerning consciousness. The first is to explain how the brain, operating within an embodied organism that is interacting continually with its environment, can have mental images of objects, events, thoughts, feelings, and actions.[1] The second problem is "how, in parallel with engendering mental patterns for an object, the brain also engenders a sense of self in the act of knowing." (Damasio 1999, 9). This sense of a unified self is our sense that our experience and ideas are *ours*, as if we "own" them. Damasio's grand hypothesis is that your sense of self involves the feeling of what is happening to you—the feeling of how "your being is modified by the acts of apprehending something" (ibid., 10).

how feeling feels

Damasio begins his account of consciousness by stressing the crucial fact that we are dynamic organisms defined by boundaries and the maintenance of balanced states within those boundaries. To live, we must continually maintain our internal milieu by monitoring and altering, when necessary, water, salts, gasses, minerals, hormones, nutrients, and so on. Damasio speculates that, whatever other purposes consciousness eventually came to serve for us, it first emerged as our way of preserving a stable internal milieu, in light of changing environmental conditions, and it never ceases to perform that most essential life-sustaining function.

So the question is, how does consciousness operate in the monitoring of our body states? The answer is, by feeling. One of Damasio's pivotal ideas is that emotions are based on neurochemical processes by which the embodied organism monitors changes in its internal situation as a result of its transactions with its surrounding, and is thereby alerted to the need for appropriate responses to changing conditions in the organism-environment interaction. Damasio distinguishes between emotions and feelings. Emotional response patterns occur automatically and mostly unconsciously in response to ever-changing interactions with the environment. He reserves the word *feeling* for those occasions when we become aware of changes in our body state that are part of the emotional response pattern. He explains: "The essential content of feelings is the mapping of a particular body state; the substrate of feelings is the set of neural patterns that map the body state and from which a mental image of the body state can emerge. . . . A feeling of emotion is an idea of the body when it is perturbed by the emoting process" (Damasio 2003, 88). In other words, we often have emotional experiences—in the form of bodily responses to how we are affected by our world—even though we remain blithely unaware of all this ongoing life-monitoring activity. Only on those occasions when we become conscious (i.e., aware) of the ebb and flow of our emotional events do we then "feel" them as ours and experience their distinctive qualities. "Feelings of emotion . . . are composite *perceptions* of what happens in our body and mind when we are emoting" (Damasio 2010, 109). In short, we are affected by objects and events both from within and outside us, we react emotionally to how things are going for us, and we sometimes feel these affections by feeling how we are being affected by these events. In this way, we develop a sense of a particular flow of experience as belonging to us.

On the basis of this account of body-state monitoring via emotions and feelings, Damasio builds a theory of types of consciousness and their relation to three types of self. He begins with the "proto-self," which is "a coherent collection of neural patterns which map, moment by moment, the state of the physical structure of the organism in its many dimensions." (Damasio 1999, 154). There is no consciousness for this proto-self, no consciousness of the body's mapping of its current physical state, even though our very life depends on such activity. We couldn't survive if we had to consciously attend to all this life-sustaining activity. Nor is the proto-self a single substantial unity, either. Rather, "it emerges dynamically and continuously out of multifarious interacting signals that span varied orders of the nervous system." (ibid., 154).

Consciousness first emerges as what Damasio calls a "core consciousness" (with its correlative "core self"), which adds to the proto-self an *awareness* of how we are being affected by aspects of our environment at the present moment in time. Here, too, this is a matter of feeling ourselves being affected by something. What we are feeling in this case are changes in our bodily state in the present moment of experience (as "here and now"), and we are feeling these feelings as ours. In Damasio's words, "Core consciousness occurs when the brain's representation devices generate an imaged, nonverbal account of how the organism's own state is affected by the organism's processing of an object, and when this process enhances the image of the causative object, thus placing it saliently in a spatial and temporal context" (1999, 169). To translate: the core self thus makes use of the proto-self's body-state mapping in order to become aware of how the body is being affected by objects, events, and internal images and occurrences. This "nonverbal account" or "narrative" that we develop is not linguistic. Instead, it involves a mapping in the brain of images, feelings, and emotions. It is the organism's nonlinguistic felt awareness of the "act of representing its own changing state as it goes about representing something else" (ibid., 170). It is the *feeling* of what is happening to us at the present moment, just as Cowboy Bill said a century ago.

However, our experience of the mere present moment is not—except in cases of extreme psychological dysfunction—an isolated event.[2] Successive moments of core consciousness are bound together in what Damasio calls "extended consciousness"; that is, our capacity to connect the present with the remembered past and an anticipated future. Extended consciousness is what makes possible our "autobiographical self," our sense of ourselves as extended continuously over a span of time and thereby living out a narrative drama. Damasio does not pretend to have a fully adequate explanation of extended consciousness, but he makes it quite clear that two basic "tricks," as he calls them, are required to accomplish extended consciousness. The first trick is to build up memories of the felt images of prior experiences of the organism, as they unfolded in its past history. The second trick is what neuroscientists call a "binding problem"—namely, to "hold active, simultaneously and for a substantial amount of time, the many images whose collection defines the autobiographical self and the images which define the object. The reiterated components of the autobiographical self and the object are bathed in the feeling of knowing that arises in core consciousness" (Damasio 1999, 198).

I believe that what Damasio is describing here as "the feeling of what happens" to us is precisely the phenomenon Cowboy Bill described as a "feeling of warmth and intimacy" in the process by which a present moment (of core consciousness) enfolds within it previous moments of the embodied organism. Both James and Damasio think that there is only a stream of consciousness and that "consciousness is not a monolith." (Damasio 1999, 121). Nonetheless, consciousness does involve a set of real phenomena that cannot be reduced simply to memory, wakefulness, low-level attention, language, or reasoning, even though in humans it is intimately connected to all these crucial functions at the level of extended consciousness. None of this can exist without emotion, since all monitoring of our changing states and images (arising both internally and externally) occurs as part of emotional response processes.

The parallels between Damasio's, James's, and Dewey's accounts of feeling, consciousness, self, and thought are quite striking. For all of them, there is no single self that is the locus of consciousness; instead, there is a vast orchestration of processes at multiple levels that conjointly give rise to our "feeling of what happens." This mostly nonconscious and nonlinguistic narrative of self-processes is only sometimes brought to conscious awareness and expressed in a linguistic narrative of our lives. However, our many self-processes most often operate in unspoken—and even unconscious—dramatic narratives of how our self-identity is continuously both sustained and reconstructed at a bodily level. James thinks that what binds our successive awarenesses (of self) together is our present thought-feeling as it appropriates, through its feeling of its bodily states, prior thought-feelings. Within his novel metaphor, each cow is a thought-feeling connected with other thought-feelings because they graze and move together on a range of consciousness—a "range" that is circumscribed by the permeable boundaries of a particular human body. In his words, the present thought's "appropriations are therefore less to *itself* than to the most intimately felt *part of its present Object, the body, and the central adjustments, which accompany the thinking, in the head. These are the nucleus of our personal identity*" (James [1890] 1950, 1:341, italics in the original). There is no substantial self available or even possible that might hold our self-processes together "as mine" (to quote Kant [1781] 1968, B133/34). Instead, each present phase of the core and extended self is connected to what has gone before and what may come in the future through the temporally and spatially related processes by which an embodied creature continues to engage aspects of its world (surroundings/environment). To the extent that there is any continuity between prior and current enactments of the self, that continuity depends on the fact that a particular body is having a flow of experiences tied to affordances provided by a relatively stable environment.

Reflecting on James's and Damasio's remarkably parallel accounts of the role of emotions in the unity of consciousness also sheds light on something in Dewey that has always puzzled and irritated me. I refer to his wild claim that it is properly *situations* that are characterized by emotionality, rather than merely a person's mind or psychic state (Dewey [1925] 1981, [1934] 1987). How can *situations* be fearful, where there is no consciousness possessed by the situation that could experience the fear?

Well, the answer, we see, is that consciousness is *in* and *of* the situation as it is felt. It resides neither in organism nor environment separately, but rather in the process of interactions that jointly constitutes an organism and its environment. As Damasio argues, we are typically not aware of the process of the body forming images of things it is experiencing. We don't *feel* that unconscious experiencing directly. But what we can and do feel is "how the organism's own state is affected by its processing of an object." (Damasio 1999, 169). Note that we feel our being affected, and we feel this as connected to our own *body*. It is only our embodiment that can hold core (or even extended) consciousness together in a moment of our experience and give us the basis for a unified identity.

At this deep level, I submit, it makes no sense to radically distinguish "mind" from "body." Our feeling of how we are affected by images is neither in the external environment nor in our psychic state, each taken in isolation from the other; rather, it dwells in both at once. It is in and of the process of interaction. That is, this feeling dwells in the body as it experiences the world, and in the world as it is felt through its influence on the organism. The feeling is the contact of our bodily state with the affordances provided by our surroundings. We incorporate those experiences into our selfhood. The reason that Dewey can think of feelings as objective qualities of entire situations is that the situation is what and how it is only in and through the pervading felt quality that distinguishes it. As Dewey says in his important essay "Qualitative Thought" ([1930] 1988, 242–62), the quality is not a mere property or affection of some aspect of the situation. To think of it that way is a mistake based on trying to abstract the quality from the situation. Dewey explains this by reference to the pervasive quality that distinguishes a particular work of art: "Its quality is not a property which it possesses in addition to its other properties. It is something which externally demarcates it from other paintings, and which internally pervades, colors, tones, and weights every detail and every relation of the work of art" (ibid., 245).

Dewey and James saw that we are not conscious of generic experiences. We are conscious of particular situations, as we feel them with all their peculiarities at the level of our embodied interactions with our environment. What Damasio adds to this is the beginnings of an account of the neurochemical processes that make possible our felt sense of the quality of a particular situation. In short, our first and most primordial encounter with the world is emotional through and through. Our world is as it is for us, insofar as we feel it and feel ourselves as affected by it. This is as close as I can come to Dewey's idea of locating the felt quality as demarcating and pervading the whole situation at a given movement.

What is most stunning about all of this, for me, is its recognition of the crucial role of emotion and feeling in everything we experience, think, and do. Our world and our self are conjointly bound together in an inseparable way via embodied feeling. The abstractions that populate our thinking do not transcend such feelings; rather, they are selections of discriminable felt qualities and patterns abstracted from the much-at-once-ness (James 1911) of any given experience. And so we all know that our thought can never do full justice to our feelings or to the pervasive qualities that characterize situations. This is the fact capitalized on by philosophers fascinated by antireductivist "qualia" arguments. None of this should lead us to some of the more mystical claims about qualia that populate the contemporary debate on the subject of consciousness. It should only make us humble in the face of the fact that our abstractions cannot present the fully embodied felt sense of a situation that makes both situation and ourselves what and who they are.

So, we ride off into the sunset on the range of consciousness. In the last analysis, what is misleading about Cowboy Bill's metaphor of the herd is that it postulates the "cowboy" who rides herd. There is no substantial cowboy-self who rides herd and recognizes brands. The cowboy can only be the present moment that enfolds, via feeling, some of its past body states within itself and projects possibilities for future experience. Cowboy Bill, you are at once nobody and the only somebody there is. You seem to be one of the cows, one of the little doggies, who, in the next moment, will be recognized with warmth and intimacy by another little doggy roaming the vast range of consciousness. It is the only self we have, and it will perhaps be a little scary for us as we feel the chill of the high desert night air and hear the lonely howling of the coyotes somewhere out beyond the dim light of the campfire.

CHAPTER 3

We Are Live Creatures

Embodiment, American Pragmatism, and the Cognitive Organism

MARK JOHNSON AND TIM ROHRER

In the first two chapters I have surveyed the overarching view of mind, consciousness, and thought that arises from the conversation between classical pragmatism and second-generation (embodied) cognitive science. One of the key tenets of that naturalistic, nonreductionist theory of mind is Dewey's "continuity principle," which states that increasingly complex "higher" levels of bodily functioning and cognition emerge from "lower" levels in a continuous fashion, without a metaphysical breach that would require the positing of some new ontological reality or causal force. In this chapter, we take a closer look at how this continuity principle might work as a way of explaining how we move from single-celled animals all the way up to the highest cognitive achievements of humans. The result is an embodied realism that explains how higher cognitive functions recruit sensory, motor, and affective processes that make up our basic bodily interactions with our environment. If this emergentist view is adequate, then there is no need for a representational theory of mind—no need for "inner" mental entities that are supposed to bridge the gap between mind and world. According to embodied realism, there never was such a gap in the first place, because thinking is a form of bodily action in the world with which we are in touch through our bodies.

What Difference Does Embodiment Theory Make?

When a young child crawls toward the fire in the hearth and a mother snatches it up before it can get burned, is that cognition? When a team of British mathematicians decodes enemy cyphers during wartime, is that cognition? When ants carrying food back to their nest lay down chemical signals and thereby mark trails to a food source, is that cognition?

Note the commonalities among these situations. In each case the body (individual and social) is in peril. The well-being and continued successful functioning of various organisms is at risk. To survive and flourish, the organism must make adjustments in its way of acting, both within its current environment and in its relations with other creatures. The child must be snatched from the imminent danger of the flames, the mathematicians desperately work to prevent their country from being overrun by the enemy, and the ants must find food and bring it back to the queen in order for the colony to survive. Second, note that in each case, the cognition is social, composed of multiple organisms acting cooperatively together in response to problems posed by the current environment. And finally, note that each of these situations have been taken by theorists as emblematic of cognition par excellence (Dewey [1925] 1981; Hodges 1983, 160–241; Deneubourg, Pasteels, and Verhaeghe 1983; Brooks and Flynn 1989).

The importance of embodiment in cognition is now widely appreciated in the cognitive sciences, yet there remains considerable debate as to what the term *embodiment* actually means (Rohrer 2001a, 2007; Ziemke 2003; Anderson 2003). Is "the body" merely a physical, causally determined entity? Is it a set of organic processes? Is it a felt experience of sensations and movement? Is it the individual physical body, or does it include the social networks (such as families) without which it would cease to exist? Or is the body a socially and culturally constructed artifact? In this chapter, we argue that each of these views contributes something important to an adequate theory of embodied cognition, and that a proper understanding of embodiment can be found within the philosophical context first elaborated in early American pragmatism in the works of thinkers such as William James and John Dewey. As we see it, embodiment theory inherits several key tenets of how these pragmatist philosophers viewed cognition:

1. Embodied cognition is the result of the evolutionary processes of variation, change, and selection.
2. Embodied cognition is situated within a dynamic, ongoing organism-environment relationship.

3. Embodied cognition is problem centered, and it operates relative to the needs, interests, and values of organisms.
4. Embodied cognition is not concerned with finding some allegedly perfect solution to a problem, but one that works well enough relative to the current situation.
5. Embodied cognition is often social and carried out cooperatively by more than one individual organism.

Note that the classical pragmatists advance a radically different view of cognition than the one we are most familiar with from "classical" cognitive science, where it is assumed that cognition consists of the application of universal logical rules that govern the manipulation of "internal" mental symbols, symbols that are supposedly capable of representing states of affairs in the "external" world. Fodor summarizes this theory as follows: "What I am selling is the Representational Theory of Mind. . . . At the heart of the theory is the postulation of a language of thought: an infinite set of 'mental representations' which function both as immediate objects of propositional attitudes and as the domains of mental processes" (1987, 16–17). These internal representations in the "language of thought" supposedly acquire their meaning by being "about"—or referring to—the states of affairs in the external world. Fodor acknowledges that his representational theory of meaning requires "a theory that articulates, in nonsemantic and nonintentional terms, sufficient conditions for one bit of the world to *be about* (to express, represent, or be true of) another bit" (ibid., 98). Typically the first "bit" would be a symbol in the internal language of thought, while the second "bit" that it represents might be either some thing or event in the external world or else a brain state underlying a conception of some fictive entity or scene.

The internal/external split that underlies this view presupposes that cognition could be detached from the nature and functioning of specific bodily organisms, from the environments they inhabit, and from the problems that provoke cognition. Given this view, it would follow that cognition could take place in any number of suitable media, such as a human brain or a machine. This theoretical viewpoint was instrumental in the development of the first electronic calculating machines and general-purpose computers. In fact, these machines were originally developed by the British military to reduce the tedious workload of military mathematicians (or human "computers"—in the sense of humans who compute). But this thought experiment did not end merely with off-loading the tedium of calculation onto electronic machines. From its original conception in the work of Alan Turing (1937), the idea of a universal computing machine became the metaphor of choice for future models of the brain. For example, in Newell and Simon's (1976) conception of the brain as a physical symbol system, they consider the human brain to be just a specific instance of a Turing-style universal machine. In short, for classical cognitive science cognition is defined narrowly as mathematical and logical computation with intrinsically meaningless internal symbols that can supposedly be placed in relation to aspects of the external world.

The pragmatist challenge to classical cognitive science should come as no surprise, since one of the pragmatists' chief targets was the tendency within traditional philosophy to assume that what demarcates "rational" humans from "lower" animals is the supposedly unique ability of humans to engage in symbolic representation between internal thoughts/language and the external world. The remedy offered by the pragmatists is based on their realization that *cognition is action*, rather than mental mirroring of an external reality. Moreover, cognition is a particular kind of action—a response strategy that applies some measure of forethought in order to solve some practical real-world problem. During World War II the practical problem of breaking the German codes was of utmost importance to the British war effort, and this led to the development of a series of machines (the Bombe) that could try a vast number of possible cipher keys against intercepted German communications. These decoding machines were among the predecessors of the modern computer. Early computers were designed to model human action—*computing* possible cipher keys—so that machines would replace human labor (Hodges 1983, 160–241).

However, this success in the modeling of a very specific intellectual operation was soon mistakenly regarded as the key to understanding cognition in general. If one thinks that mathematical and logical reasoning are what distinguish human beings from other animals, one might erroneously assume that any computational machine that could model aspects of this peculiarly human trait could also be used to model cognition in general. Hence the MIND AS COMPUTER PROGRAM metaphor swept early (first-generation) cognitive science. This is a disembodied view of rationality. By contrast, on the pragmatist view, our rationality emerges from, and is shaped by, our embodied nature. Thus,

John Dewey famously asserted that "to see the organism *in* nature, the nervous system in the organism, the brain in the nervous system, the cortex in the brain is the answer to the problems which haunt philosophy" ([1925] 1981, 198).

In the following sections we show how the pragmatist view of cognition as action provides an appropriate philosophical framework for the cognitive science of the embodied mind. We begin by describing the nondualistic, nonrepresentational view of mind developed by William James and John Dewey. Their understanding of situated cognition is reinforced by recent empirical research and developments within the cognitive sciences. We cite evidence from comparative neurobiology of organism-environment coupling ranging from the amoeba all the way up to humans, and we argue that in humans this coupling process becomes the basis of meaning and thought. We describe the patterns of these ongoing interactions as *image schemas* that ground meaning in our embodiment and yet are not internal representations of an external reality. This leads to an account of an emergent rationality that is embodied, social, and creative.

James and Dewey: The Continuity of Embodied Experience and Thought

In many ways the American pragmatist philosophers James and Dewey provide us today with exemplary nonreductionist and nonrepresentationalist models of embodied mind. Their models combined the best current biological and cognitive science of their day with nuanced phenomenological description and a commitment that philosophy should address the problems that arise in our daily lives. James and Dewey understood something that is taken for granted in contemporary biological science: that cognition emerges from the embodied processes of the constantly developing relationship between an organism and its environment. One problem for such a naturalistic account of mind is to explain how meaning, abstract thinking, and formal reasoning could emerge from the basic sensorimotor capacities of organisms as they interact with the environment and each other.

The fundamental assumption of the pragmatists' naturalistic approach is that everything we attribute to "mind"—perceiving, conceptualizing, imagining, reasoning, desiring, willing, dreaming—has emerged (and continues to develop) as part of a process in which an organism seeks to survive, grow, and flourish within different kinds of situations. As James puts it:

> Mental facts cannot be properly studied apart from the physical environment of which they take cognizance. The great fault of the older rational psychology was to set up the soul as an absolute spiritual being with certain faculties of its own by which the several activities of remembering, imagining, reasoning, and willing, etc. were explained, almost without reference to the peculiarities of the world with which these activities deal. But the richer insight of modern days perceives that our inner faculties are *adapted* in advance to the features of the world in which we dwell, adapted, I mean, so as to secure our safety and prosperity in its midst. (1900, 3)

This evolutionary embeddedness of the organism within its changing environments (and the development of thought in response to such changes) ties mind inextricably to body and environment. The changes entailed by such a view are revolutionary. From the very beginning of life, the problem of knowledge is *not* how so-called internal ideas can *re*-present external realities. Instead, the problem of knowledge is to explain how structures and patterns of organism-environment interaction can be transformed in the face of changing circumstances that pose new problems, challenges, and opportunities for the organism. On this view, mind is never separate from body, for it is always a series of bodily activities immersed in the ongoing flow of organism-environment interactions that constitutes experience. In Dewey's words, "Since both the inanimate and the human environment are involved in the functions of life, it is inevitable, if these functions evolve to the point of thinking and if thinking is naturally serial with biological functions, that it will have as the material of thought, even of its erratic imaginings, the events and connections of this environment" ([1925] 1981, 212–13).

Another way of expressing this rootedness of thinking in bodily experience and its connection with the environment is to say that there is no rupture in experience between perceiving, feeling, and thinking. In explaining more complex "higher" functions, such as consciousness, self-reflection, and language use, we do not postulate new ontological kinds of entities, events, or processes that are nonnatural or supernatural. More levels of organic functioning are just that—levels—and nothing more, although there are emergent properties of "higher" levels of functioning. Dewey names this connectedness of all cognition the "principle of continuity," which states that "there is no breach of continuity between operations of inquiry and biological operations and physical operations. 'Continuity' . . . means that rational operations *grow out of* organic activities, without being identical with that from which they emerge" ([1938] 1991, 26).

What the continuity thesis entails is that any explanation of the nature and workings of mind—even the most abstract conceptualization and reasoning—must have its roots in our organismic capacities for perception, feeling, object manipulation, and bodily movement. Furthermore, social and cultural forces are required to develop these capacities to their full potential, including language and symbolic reasoning. Infants do not speak or discover mathematical proofs at birth; Dewey's continuity thesis requires both evolutionary and developmental explanations. For James and Dewey, this means that a full-fledged theory of human cognition must have at least three major components:

1. There must be an account of the emergence and development of meaningful patterns of organism-environment interactions—patterns of sensory-motor experience shared by all organisms of a certain kind and meaningful for those organisms. Such patterns must be tied to the organism's attempts to function within its environment.

2. There must be an account of how we can perform abstract thinking using our capacities for perception and motor response. There would need to be bodily processes for extending sensory-motor concepts and logic for use in abstract reasoning, as well as an account of how the processes embodying such abstract reasoning capacities are learned during organismic development. This story has at least two parts: (1) an evolutionary and physiological account explaining how an adult human being's abstract reasoning utilizes the brain's perceptual and motor systems, and (2) a developmental and anthropological account of how social and cultural behaviors educate the sensorimotor systems of successive generations of children so that they may speak and perform abstract reasoning.

3. There must be an account of how values and behavioral motivations emerge from the organism's ongoing functioning. This explanation will include (1) the physical and social makeup of organisms, (2) the nature of their emotional responses, and (3) the kinds of environments (e.g., material, social, cultural) they inhabit. In the present space we are able to offer only a very compressed and partial treatment of such an account.

Organism-Environment Coupling

Maturana and Varela: From Chemotaxis to the Nervous System

Dewey's principle of continuity states that there are no ontological gaps between the different levels of an organism's functioning. One way to see what this entails is to survey a few representative types of organism-environment couplings, starting with single-celled organisms and moving up by degrees to more complex animals. In every case we can observe the same adaptive process of interactive coordination between a specific organism and recurring characteristics of its environment. But does that mean that we can trace human cognition all the way back to the sensorimotor behavior of single-celled organisms? On the face of it, this seems preposterous—viewed from an evolutionary biologist's perspective, there are clear differences in the size, complexity, and structural differentiation of human beings as compared with single-celled organisms like bacteria. Single-celled organism behavior is not ordinarily relevant to the behavior of multicelled organisms—except insofar as there might be structural morphological analogies between the sensorimotor activity of single-celled organisms and particular sensorimotoric cells within the multicelled body.

Just this sort of morphological analogy plays a key role in Maturana and Varela's (1998, 142–63) argument that central nervous systems evolved in multicelled organisms to coordinate sensorimotor activity. In a single-celled organism, locomotion is achieved by dynamically coupling the sensory and motoric surfaces of the cell membrane. When an amoeba engulfs a protozoan, its cell membranes are responding to the presence of the chemical substances that make up the protozoan, causing changes in the consistency of the amoeba's protoplasm. These changes manifest as pseudopods—digitations which the amoeba appears to extend around the protozoan as it prepares to feed on it. Similarly, certain bacteria have a tail-like membrane structure called a flagellum that is rotated like a propeller to move the bacterium. When the flagellum is rotated in one direction, the bacterium simply tumbles, while reversing the direction of rotation causes the bacterium to move. If a grain of sugar is placed into the solution containing this bacterium, chemical receptors on the cell membrane sense the sugar molecules. This causes a membrane change in which the bacterium changes the direction of rotation of its flagellar propeller and gradually moves toward the greatest concentration of the sugar molecules (chemotaxis). In both cases, changes in the chemical environment cause sensory perturbations in the cellular membrane, which invariably produces movement. The key point here is that, without anything like an internal representation, single-celled organisms engage in sensorimotor coordination in response to environmental changes. Even at this apparently primitive level, there is a finely tuned ongoing coupling of organism and environment.

Multicelled organisms also accomplish their sensorimotor coordination by means of changes in cell membranes. However, the cellular specialization afforded by a multicelled organism means that not every cell needs to perform the same functions. Maturana and Varela (1998) discuss the example of an evolutionarily ancient metazoic organism called the hydra (a coelenterate). The hydra, which lives in ponds, is shaped like a two-layered tube with four or six tentacles emanating from its mouth. On the inside layer of the tube, most cells secrete digestive fluids, while the outside layer is partly composed of radial and longitudinal muscle cells. Locomotion is accomplished by contracting muscle cells along the body of the organism, some of which cause changes in the hydrostatic pressure within the organism, changing its shape and direction of locomotion.

Between the two layers of cells, however, are specialized cells—neurons—with elongated membranes that can extend over the length of the entire organism before terminating in the muscle cells. These tail-like cellular projections are the axons, and evolutionarily speaking they are the flagella of the multicelled organism. Changes in the electrochemical state in other, smaller cellular projections of the cells (the dendrites) cause larger changes in the electrochemical state of the axonal membrane, which in turn induces the muscle cells to contract. These neural signals typically originate in either the tentacles or the "stomach" of the hydra, such that their electrochemical state responds to the molecules, indicating the presence or absence of food and/or excessive digestive secretions. These neurons consistently terminate in the longitudinal and radial muscles that contract the hydra body for locomotion or for swallowing. The topology of how the nerve cells interconnect is crucially important: when touched, a chain of neurons fire sequentially down a hydra tentacle toward its mouth and cause the muscle cells to curl the tentacle about its prey. This structural coupling reflected between organism and environment is what allows the hydra to contract the correct muscles to swallow, to move up and left, or right and down. Like the hydra opening its mouth as a reflexive part of bringing food to it with its tentacles, we humans think in order to act and we act as *part of our thinking*—cognition is action. But how is that we humans can learn new behaviors, while the hydra generally cannot?

From Neural Maps to Neural Plasticity

Although still surprisingly continuous with the hydra, human cognition is a little more like what happens in frogs, owls, and monkeys, in that all these organisms have nervous systems that include neural maps and adaptive neural plasticity. Frogs have a certain regularly occurring pragmatic problem—they need to extend their tongues to eat a fly—which was the subject of a classic experiment in the early history of neurobiology (Sperry 1943). When a frog is still a tadpole, it is possible to rotate the frog's eye 180 degrees, making sure to keep the optic nerve intact. The tadpole is then allowed to develop normally into a frog. The frog's tongue extends to exactly the opposite point of the frog's visual field than where the fly is located. No amount of failure will teach the frog to move its tongue differently; the nervous system acts entirely on the basis of the connections between the retinal image and the tongue muscles. Maturana and Varela conclude that *for the frog*, "there is no such thing as up or down, front and back, in reference to an outside world, as it exists for the observer doing the study" (1998, 125–26). The frog has no access to our notion of the external world and our 180-degree rotation of its eye; it has only an environmentally induced change of state in the neurons comprising its (extremely inverted) retinal map.

One of the most profound findings in neuroscience is that nervous systems exploit topological and topographic organization. In other words, organisms build neural "maps." In neural maps, adjacent neural cells (or small groups of neural cells) fire sequentially when a stimulus in adjacent positions within a sensory field moves. For example, scientists have manipulated the frog's visual field and measured the electrical activity of a region of its brain to show that as one stimulates the frog's visual field, the neurons of its optic tectum will fire in coordination with the visual stimulus. Fraser (1985) covered the frog's optic tectum with a twenty-four-electrode grid, with each electrode recording electrical activity that was the sum of the signals from a receptive field containing many optic nerve–fiber terminals. When a point of light was moved in a straight line from right to left and then from bottom to top in the frog's right visual field, the electrode grid recorded neuronal activity in straight lines, firing sequentially, first from the rostral (front) to the caudal (back) and then from the lateral to the medial. We call this the frog's retinal map (or retinotectal map) because it encodes environmental visual stimuli in a topographically consistent manner. The spatial orientation of this topography is rotated in various ways (thus visual right-to-left has become front-to-back, etc.), but the topographic mapping between movement in the vertical visual plane and the plane of the retinotectal map remains consistent. Even though there is considerable spatial distortion in the neural map, the key relational structures are preserved. In some other cases—such as some auditory maps and color maps, where the correspondences are less about shape and position—the organization is more properly called "topologic" than "topographic," but the organizing principle of the neural mapping of sensation still holds.

The degree to which such neural maps might be plastic has been the subject of much recent study. It is important to remember that in the case of the frog, Sperry performed a radical and destructive intervention that is outside the realm of "normal" Darwinian deviation—in other words, if this were to occur by natural selection, such a frog would die quickly without passing on its genes. However, interventions that are more subtle and perhaps more likely to occur in nature—such as cutting the optic nerve and destroying part of the optic tectum of a goldfish—result in a recovery of function in which the optic nerve axons regenerate and make a complete retinal map in the remaining part of the tectum (Gaze and Sharma 1970). Although radical interventions can "break" the neural maps, even the more evolutionary determined neural networks exhibit some range of adaptive neural plasticity to environmental factors.

Plasticity is particularly profound in cross-modal neural maps. Consider another even more subtle intervention: suppose we were to have an owl wear glasses that changed its perception of the visual field. Similar to frogs, owls have developed an extremely accurate method of attacking prey. The owl hears a mouse rustling on the ground and locates the mouse primarily using the tiny difference in time it takes for a sound to pass from one ear to another. This establishes the mouse's approximate position in the owl's retinotectal map, and the diving owl then looks to find the exact location of its prey before it strikes. Knudsen and colleagues (Knudsen 1998, 2002) put prismatic glasses on adult and juvenile owls which distorted the owls' vision by 23 degrees. After eight weeks with glasses, adults raised normally never learned to compensate, but juveniles were able to learn to hunt accurately. Moreover, when the glasses were reintroduced to the adult owls who had worn them as juveniles, they were able to readjust to the glasses in short order; in other words, the prism-reared owls could successfully hunt with or without glasses.

These behavioral adaptations have anatomical underpinnings in the organization of the neural maps. When injected with an anatomical tracing dye, comparison of the neural arbors from normally reared and prism-reared owls revealed a much different pattern of axonal projections between auditory and spatial neural maps, "showing that alternative learned and normal circuits can coexist in this network" (Knudsen 2002, 325). In other words, in order to deal with wearing glasses, the owl brain had grown permanent alternative axonal connections in a cross-modal neural map of space located in the external nucleus of the inferior colliculus (ICX). The ICX neural arbor is significantly more dense than in normally developing owls, with arbors typically having at least two distinct branches of axons (DeBello, Feldman, and Knudsen 2001). By contrast, the retinotectal maps of the visual modality alone do not quite seem to exhibit the same plasticity, either in owls (whose retinotectum did not change) or in frogs. Anatomical research on frogs reared and kept alive with surgically rotated eyes has shown that after five weeks, the retinotectal neural arbors initially exhibited a similar pattern of "two-headed axons"—that is, they had two major axonal branches. However, after ten weeks, the older axonal connections were starting to decay and disappear, while after sixteen weeks, no two-headed axons could be traced (Guo and Udin 2000). Apparently, the frog's single-modal retinotectal maps did not receive enough reentrant neural connections from other sensory modalities to sustain the multiple branching neural arbors found in the cross-modal map of the prism-reared owls.

Working on neural plasticity in adult squirrel and owl monkeys, Merzenich and colleagues (Merzenich et al. 1987; reviewed in Buonomano and Merzenich 1998) have shown that it is possible to dynamically reorganize the somatosensory cortical maps subject to certain bodily constraints. Similar to the owls and frogs who grew dual arborizations, these monkeys exhibited a plasticity based on their brains' ability to select which parts of their neural arbors to use for various kinds of input. In a series of studies, Merzenich and colleagues altered the monkey's hand sensory activity by such interventions as (1) cutting a peripheral nerve such as the medial or radial nerve and (1a) allowing it to regenerate naturally or (1b) tying it off to prevent regeneration; (2) amputating a single digit; and (3) taping together two digits so that they could not be moved independently. The results show that cortical areas now lacking their previous sensory connections (or independent sensory input in the third condition) were "colonized" in a couple of weeks by adjacent neural maps with active sensory connections. In other words, the degree of existing but somewhat dormant neural arbor overlap was large enough that the cortex was able to reorganize. And where the nerve was allowed to regenerate, the somatosensory map gradually returned to occupy a similar-sized stretch of cortex, albeit with slightly different boundaries. Learning in adults is accomplished in part by neural switching between redundant and overlapping neural arbors.

All these examples of ontogenetic neural change suggest that there is a process of neural arbor selection akin to natural selection taking place in concert with specific patterns of organism-environment interactions. On precisely these grounds, the neurobiologist Gerald Edelman (1987) has proposed a theory of "neural Darwinism," or "neuronal group selection," to explain how such neural maps are formed in the organism's embryonic development. Different groups of neurons compete to become topological neural maps as they migrate and grow during neural development. Successful cortical groups—driven primarily by regularities in the environment passed on from those neurons that are closer to the sensory apparatus—will fire together and wire together in a process of axonal sprouting and synaptogenesis. Some neuronal groups will fail to find useful topological connections, and they eventually die and are crowded out by the successful neuronal groups, while others will hang on in something of an intermediate state of success (Edelman 1987, 127–40). In the adult organism, the latent axonal arbors from only partly successful attempts to wire together lay dormant, ready to reorganize the map as needed by means of further synaptogenesis. Edelman (ibid, 43–47) calls these latent reorganizations of the neuronal groups "secondary repertoires," as distinguished from their normal "primary repertoires."

Like frogs, owls, and monkeys, humans have sets of visual, auditory, and somatosensory maps. The more obvious of these map perceptual space in fairly direct analogs—preserving topologies of pitch, the retinal field, color, the parts of the body, and so on—but subsequent maps preserve increasingly abstract topological structure (or even combinations of structure) such as object shape, edges, orientation, direction of motion, and even the particular degree of the vertical or horizontal. *Like the frog, we live in the world of our maps. Topologically speaking, our bodies are in our minds, in the sense that our sensorimotor maps provide the basis for conceptualization and reasoning.* We perceive the patterns of our daily organism-environment interactions in image-like fashion, constantly seeking out various topological invariances in those patterns that prove useful to us. In the following sections, we will explore how our imagination and our reason are constituted by patterns of activation within these neural maps. But before proceeding to human cognition, we must first address why neural "maps" are not classical representations.

Neural Maps Are Not Internal Representations

Some people might suppose that talk of neural maps would necessarily engender representational theories of cognition. On this view, the map would be construed as an internal representation of some external reality. But the account we have been giving *does not* entail any of the traditional metaphysical dualisms that underlie representationalist views—dichotomies such as inner/outer, subject/object, mind/body, self/world. Such dichotomies might describe aspects of organism-environment interactions, but they do not indicate different ontological entities or structures. According to our interactionist view, maps and other structures of organism-environment coordination are prime examples of nonrepresentational structures of meaning, understanding, and thought. Maturana and Varela (1998, 125–26) make this important philosophical point quite clear. We must not read our scientific or philosophical perspectives (i.e., our theoretical stance) on cognition into the experience itself that we are theorizing about. This is an error James ([1890] 1950) termed the "psychologist's fallacy." In observing something scientifically, one must always consider the standpoint of the scientist in relation to the object of study. When we use terms such as *retinal map, pitch maps, sensorimotor maps, color maps,* and so on, to describe the operations of various neural arrays in a frog's nervous system—or in human nervous systems—we are doing so from our standpoint as observers and theorists who can see mappings between the neural world and our own experience of the "external world." But for the frog, and for the human in the act of perceiving, that map is the basis for its experience of the world. The frog's neural map itself has its origin not in the immediate mappings that we observers see in the moment, but in a longitudinal evolutionary and developmental process during which those neural connections were "selected for" by Darwinian or neo-Darwinian mechanisms.

In short, what we (as scientists) theoretically recognize and describe as an organism's "maps" are *not, for that organism,* internal representations.

Rather, what we call sensorimotor and somatosensory maps (whether in multicelled organisms, monkeys, or humans) are *for that organism* precisely its structures of its experienced world! Consequently, we must be careful not to be misled by philosophers of mind and language who would treat these maps as internal representations of external realities, thereby surreptitiously reintroducing an "inner/outer" split that does not exist in reality for the organism.

Ontological Continuity and Human Thought: Image Schemas and Modal Perception

Since the earliest episodes of ancient Greek philosophy, humans have distinguished themselves from "brute" animals and all lower organisms by their supposedly unique capacity for abstract conceptualization and reasoning. According to this view, what is so distinct about human reason is that it makes it possible for us to form abstract representations that stand for and point to states of affairs that are either external to us or are not currently present in our experience (i.e., are past or future). But the pragmatist continuity thesis denies the inner/outer dichotomy on which representationalist theories are grounded. Consequently, the problem for an embodied view of cognition is how to explain our marvelous human feats of abstraction, reasoning, and symbolic interaction, yet without positing an ontological rupture between "lower" animals and humans.

The key, once again, is the coupling (the interactive coordination) of an organism (here, a human one) and its environment. Recurring adaptive patterns of organism-environment interaction are the basis for our ability to survive and flourish. In humans, these patterns are no more "internal" representations than they are in other creatures. Let us consider briefly some of the most basic kinds of structural couplings that make up a human's experience of its world.

Image Schemas and Cross-Modal Perception

The character of our experience is delineated in large part by the nature of our bodies and brains, the kinds of environments we inhabit, and the values and purposes we have. The patterns of our ongoing interactions (or "enactions," as Varela, Thompson, and Rosch [1991] have called them, to stress their active, dynamic character) define the contours of our world and make it possible for us to make sense of, reason about, and act reliably within this world. Thousands of times each day we see, manipulate, and move into and out of containers, so containment is one of the most fundamental patterns of our experience. Because we have two legs and stand up within a gravitational field, we experience verticality and up/down orientation. Because the qualities (e.g., redness, softness, coolness, agitation, sharpness) of our experience vary continuously in intensity, there is a scalar character to each of the qualitative dimensions of our world. For example, lights can grow brighter or dimmer, stoves get hotter or cooler, iced tea gets sweeter as we add sugar. We are subject to forces that move us, change our bodily states, and constrain our actions, and all these forces have characteristic patterns and qualities. We are bound inextricably to our world interactively (enactively) by means of these recurring patterns that are the very conditions for us to survive, grow, and find meaning. Without such patterns, and without neural maps of such characteristic patterns, each moment of our experience would be utterly chaotic, as though we had to make sense of our world from scratch, over and over again as each new moment arose.

What I (M. Johnson 1987) and Lakoff (1987) have called "image schemas" are precisely these recurring patterns of sensorimotor experience by which we encounter a world that we can understand and act within to further our purposes. There are numerous sources of evidence for image schemas, ranging from experimental psychology to linguistics to developmental psychology. We hypothesize that these image schemas are neurally embodied as patterns of activation in our topological neural maps. Image schemas are thus part of our nonrepresentational coupling with our world, just as barn owls and squirrel monkeys have image schemas that define their types of sensorimotor experience.

Image-schematic structure is the basis for our understanding of spatial terms and all aspects of our perception and motor activities. An example from Lakoff and Núñez (2000) illustrates this image-schematic basis of spatial concepts in humans. What we call our concept *in* is defined for us by a CONTAINER image schema that consists generically of (1) a boundary, that demarcates (2) an interior from (3) an exterior.

When we say, "The car is in the garage," we understand the garage as a bounded space, we profile (Langacker 1987–91) the interior of that space, and we regard the car as a *trajector* within that space, with the garage (as container) serving as a *landmark* in relation to which the trajector is located. Similarly, when we hear the sentence "Grandpa walked from the outhouse into the garage," we understand that situation via a SOURCE-PATH-GOAL schema that consists of (1) a starting point,

(2) a destination (endpoint), and (3) a path from the starting location to the destination. In other words, the *from/to* construction is image-schematic. The English word *into* is understood via a superimposition of the CONTAINER schema and the SOURCE-PATH-GOAL schema, as follows:

- The word *in* activates a CONTAINER schema with the interior profiled.
- The word *to* activates a SOURCE-PATH-GOAL schema with the destination (endpoint) profiled.
- The destination (endpoint) is mapped onto the interior of the CONTAINER schema.
- We thus understand Grandpa's (as trajector) movement as beginning outside the garage (container) and terminating inside the garage (as landmark), as a result of motion along a path from the exterior to the interior.
- The word *into* in English is thus an elementary composition of two image schemas.

Image schemas, according to our view, are realized as activation patterns (or "contours") in human topological neural maps. As with much interdisciplinary research in the neurosciences, this finding was first discovered by intracranial neuronal recordings in monkeys that were later extended by analogous neuroimaging studies. When Rizzolatti and colleagues (Fogassi et al. 2001; see review in Rizzolatti, Fogassi, and Gallese 2002) showed macaque monkeys visual imagery of another monkey grasping a banana with their hands, they were able to record activity from "mirror" neurons in the same secondary somatomotor maps that would be implicated if the monkey himself were performing the particular grasping action. Analogous human neuroimaging experiments (Buccino et al. 2001), in which participants watched a video clip of another person performing an action, showed increased activation in the human secondary somatomotor cortices that are known to map hand and arm grasping motions. Along with Rizzolatti's colleague Gallese, we interpret these and related results as having shown that these neural maps contain image-schematic sensorimotor activation patterns for grasping (Gallese and Lakoff 2005).

An explicit attempt to model image schemas using known facts about our neural maps can be found within the neurocomputational modeling literature. Regier (1996) has developed what he calls "structured" or "constrained" connectionist neural models for a number of image schemas. "Constrained" neurocomputational connectionism builds into its neural models a small number of structures that have been identified in research on human visual and spatial processing (Feldman 2006). These include center-surround cell arrays, spreading activation, orientation-sensitive cells, and neural gating. Regier has shown how these constrained connectionist models of image schemas can learn spatial-relations terms.

There is also a growing body of research from developmental psychology suggesting that infants come into the world with capacities for experiencing image-schematic structures. Stern (1985) describes certain types of experiential structures that infants are able to detect, and he argues, first, that these capacities form the basis for meaning and the infant's sense of self; and, second, that these capacities continue to play a central role in meaning, understanding, and thinking even in adults who are capable of propositional thinking. Let us briefly consider two of these basic structures: (1) cross-modal perception and (2) vitality affect contours.

Stern begins with a well-known experiment (Meltzoff and Borton 1979) in which blindfolded infants were given one of two pacifiers to suck. One was the typical smooth pacifier, while the other had protruding nubs. When the blindfolds were removed and smooth and nubbed pacifiers were placed on either side of the infant's head, most of the time (roughly 75 percent) the infant would attend to the nipple of the pacifier just sucked. Based on this and other studies (e.g., Lewkowicz and Turkewitz 1981), Stern suggests that

> infants thus appear to have an innate general capacity, which can be called *amodal perception*, to take information received in one sensory modality and somehow translate it into another sensory modality. . . .
>
>   These abstract representations that the infant experiences are not sights and sounds and touches and nameable objects, but rather shapes, intensities, and temporal patterns—the more "global" qualities of experience. (1985, 51)

Although Stern speaks of these structures of cross-modal perception as abstract "representations," Stern also makes it clear that these perceptual structures are not inner mirrorings of external things but rather are the contours of the infant's experience: the cross-modal shapes, intensities and temporal patterns that we call image schemas.

Like infants, we adults have a ROUGH/SMOOTH image schema, which we use as we anticipate the change in surface texture as we walk. For example, we can see where we will step from the rough carpet of the hallway onto the slippery tile of the bathroom, and we transfer this information from the visual to the somatomotor system so that our feet will not slip. Such patterns of cross-modal perception are especially clear examples of how image schemas differ from being just a topographically mapped image in a neural map; they are sensorimotoric patterns of experience which are instantiated in and coordinated between the neural maps. Our image-schematic experience may, as in the case of the owls, become instantiated in its own cross-modal neural map; or, as in the case of the monkeys, it might consist of coordinated activation patterns between a network of more modal neural maps, including possibly calling on the secondary rather than primary repertoires of those maps. We predict that cases analogous to each will be observed in human neuroanatomical studies.

A second type of pattern that makes up the infant's (and adult's) image-schematic experience is what Stern (1985) calls "vitality affect contours." Stern illustrates this with the notion of a "rush," or the swelling qualitative contour of a felt experience. We can experience an adrenaline rush, a rush of joy or anger, a drug-induced rush, or the rush of a hot flash. Even though these rushes are felt in different sensory modalities, they are all characterizable as a rapid, forceful building up or swelling contour of the experience across time. Stern notes that understanding how such affect contours are meaningful to creatures like us gives us profound insight into meaning generally, whether that meaning comes via language, vision, music, dance, touch, or smell. We crave the emotional satisfaction that comes from pattern completion, and witnessing even just a portion of the pattern is enough to set our affect contours in motion. The infant just needs to see us *begin* to reach for the bottle, and it already begins to quiet down—the grasping image schema does not even need to be completely realized in time before the infant recognizes the action. When as adults we hear a musical composition building up to a crescendo, this causes increasing emotional tension that is released at the musical climax. The emotional salience of the vitality affect contours in image schemas shows that image schemas are not mere static "representations" (or "snapshots") of one moment in a topographic neural map. Instead, image schemas proceed dynamically in and through time.

To summarize, image schemas can be characterized more formally as:

1. recurrent patterns of bodily experience;
2. "image"-like in that they preserve the topological structure of the perceptual whole, as evidenced by pattern completion;
3. operating dynamically in and across time;
4. instantiated as activation patterns (or "contours") in topologic neural maps;
5. structures that link sensorimotor experiences to conceptualization and language; and
6. structures that afford "normal" pattern completions that can serve as a basis for inference.

Image schemas constitute a preverbal and pre-reflective emergent level of meaning. They are patterns found in the topologic neural maps we share with other animals, though we as humans have particular image schemas that are more or less peculiar to our types of bodies. However, even though image schemas typically operate without our conscious awareness of how they structure our experience, it is sometimes possible to become reflectively aware of the image-schematic structure of a certain experience, such as when I am consciously aware of my cupped hands as forming a container, or when I feel my body as being off-balance.

Abstract Conceptualization and Reasoning

Pragmatism's continuity thesis claims that we must be able to move, without any ontological or epistemological rupture, from the body-based meaning of spatial and perceptual experience that is characterizable by image schemas and affect contours, all the way up to abstract conceptualization, reasoning, and language use. Although there is not yet any fully worked-out theory of how all abstract thought works, some of the central mechanisms are becoming better understood. One particularly important structure is *conceptual metaphor* (Lakoff and Johnson 1980, 1999). The most sweeping claim of conceptual metaphor theory is that what we call "abstract" concepts are defined by systematic mappings from a bodily based sensorimotor source domain onto the abstract target domains. These metaphor mappings are found in patterns motivated by image-schematic constraints—for example, if we map an interior from the source domain, we can expect to map the exterior as well; if we have source and destination mappings, we can expect a path mapping.

Consider, for example, how we understand the expression *We have a long way to go before our theory is finished*. Why can we use the phrase *a long way to go*, which is literally about distance in motion through space, to talk about the completion of a mental project (i.e., developing a theory)? The answer is that there is a conceptual metaphor PURPOSEFUL ACTIVITIES ARE JOURNEYS, via which we understand progress toward some nonphysical goal as progress in moving toward some destination. The metaphor consists of the following conceptual mapping:

The PURPOSEFUL ACTIVITIES ARE JOURNEYS Metaphor

Source domain (motion in space)		Target domain (mental activity)
Starting Point *A*	→	Initial State
Ending Location *B*	→	Final State
Destination	→	Purpose To Be Achieved
Motion From *A* to *B*	→	Process Of Achieving Purpose
Obstacles To Motion	→	Difficulties In Achieving Goals

This conceptual mapping also makes use of one of our most basic metaphors for understanding the passage of time, in which temporal change is understood metaphorically as motion along a path to some location. In this metaphor, the observer moves along a time line, with the future arrayed as the space in front of her and the past as the space behind. Consequently, when we hear "We have a long way to go until our campaign drive is finished," we understand ourselves metaphorically as moving along a path toward the destination (completion of the fund drive), and we understand that there can be obstacles along the way that would slow our progress.

Conceptual metaphor theory proposes that abstract conceptualization works via conceptual metaphor, conceptual metonymy, and a few other principles of imaginative extension. To date there is a rapidly growing body of metaphor analyses of key concepts in nearly every conceivable intellectual field and discipline, including the physical and biological sciences, economics, morality, politics, ethics, philosophy, anthropology, psychology, religion, and more. For example, Lakoff and Núñez (2000) have carried out extensive analyses of the fundamental metaphorical concepts that underlie mathematics from simple models of addition all the way up to concepts of the Cartesian plane, infinity, and differential equations. Winter (2001) analyzes several key metaphors that define central legal concepts and are the basis for legal reasoning (see also Bjerre 2005). Grady (1997) examines "primary metaphors" (such as PURPOSES ARE DESTINATIONS) that are combined systematically into more complex metaphors (such as PURPOSEFUL ACTIVITIES ARE JOURNEYS).

The reason that conceptual metaphor is so important is that it is our primary means for abstract conceptualization and reasoning. Pragmatism's principle of continuity claims that abstract thought is not disembodied; rather, it must arise from our sensorimotor capacities and is constrained by the nature of our bodies, brain architectures, and environments. From an evolutionary perspective, this means that we have *not* developed two separate logical and inferential systems, one for our bodily and spatial experiences and one for our abstract reasoning (as a pure logic). Instead, the logic of our bodily experience provides all the logic we need in order to perform every rational inference that we make. In our metaphor-based reasoning, the inferences are carried out via the corporeal logic of our sensorimotor capacities; and then, via the source-to-target domain mapping, the corresponding logical inferences are drawn in the target domain.

For example, there is definite spatial or bodily logic of containment that arises in our experience with containers:

a. An entity is either inside the container or outside it, but not both at once.
b. If I place an object O within a physical container C and then put container C inside of another container D, then O is in D.

In other words, our bodily encounters with containers and objects that we observe and manipulate teach us the spatial logic of containers.

Next, consider the common conceptual metaphor CATEGORIES ARE CONTAINERS, in which a conceptual category is understood metaphorically as an abstract container for physical and abstract entities. For example, we may say: "The category 'human' is *contained in* the category 'animals,' which *is contained* in the category 'living things.'" Similarly, we may ask, "Which species category is this tree *in*?" Based on the inferential image-schematic structure of the source domain, and via the source-to-target mapping, we then have corresponding inferences about abstract concepts:

a'. An entity either falls within a given category or falls outside it, but not both at once (e.g., Charles cannot be a man and not a man at the same time, in the same place, and in the same manner; the law of the excluded middle).

b′. If an entity *E* is in one category *C′*, and *C′* is in another category *D′*, then that entity *E* is in category *D′* (e.g., all men are mortal [*C′* is in *D′*] and Socrates is a man [*E* is in *C′*], therefore Socrates is mortal [*E* is in *D′*]).

Thus, according to conceptual metaphor theory, we would then predict that the abstract inferences are "computed" using sensorimotor neural maps, and those inferences are activated as target-domain inferences because there are neural connections from sensorimotor areas of the brain to other areas that are responsible for so-called "higher" cognitive functions. We don't run an inferential process at the sensorimotor level and then perform an entirely different inferential process for abstract concepts; rather, human beings utilize the inference patterns found in the sensorimotor brain regions to do our "abstract" reasoning. Just as the pragmatist principle of continuity requires, there is no need to introduce a new kind of reasoning (with a different ontological basis) to explain logical reasoning with abstract concepts.

Evidence for Metaphor and Abstract Reasoning Using Conceptual Metaphors

Recently several new sources of evidence have become available to explain the possible neural bases for the image-schematic mappings that operate in conceptual metaphors. The new evidence comes from both the patient-based neurological literature and neuroimaging studies of normal adults. While we have long known that patients can develop anomias reflecting selective category deficits for animals, tools, and plants (Warrington and Shallice 1984), two studies have reported a selective category deficit for body-part terms (Suzuki, Yamadori, and Fuji 1997; Shelton, Fouch, and Caramazza 1998; Coslett, Saffran, and Schwoebel 2002). The deficit work suggests that lesions in the secondary motor cortices—in regions that likely contain both somatotopic and egocentric spatial maps—can cause difficulties in tasks such as body-part naming, naming contiguous sections of the body, and so on. This finding suggests that the comprehension of body-part terms requires the active participation of these neural maps.

Two other neuroimaging studies also show that we can drive the human somatomotor maps with both metaphoric and literal linguistic stimuli relating to the body. In an fMRI study, Hauk, Johnsrude, and Pulvermuller (2004) have shown that single word terms such as *smile*, *punch*, and *kick* differentially activate face, arm/hand, and leg regions within the somatomotor maps, suggesting that literal language can differentially activate *body-part related* somatomotor neural maps. Similarly, an fMRI neuroimaging study by Rohrer (2001b, 2005) shows that both literal and metaphoric sentences using hand terms (e.g., *She handed me the apple* and *He finally grasped the theory*) activate primary and secondary hand regions within the primary and secondary sensorimotor maps. After the presentation of the linguistic stimuli, Rohrer also mapped the hand somatic cortex of each study participant using a tactile hand-stroking task. A comparison between the tactile and the sentential conditions shows a high degree of overlap in the primary and secondary somatomotor cortex for both language tasks.

There is also evidence from neurocomputationally inspired models of conceptual metaphor and abstract reasoning. Building on Regier's work on modeling the image-schematic character of spatial-relation terms, Narayanan (1997; Feldman and Narayanan 2004) developed a constrained connectionist network to model how the bodily logic of our sensorimotor systems enables us to perform abstract reasoning about international economics using conceptual metaphors. For example, the system was able to successfully interpret both "*In 1991, the Indian government deregulated the business sector*" and "*In 1991, the Indian government loosened its stranglehold on business*" (Feldman and Narayanan 2004, 389). Narayanan's model can perform inferences either entirely within the sensorimotoric domain or in the linguistic domain using common conceptual metaphor mappings. Taken together with the neurophysiological evidence for image schemas and conceptual metaphors, these neurocomputational models support the metaphoric and image-schematic basis of our language and abstract reasoning.

The Continuity of Embodied Social and Cultural Cognition

In this chapter, we have been presenting evidence for the embodied character of cognition, and we have suggested an appropriate pragmatist philosophical framework for interpreting that evidence. Contra representationalism, we have argued that cognition is not some inner process performed by "mind," but rather is a form of embodied action. We argued this by giving examples of how cognition is located in organism-environment interactions, instead of being locked up in some allegedly private mental sphere of thought. However, an exclusive focus on the organism's engagement and coupling with its environment can lead to the mistaken impression that thought is individual, not social. Therefore, we must at least briefly address the crucial fact that language and abstract reasoning are socially and culturally situated activities.

Thus far, we have discussed only one sociocultural dimension, albeit a crucially important one—namely, development. Our brief discussion of development was framed more within the context of nervous systems than within sociocultural interactions. We stressed the point that epigenetic bodily interactions with the world are what shape our neural maps and the image schemas in them. For humans, a very large and distinctive part of that involves interacting with other humans. In other words, human understanding and thinking is social. This raises the question: How do socially and culturally determined factors come to play a role in human cognition?

Perhaps the skeptic might say that the locus of the distinctively human lies in a socially and culturally learned capacity for classical representationalism. Once again, however, the representationalist proposal rests on two mistakes. First, there is not a radical ontological break from the rest of the animal kingdom with respect to socially and culturally transmitted behaviors, both in general and specifically in the cases of linguistic and symbolic communication. Second, having challenged the "inner-mind" versus "outer-body" split, we must not then proceed to replace it with another equally problematic dichotomy—that between the "individual" and the "social." We must recognize that cognition does not take place only within the brain and body of a single individual, but instead is partly constituted by social interactions and relations. The evidence to which we now turn comes from cognitive ethology and distributed cognition. Of course there are ways in which our sociocultural behaviors are peculiarly human; but the story is once again much more complex and multidimensional than classical representationalists suppose.

Following Maturana and Varela (1998, 180–84), we would define *social phenomena* as those phenomena arising out of recurrent structural couplings that require the coordinated participation of multiple organisms. They argue that just as the cell-to-cell interactions in the transition from single- to multicelled organisms afford a new level of *intercellular* structural coupling, so also recurrent interactions between organisms afford a new level of *interorganism* structural coupling.

The social insects are perhaps the most basic example of this kind of recurrent interorganismic behaviors. For example, ants must feed their queen for their colony to remain alive. Individual workers navigate their way to and from the nest and food sources by leaving trails of chemical markers, but these markers are not distinctive to the individual ant. When seeking food, an individual ant moves away from markers dropped by other ants. Naturally the density of such markers decreases in proportion to the distance from the nest. But when one finds food, it begins to actively seek denser clusters of markers, thus leading it back to the nest. Furthermore, whenever a worker ant eats, its chemical markers change slightly. These chemical markers attract, rather than repel, other ants. Thus the ants gradually begin to form a column leading from a food source to a nest. Note that the ants' cognition is both social (in that it takes place between organisms) and distributed (in the sense that it off-loads much of the cognitive work onto the environment). No single ant carries around either an "internal representation" or a neural map of where the ant colony is. Ant cognition is thus nonrepresentational in that it is both intrinsically social and situated in organism-environment interactions.

The social cognition of insects, however, does not include the capacity for spontaneous imitation, which is so central to human cognition. For a social behavior to become a learned behavior and then continue across generations, a capacity for spontaneous imitation is crucial. However, zoological ethologists have shown that this imitative capacity is not unique to humans. Researchers studying macaque monkeys left potatoes on the beach for a colony of wild monkeys who normally inhabit the jungle near the beach. After gradually becoming habituated to the beach and becoming more familiar with the sea, one monkey discovered that dipping the potatoes in a tide pool would cleanse them of the sand that made them unpalatable. This behavior was imitated throughout the colony in a matter of days, but the researchers observed that older macaques were slower to acquire the behavior than the younger ones (Kawamura 1959; McGrew 1998). Maturana and Varela (1998, 203) define *cultural behavior* precisely as this kind of relatively stable pattern of such transgenerational social behavior.

The culturally acquired behavior most often held up by classical representationalists as the hallmark of the distinctively human is language. However, even here there is not a clear break from the animal kingdom in terms of basic cognitive capabilities, as we see when considering the results of researchers who have been trying to teach symbolic communication to other primates. Instead, their observations are consonant with our theory of how language and image schemas emerge from bodily processes involving cross-modal perception. In experiments done by Savage-Rumbaugh, Sevcik, and Hopkins (1988), three chimpanzees who had been trained in symbolic communication were able to make not only cross-modal associations (i.e., visual to tactile), but were able to make symbolic-to-sensory-modal associations. For example, Kanzi was able to hear a spoken English word and accurately (100 percent of the time) choose either the corresponding visual lexigram or a visual picture of the word. Sherman and Austin were able to choose the appropriate object by touch when presented with a visual lexigram (100 percent correct), and conversely they were also able to choose the appropriate visual lexigram when presented with a tactile-only stimulus (Sherman, 96 percent correct; Austin, 100 percent correct) or olfactory-only stimulus (Sherman, 95 percent correct; Austin, 70 percent correct). Their ability to perform such symbolic-to-sensory-modality coordination enhanced their performance on tasks measuring solely cross-modal coordination; as Savage-Rumbaugh, Sevcik, and Hopkins observe: "These symbol-sophisticated apes were able to perform a variety of cross-modal tasks and to switch easily from one type of task to another. Other apes have been limited to a single cross-modal task" (1988, 623). Although these apes will never approach the linguistic capabilities of humans, these results show the continuity of our human capacity for abstract cross-modal thought is shared by at least some members of the animal kingdom.

In fact, related recent research on primates has shown that it is the distinctively human sociocultural environment (and not some great discontinuity in comparative cognitive capacity) that facilitates the cross-modal capabilities underlying language and abstract reason. We have already noted that the neural development of the cross-modal maps of juvenile owls can be modified by epigenetic stimulation; but it is equally important to realize that the cross-modal basis for many of our image schemas requires epigenetic stimulation of the kind presented by human parents. Tomasello, Savage-Rumbaugh, and Kruger (1993) compared the abilities of chimpanzees and human children to imitatively learn how to perform novel actions with novel objects. They tested three conspecific (mother-reared) chimpanzees and three enculturated chimpanzees, along with eighteen- and thirty-month-old human children. They introduced a new object into each participant's environment, and after observing the participant's natural interactions with the object, the experimenter demonstrated a novel action with the object with the instruction "Do what I do." Their results showed that the mother-reared chimpanzees were much poorer imitators than the enculturated chimpanzees and the human children, who did not differ from one another. A human-like sociocultural environment is an essential component not only for the development of our capacity for imitation, but also for the development of our capacities for the cross-modal image schemas that underlie language and abstract reasoning (see also Fouts, Jensvold, and Fouts 2002).

Finally, there is also considerable evidence from cognitive anthropology that adult humans do not think in a manner consistent with the dichotomies posed by classical representationalism. Like the social insects, we tend to off-load much of our cognition onto the environments we create. We tend to accomplish this in two ways—first, we make cognitive artifacts to help us engage in complex cognitive actions; and second, we distribute cognition among members of a social organization. As an example of the first, Hutchins (1995, 99–102) discusses how medieval mariners used the thirty-two-point compass rose to predict tides. By superimposing onto the compass rose the twenty-four-hour day (in forty-five-minute intervals), the mariners could map the lunar "time" of the high tide (the bearing of the full moon when its pull causes a high tide) to a solar time of day. As long as we know two facts—the number of days since the last full moon and the lunar high tide for a particular port—we simply count off a number of points on the compass rose equal to the days past the full moon to compute the time of next high tide. Without the schema provided by the cognitive artifact, computing the next high tide is a much more laborious cognitive task. As an example of the second, Hutchins (ibid., 263–85) discusses how the partially overlapping knowledge distributions of a group of three navy navigation personnel are distributed among the team. Although no single team member is expected to constantly maintain a complete internal representation of all the navigational data, Hutchins shows how the social distribution of the cognitive tasks functions as a brake on serious navigational errors that could imperil the ship, because the participants each know some of the spatial relations and procedures immanent to another team member's job. In short, the off-loading of some of the cognitive load onto the environment—as found both in cognitive artifacts and the social distribution of cognitive tasks—is crucial to many of our daily cognitive activities.

A fully adequate treatment of the social dimension of thought would require substantially more evidence and analysis than we can provide here. We have only attempted to suggest that sociocultural cognition in general is not unique to humankind, that the common cases for cross-modal cognition and symbolic/linguistic communication are not unique to humans, and that human cognition cannot be locked up within the private workings of an individual mind. Since thought is a form of coordinated action, it is spread out in the world, coordinated with both the physical environment and the social, cultural, moral, political, and religious environments, institutions, and shared practices. Language — and all forms of symbolic expression — are quintessentially social behaviors. Dewey nicely summarizes the intrinsically social character of all thought in his argument that the very idea of thinking as a kind of inner mental dialogue is only possible because of socially established and preserved meanings, values, and practices:

> When the introspectionist thinks he has withdrawn into a wholly private realm of events disparate in kind from other events, made out of mental stuff, he is only turning his attention to his own soliloquy. And soliloquy is the product and reflex of converse with others; social communication not an effect of soliloquy. If we had not talked with others and they with us, we should never talk to and with ourselves. Because of converse, social give and take, various organic attitudes become an assemblage of persons engaged in converse, conferring with one another, exchanging distinctive experiences. . . . Through speech a person dramatically identifies himself with potential acts and deeds; he plays many roles, not in successive stages of life but in a contemporaneously enacted drama. Thus mind emerges. ([1925] 1981, 135)

"Thus mind emerges"! It emerges as, and is enacted through, social cognition. There is no radical rupture with our bodily experience of meaning; instead, that meaning is carried forward and given voice through language and other forms of social symbolic interaction and expression.

Embodied Meaning, Thought, and Language

We have been arguing against disembodied views of mind, concepts, and reasoning, especially as they underlie representationalist theories of mind and language. Our alternative view — that cognition is embodied — has roots in American pragmatist philosophy and is being supported and extended by recent work in second-generation cognitive science. Pragmatists like James and Dewey understood that philosophy and empirical science must develop in mutual cooperation and criticism, if we are ever to have an empirically responsible understanding of the human mind and all its marvelous capacities and acts. Pragmatism is characterized by (1) a profound respect for the richness, depth, and complexity of human experience and cognition; (2) an evolutionary perspective that appreciates the role of dynamic change in all development (as opposed to fixity and finality); and (3) recognition that human cognition and creativity arise in response to problematic situations that involve values, interests, and social interaction. The *principle of continuity* encompasses the fact that apparently novel aspects of thought and social interaction arise naturally via increased complexity of the organism-environment interactions that constitute experience. Pragmatists thus argue that all our traditional metaphysical and epistemological dualisms (e.g., mind/body, inner/outer, subject/object, concept/percept, reason/emotion, knowledge/imagination, and theory/practice) are merely abstractions from the interactive (enactive) process that is experience. Such distinctions are not absolute ontological dichotomies. Sometimes they serve us well, but oftentimes they serve us quite poorly, depending on what problems we are investigating, what values we have, and what the sociocultural context is.

In recent years the number of researchers engaged in some variation of "embodied cognition" has swelled prodigiously. Once upon a time, cognitive science seemed defined by the representationalist view that the body is inconsequential to the study of the mind. But that has changed dramatically. Some representationalists have recently argued for a very limited sense of embodiment that would keep intact much of the first generation of cognitive science's representational baggage (Clark 1998). Today we are witnessing a new generation of cognitive science emerging that defines "embodied cognition" as a fundamentally nonrepresentational project. Contributions to a radical theory of embodied cognition are being made by dynamic systems theorists who argue that cognition, though amenable to mathematical description, is not computational (van Gelder 1995); by neurobiologists whose experiments show us how metaphors of information transfer mislead us as we struggle to understand the population dynamics behind neural organization (Edelman 1992; Edelman and Tononi 2000); and by cognitive roboticists who understand that having a body is perhaps not such a bad thing after all (Brooks 1991; Brooks and Stein 1994). Even Alan Turing— a leader among that lost first generation who so errantly steered cognitive science toward disembodiment—was willing to admit he might be wrong when it came to how we might teach a robot language: "It can also be maintained that it is best to provide the machine with the best sense organs that money can buy, and then teach it to understand and speak English. That process could follow the normal teaching of a child. Things would be pointed out and named, etc. Again, I do not know what the right answer is, but I think both approaches should be tried" (1950, 460). We have already tried the disembodied approach, and its failures have breathed new life into the pragmatist approach to embodied cognition.

The themes we have been tracing throughout this chapter—our animal engagement and cognition, our ongoing coupling and our falling in and out of harmony with our surroundings, our active value-laden inquiry to reestablish harmony and growth, and our community of social interactions—are beautifully encapsulated by Dewey in his attempt to recover the value of the aesthetic dimensions of meaning in human life:

> At every moment, the living creature is exposed to dangers from its surroundings, and at every moment, it must draw upon something in its surroundings to satisfy its needs. The career and destiny of a living thing are bound up with its interchanges with environment, not externally but in the most intimate needs.
>
> The growl of a dog crouching over his food, his howl in time of loss and loneliness, the wagging of his tail at the return of his human friend are expressions of the implication of a living in a natural medium which includes man along with the animal he has domesticated. Every need, say for hunger for fresh air or food, is a lack that denoted at least a temporary absence of adequate adjustment with surroundings. But it is also a demand, a reaching out into the environment by building at least a temporary equilibrium. Life itself consists of phases in which the organism falls out of step with the march of surrounding things and then recovers unison with it—either through effort or some happy chance. . . .
>
> These biological commonplaces are something more than that [mere biological consequences]; they reach to the roots of the esthetic in experience. ([1934] 1987, 13–14)

We humans are live creatures. We are acting when we think, perhaps falling in and out of step with the environment, but never are our thoughts outside of it. Via our bodily senses, the environment enters into the very shape of our thought, sculpting our most abstract reasoning from the granite of our embodied interactions with the world.

CHAPTER 4

The Meaning of the Body

We humans are incarnate. Our embodiment shapes both *what* and *how* we experience, think, mean, imagine, reason, and communicate. This claim is a bold one, and it challenges our received wisdom that what we call "mind" and "body" are not one and the same, but rather are somehow fundamentally different in kind. From a philosophical point of view, one of the hardest tasks you'll ever face is coming to grips with the fact of your embodiment. What makes this task so very difficult is the omnipresent idea of disembodied mind and thought that shows itself throughout our intellectual tradition, from claims about pure logical form to ideas of noncorporeal thought, to spectator views of knowledge, to correspondence theories of truth. Everywhere you turn, the mysterious exotic snail of disembodied mind leaves its shiny, slippery trail through our views of thought, language, and knowledge.

In the previous chapters, I developed the embodied view of mind and thought that comes from blending pragmatist philosophy with second-generation cognitive science. What is needed now is a more detailed account of how human meaning is embodied at all levels, from perception and action all the way up to abstract conceptualization and reasoning. My modest efforts to counteract our inherited cultural habit of conceiving of mind as disembodied consist primarily in trying to show some of the ways that meaning, concepts, logic, and inferential patterns are grounded in our bodies and in bodily activities. In a nutshell, to say that meaning is embodied is to say that meaning, understanding, and reasoning depend directly on how our bodies and brains work and on the patterns of our bodily interactions with the world. This is not merely the obvious claim that we need bodies and brains in order to think. It is the much-stronger claim that the nature of conceptualization and even reason itself are shaped by the ways our bodies work and by the nature of our bodily encounters with our environments.

In this chapter I argue that meaning emerges in our sensory-motor and affective experiences, where it is organized by recurring patterns of bodily perception and action known as "image schemas." Image schemas support body-based thinking and inference, but this occurs mostly beneath the level of conscious awareness. This body-based meaning is extended, via imaginative processes like conceptual metaphor, to structure our abstract concepts. Conceptual metaphors allow us to understand and reason about abstract entities and domains, without losing the bodily grounding of meaning. I will suggest that our bodily experience thus provides a pre-reflective fund of meaning that makes it possible for us to think abstractly and to carry out all forms of meaningful human symbolic interaction, expression, and communication.

Where Does Meaning Come From?

Human beings are embodied organisms engaged in ongoing patterned interactions with their ever-changing environments. Those environments are not just physical—not just earth, air, fire, and water—but are also always social, economic, moral, political, and spiritual. Experience is therefore never just bodily or just mental, but rather both at once. Experience is neither merely subjective nor merely objective, but rather is a more continuous process out of which what we call "subjects" and "objects" emerge. Experience doesn't separate itself into emotional versus rational components; rather, our rationality is at once embodied and emotional, full of eros.

Our experiences are always structured by a large number of recurring interactional patterns that make up our intercorporeal communal experience. Such flesh-and-blood patterns are the bodily basis of our shared world, given our present state of evolutionary development. What these patterns are and how they blend depends on a number of factors: the nature and limits of our perceptual systems, the architecture of our brains, the character of the environments we inhabit (including the "affordances" available to us for our experience), the kinds of motor programs we can execute, the needs we have, the purposes we seek to realize through our actions, the range of emotions we are capable of experiencing, and the values we have because of our overall makeup and evolutionary history. Thus, the characteristics of our bodies, our neural makeup, and our environments constrain not only *what* it is possible for us to think, but more important, *how* we think about it.

If you think, as I do, that there is no mind without a body—a body in continuous interaction with ever-changing environments—then you've got to explain how this bodily activity gives rise to all our glorious abstract thought and symbolic interactions. I want to give a sketch of certain key parts of this account of embodied meaning and thought; in particular, (1) image schemas, (2) controller executing schemas, and (3) primary conceptual metaphors.

Image Schemas

Let us start with the fact that our experience is permeated with hundreds of recurring sensory-motor patterns, known as "image schemas," that give shape, connection, and significance to what we experience (M. Johnson 1987; Lakoff 1987; Lakoff and Johnson 1999). To illustrate this kind of meaningful structure, consider the CONTAINER schema, examined in the previous chapter. Thousands of times each day we perceive, manipulate, and interact with containers, such as cups, boxes, briefcases, rooms, vehicles, and even our own bodies. Via these recurrent vital interactions, we come to learn the meaning and logic of containment. The CONTAINER schema consists of the following minimal structure:

1. a boundary
2. an interior
3. an exterior

To get schemas for concepts like *in* and *out*, you must add structure that profiles various parts of the CONTAINER schema. The concept *in* profiles (highlights or activates) the interior of the CONTAINER schema, whereas the concept *out* profiles the exterior that surrounds the boundary. *In* and *out* also require identification of a figure/ground (or trajector/landmark) structure relative to the CONTAINER schema. When we say, "The horse left the barn," the horse is the trajector relative to the barn (landmark).

Even for image schemas as elementary and simple as the CONTAINER schema, there is already a definite spatial or bodily logic (summarized earlier, in chap. 3) that is learned from our sensory-motor experience and that constrains our inferences about containers:

1. If an object *X* is in a container *A*, then that object is not outside that container.
2. If an object *X* is within container *A*, and container *A* is within container *B*, then object *X* is within container *B*.
3. If an object *X* is outside of container *B*, and container *A* is inside container *B*, then object *X* is outside of container *A*.

To emphasize just how much internal structure—and thereby how much constraint on spatial logics there can be for even our most elementary image schemas—consider the SOURCE-PATH-GOAL schema mentioned briefly in the previous chapter. The schema consists of at least the following minimal structure:

1. a source point, from which the path begins
2. a path leading in some direction
3. a goal; that is, an endpoint for the path

Described in this minimal way, it might seem as though the image schema does not have enough internal structure to support extensive inferences. However, actual SOURCE-PATH-GOAL schemas usually have considerable additional structure that can serve as the basis for a wide range of inferences. For example:

- a trajector that moves
- a source location (the starting point)
- a goal (the intended destination for the trajector)
- a route from the source to the goal
- the actual trajectory of motion
- the position of the trajector at a given time
- the direction of the trajector at that time
- the actual final location of the trajector when the motion is terminated, which may be different from the intended destination

Typically, there is even more structure available within this image schema, for the above list leaves out other possible dimensions that might play a role in various events, including the speed of the trajector, the trail left by the trajector, obstacles to motion, aids to motion, forces that move the trajector, multiple trajectors, and so on.

An important feature of image schemas is their topological character, in the sense that they can undergo a wide range of distortions or transformations while still retaining their image-schematic structure and logic. For example, a path can be straight, or it can twist and turn back on itself, or it can involve stop-and-go motion, without losing its characteristic SOURCE-PATH-GOAL structure and without violating its characteristic spatial logic.

Another crucial property of image schemas is their compositionality, that is, their ability to combine to produce other image schemas. Via such composition, vast expanses of our experience and understanding of our mundane bodily experience are structured image-schematically. For example, as Lakoff and Núñez (2000) have shown, the concepts *into* and *out of* are blendings of the CONTAINER schema with the SOURCE-PATH-GOAL schema.[1] The INTO schema is a composition of the IN schema and the TO schema, whereas the OUT OF schema combines the OUT schema and the FROM/TO schema.

INTO Schema

- *The* IN *schema*: consisting of a CONTAINER schema, with the interior profiled and taken as landmark
- *The* FROM/TO *schema*: consisting of a SOURCE-PATH-GOAL schema, with the goal profiled and taken as landmark
- *Correspondences*: (interior; goal) and (exterior; source)

OUT OF Schema

- *The* OUT *schema*: consisting of a CONTAINER schema, with the exterior profiled and taken as landmark
- *The* FROM/TO *schema*: consisting of a SOURCE-PATH-GOAL schema, with the source profiled and taken as landmark
- *Correspondences*: (interior; source) and (exterior; goal)

A full accounting of the image-schematic structure of our experience and understanding might extend to thousands of structures. However, most of these would be complex combinations of a smaller number of more basic image schemas.

In summary, there are four major points to keep in mind concerning the nature and activation of image schemas:

1. Image schemas characterize the recurring structure of much of our sensory-motor experience, and they are the basis for much of our embodied pre-reflective meaning.
2. They are learned automatically—and usually unconsciously—through our bodily interactions with aspects of our environment, given the nature of our brains and bodies in relation to the possibilities for experience that are afforded us within different environments. Image schemas are meaningful to us even when, as is typical, they operate beneath the level of conscious awareness.
3. They have highly determinate "spatial" or "bodily" logics that support and constrain inferences.
4. They are compositional, in that they combine and blend, yielding even more complex embodied meaning and inference patterns.

Image schemas were originally hypothesized to explain the bodily basis of meaning, language, and inference structure, and they were often illustrated via phenomenological descriptions of various dimensions of our sensory-motor experience (Lakoff 1987; M. Johnson 1987). Subsequently, empirical studies have supplied evidence of the existence of cross-modal connections of the sort that we have claimed for image schemas. A recent survey of research on the role of motor and kinesthetic capacities in the processing of mental images (Gibbs and Berg 2002) includes the following striking examples of cross-modal representational capacities:

Motor Processes in Mental Imagery

Wexler, Kosslyn, and Berthoz (1998) argue that certain motor programs are part of our capacity to rotate mental images. In one experiment, participants first learned to rotate a handheld joystick at different speeds (45 or 90 degrees per second), in both clockwise and counterclockwise directions, without being able to see their hands. They were then directed to perform a dual task that consisted of rotating the joystick at the same time as they were performing image-rotation tasks of the sort studied by Shepard and Cooper (1982). These experiments showed that clockwise rotation of the joystick facilitated clockwise rotation of mental images, while rotating the hands in the opposite direction from that in which the mental image is rotated hinders the image-rotation task. If there was no motor dimension to the mental image-rotation task, then there should be no differential interference evident when the hands and mental images were rotating in opposite directions.

The idea that motor and kinesthetic processes are involved in mental imagery is also supported by various studies of congenitally blind peoples' ability to perform a range of mental image manipulation tasks. Although blind people are typically slower at performing these tasks, they are able to rotate and scan mental images (Marmor and Zaback 1976; Carpenter and Eisenberg 1978). The explanation of this ability, given the absence of certain types of visual processing in blind people, is that they use their tactile, proprioceptive, and kinesthetic abilities to perform tactile analogues of visual inspection and rotation.

Sensory and Motor Coactivations (Mirror Neurons)

Over the past few years, a number of experiments indicate that parts of the sensory-motor cortex are weakly activated when people observe others performing motor tasks or imagine themselves doing those tasks. For example, when a person merely observes another person move his hand in a certain way (grasping a specific object, for example), the same areas of the motor cortex are activated that are also used when that person performs that same grasping motion with her own hand (di Pellegrino et al. 1992; Rizzoletti and Fadiga 1998; Gallese 2003; Rizzolatti and Craighero 2004; Gallese and Lakoff 2005; Gallese and Cuccio 2015). These are remarkable findings because they reveal connections between various perceptual, kinesthetic, and motor capacities. Cross-domain connections of this sort are exactly what is required for image schemas to be cross-modal.

These experimental results also suggest that simulation is a key part of our capacity to understand situations and events (Feldman 2006; Bergen 2012). Part of the meaning of seeing another person perform an action depends on our own simulation of that same action in the appropriate motor cortex. Moreover, when we merely imagine ourselves performing a certain bodily movement or object manipulation, the sensory-motor areas activated are those that would be involved in our actually performing those actions. Gibbs and Berg summarize key implication of such research: "Most scholars agree that the motor processes activated during perception and imagination are always a limited subset of those activated during overt movement (Ellis 1995; Ramachandran and Hirstein 1997). More generally, though, the various behavioral and neuroimagery findings highlight that motoric elements are recruited whenever the perceived or imagined object is conceptualized in action-oriented terms" (Gibbs and Berg 2002, 13).

Representational Momentum

A series of experiments performed by Freyd and colleagues argue that people have body-based models of physical momentum [called "representational momentum" by Freyd and Finke (1984)] that they use in reasoning about visual and auditory images. In one example of the experimental design, three static images of some simple object were presented, such that the object appears either to move along a linear path, or else to rotate in one direction. Then a final target position of the image is presented, and the subject is asked whether that target image location coincides with the earlier third image they have just seen. In several such experiments, researchers found a tendency for people to misremember the final (i.e., third) location as being farther along the trajectory than it actually is. If the trajectory is a linear path, they will tend to remember that the third position was farther in the direction of motion than it is. If there is rotational motion, they will tend to remember the third object location as rotated beyond where it actually was. Kelly and Freyd claim that representational momentum of this sort "reflects the internalization in the visual system of the principles of physical momentum" (1987, 369). These effects occur in linear motion, rotation, centripetal force, and spiral paths, and they are relative to object speed, acceleration, and size. Moreover, there appears to be momentum experienced in the auditory domain, such as when a third tone in an ascending pitch contour will be remembered as higher than it actually was and lower than it was in a descending pitch contour (Kelly and Freyd 1987). Although there is no settled explanation of such representational momentum phenomena, these results indicate the role of embodied structures of perception, motion, and object manipulation in our representation of events.

In general, then, experiments of the sort described above give evidence for the existence of cross-modal representations in mental imagery and image-schematic structure. The key point is that sensory-motor correlations lie at the heart of our ability to form mental images and to recognize corresponding structures of imagination across different perceptual and motor representations. Gibbs and Berg conclude: "To the extent, then, that people's mental images reflect the operation of various modalities and kinesthetic properties of the body, the experimental findings on mental imagery support the idea that image schemas play a significant role in certain aspects of perception and cognition" (2002, 26).

In addition to linguistic, phenomenological, sensory-motor, and cognitive evidence for the existence of image schemas, there are now neural models of how such image schemas might be realized in known neural architectures. Terry Regier (1996), for instance, has designed and built so-called "structured connectionist" models capable of computing a number of basic image schemas. "Structured" connectionism uses neural structures and capacities known to exist in humans (such as orientation-sensitive cell assemblies, center-surround architecture, "filling-in" mechanisms, and spreading activation) to model the topological features of selected image schemas. Such modeling is important because it suggests how image schemas might be realized neurally for creatures with brains, bodies, and environments like ours (Feldman 2006; Lakoff and Narayanan 2017).

Controller Executing Schemas

Anyone who is convinced by the evidence for the embodiment of mind must face the vexing problem of how abstract thought is tied to the body. The general form of the answer appears to be something like this: neural structures central to sensory and motor processing must be recruited to carry out the inferences that make up our abstract patterns of thinking. Structures of *perceiving and doing* must serve as structures of *thinking and knowing*.

At present, we have only speculations and some preliminary neural models of how this process might work, but they are highly instructive. David Bailey (1997) developed a model that learns how to categorize and name verbs of hand motions from various languages around the world. His model can also give orders to produce the appropriate hand motions for these verbs in a computer model of the body that can be used in robotics. Bailey's model involves high-level motor-control schemas (*X-schemas*, for "executing schemas") that operate dynamically to control and organize various motor synergies. Thus, for example, there would be a specific X-schema for a simple action like picking up a glass and drinking. The X-schema for this particular action would be a controller schema with particular kinds of bindings to certain motor synergies that are part of picking up and moving a glass (e.g., opening the fingers, forming them into an appropriate grasping configuration, closing the hand around the glass with appropriate force, lifting the glass to the lips, etc.).

Srini Narayanan (1997) worked with Bailey to model motor schemas of this sort. They soon recognized that all the motor schemas they were modeling shared a common high-level control structure with the following dimensions:

- *Readiness*: Prior to initiating a particular action, your body must satisfy certain readiness or preparatory conditions. For example, in order to lift chair, you might have to stop doing some other bodily task and reorient your body posture.
- *Starting up*: You have to begin the specific action process in an appropriate way (e.g., to lift a chair, you must grasp it with your hands in a way that will allow you to exert force in an upward direction).
- *Main process*: You then undertake the typical motor movements that constitute the particular kind of action you are performing.
- *Possible interruption and resumption*: While engaged in the main process, you might be interrupted and have to stop, and you can then consider whether to resume the same action.
- *Iteration*: Having completed one iteration of the main activity, you might choose to repeat that structure.
- *Purpose*: In cases where there is a goal or purpose for one's action, you monitor your progress toward the fulfillment of that purpose.
- *Completion*: You may then decide to terminate the action, recognizing it as completed (with perhaps the purpose or goal achieved).
- *Final state*: At this point you then enter the final state, with whatever results and consequences it brings.

These dimensions of motor schemas together constitute what linguists call "aspect." They define the temporal dimensions of actions in general, and so they are not specific only to particular motor schemas. Any action a person undertakes—from picking up a cup to preparing a salad to planning a trip—will manifest this general aspectual structure. Because even our most abstract acts of thought are *acts*, they, too, have these dimensions. Languages around the world have syntactic and semantic devices for coding these aspectual dimensions for all kinds of actions and events (Langacker 1987–91; Talmy 2000; Dodge and Lakoff 2005).

Notice also that once we have one or more actions that manifest both this generic X-schema structure and some more specific X-schema structures (such as *lifting a chair*), we can then build up an indefinite number of larger event and action structures by means of compositional processes of the following sort:

- *Iteration*: We can repeat an action, or some subroutine within an action. You can swing a golf club, swing it again, and then swing it seven times more.
- *Sequences*: Large-scale event structures can be built up via the stringing together of a series of events or actions. You can go to the store before preparing dinner, which is followed by a walk in the park, before coming back home to read a book.
- *Embedding*: One part of an X-schema can embed some other action or part of an action. For example, the *goal* of the action of packing your camping gear might become the *starting point* for your extended action of going backpacking in the mountains.
- *Conditional relations*: One action can provide the condition for the performance or occurrence of another, as in "If you pick up your dirty clothes, your girlfriend won't leave you."

In short, via structures like these for combining, embedding, and sequencing actions, we are able to construct the large-scale actions and narrative structures that make it possible for us to make sense of our actions. Moreover, insofar as the structure of motor programs can also perform abstract inferences, our abstract conceptualization and reasoning manifests sequencing, embedding, iteration, and other structures for building up actions (Lakoff and Narayanan 2017).

Narayanan hypothesizes that controller X-schemas might exist in the premotor cortex, which coordinates various motor synergies into organized actions and action sequences. What Narayanan then proceeds to show is that his neural models for X-schemas are capable of performing inferences about events and actions, even actions that that do not require bodily movements. For example, let's say that you read in the *Wall Street Journal* that Germany fell into a deep economic depression, but that it was slowly climbing out, thanks to improved international trade. Narayanan developed a model of conceptual metaphor in which structure from various sensory-motor domains (e.g., motion in space) could be recruited to perform inferences for some abstract domain (e.g., economics). Narayanan then showed that certain models of metaphoric thinking based on motor schemas could perform the appropriate abstract inferences for the domain of international economics.

We do not yet know whether the human brain actually works in precisely the same way as these neural models specify. That is, we do not yet have sufficient evidence that motor schemas are recruited for abstract reasoning. What we do have so far are some examples of neural models that can both perform appropriate motor actions within a model of the body and can also perform appropriate inferences about abstract conceptual domains (for a summary of current research, see Lakoff and Narayanan 2017). And we have evidence, as noted above, of the existence of cross-modal neural connections. There is a certain evolutionary economy to such a picture of human cognitive functioning. Instead of developing a second set of inferential operations for abstract concepts—a kind of doppelgänger of sensory-motor inference structure—it would be more efficient to recruit sensory-motor programs for so-called "higher-level" cognitive functions. However, the details of how this might work remain to be developed, and we await neuroimaging evidence that would be relevant to the assessment of this hypothesis.

Primary Conceptual Metaphors

It is not surprising that all our perceptual, spatial-relation, and bodily movement concepts are intimately tied to our embodiment. Still, even though this may seem obvious to many people, it is nonetheless a difficult task to explain just how this meaning arises and achieves symbolic expression. Image schemas are but one key part of how this happens. The most difficult problem facing any proponent of the embodied thought hypothesis is to explain how abstract conceptualization and reasoning are possible. How can we move from embodied meanings tied to our sensory-motor experience all the way to abstract concepts like love, justice, mind, knowledge, and freedom? How can we move from embodied spatial logic and inferences all the way to abstract logical relations and inferences?

There is no simple answer to these questions, but I believe that the general answer is that various imaginative structures and processes allow us to extend embodied meaning and thought to the highest level of abstraction possible for us, all the way up to science, philosophy, mathematics, and logic. Let us begin with a simple but suggestive example of how this works. Recall our earlier description of the structure and logic of the CONTAINER schema. There is a commonplace conceptual metaphor, CATEGORIES ARE CONTAINERS, that is pervasive in our culture and has its grounding in the embodied CONTAINER schema logic that I discussed earlier. The conceptual metaphor CATEGORIES ARE CONTAINERS consists of a systematic mapping of entities and relations from the domain of spatial containment onto our understanding of conceptual categorization, as follows:

The CATEGORIES ARE CONTAINERS Metaphor

Source domain (containers)		*Target domain (categories)*
Bounded regions in space	$\longrightarrow$	Categories
Objects inside bounded regions	$\longrightarrow$	Category members
One bounded region inside another	$\longrightarrow$	Subcategory

Via this conceptual mapping, we can understand categorization as metaphorical placement within a container (as a bounded space). The CATEGORIES ARE CONTAINERS metaphor underlies linguistic expressions of the following sort:

The biologist identified the newly discovered object as being *in* the category of "living thing," while other mysterious objects fall *outside* that category. A subcategory is *part of* a larger category. Logically, several subcategories can be *contained within* one larger category. Developing scientific research can *move* one organism from the "plant" category *into* the "animal" category.

Via the mapping for CATEGORIES ARE CONTAINERS, the spatial logic of the CONTAINER schema that we described earlier can carry over directly into the logic of abstract categories. This gives rise to a series of correspondences between the logic of spatial containment and that of metaphorical containment for abstract entities of the following sort:[2]

"Every object is either within a container or outside of it" (source-domain inference) yields "Every entity is either within a category C or outside of it" (target-domain inference) = the law of the excluded middle

"Given two containers A and B and an object X, if container A is in B and X is in A, then X is in B" (source-domain inference) yields "Given two categories A and B and an entity X, if A is in B, and X is in A, then X is in B" (target-domain inference) = modus ponens

"Given three containers (*A*, *B*, *C*), if *A* is in *B* and *B* is in *C*, then *A* is in *C*" (source-domain inference) yields "Given three categories (*A*, *B*, *C*), if *A* is in *B* and *B* is in *C*, then category *A* is in *C*" (target-domain inference) = the hypothetical syllogism

"Given two containers *A* and *B* and an object *Y*, if *A* is in *B* and *Y* is outside *B*, then *Y* is outside *A*" (source-domain inference) yields "Given two categories *A* and *B* and an entity *Y*, if *A* is in *B* and *Y* is outside of *B*, then *Y* is outside of *A*" (target-domain inference) = modus tollens

What this *metaphorical logic of containment* illustrates is the general principle that there are metaphorical and other imaginative structures that make it possible for us to understand abstract concepts and to reason about them using the spatial logics of various body-based source domains. For example, when we hear someone say, "Whales fall *outside* the category of fish," *outside* activates the source-to-target mapping of the conceptual metaphor Categories Are Containers, and we thereby enlist the logic of containers as we process the next utterances of the speaker.

One of the most pressing questions raised by the existence of conceptual metaphors is why we have the ones we do and how we acquire them. When Lakoff and I (1980) first described conceptual metaphors of this sort, we did not have satisfactory answers to such questions about grounding. However, over the past three decades, a substantial and growing body of empirical research has shed increasing light on the experiential grounding issue.

Joseph Grady (1997) has proposed a theory of "primary metaphors" that offers a way of explaining how more complex systems of conceptual metaphors arise from and are built out of more primitive body-based metaphors. Grady's work drew on Chris Johnson's (1997) study of metaphor acquisition in young children. Johnson hypothesized that young children go through a *conflation stage*, in which certain subjective experiences and judgments are conflated with—and therefore are not differentiated from—certain sensory-motor experiences. An infant that is being held in its mother's arms, for instance, will experience simultaneously affection and warmth. During this conflation period, the young child will automatically acquire a large number of associations between these two different domains of affection and warmth, since they are co-active domains. Later, the child enters a *differentiation stage*, in which it can conceptually distinguish the different domains, even though they remain coactivated and associated. These cross-domain associations are the basis of mappings that define a large number of primary metaphors, such as AFFECTION IS WARMTH. The AFFECTION IS WARMTH metaphor underlies such expressions as "She was *cool* toward me all afternoon," "The ambassador was *warmly* greeted by her new staff," "He shot her an *icy* glare," "She's *warming* to me slowly," and "Relations between the two nations have *thawed* since the Cold War ended." Prior to the differentiation stage, a child would use terms like *warm, cool, hot,* and *cold* only for cases where there is an actual temperature change for some object or person. After the differentiation stage, such terms have metaphoric applications to states of temperament and character.

Grady (1997) has analyzed a large number of primary metaphors that result from basic cross-domain correlations in our shared bodily experience. What follows are some representative examples of primary metaphors, along with their grounding and examples of linguistic manifestations of the underlying mapping.[3]

AFFECTION IS WARMTH
Subjective judgment: Affection
Sensory-motor domain: Temperature
Experiential basis: Feeling warmth while being held affectionately
Examples: "I received a *warm* reception in Norway." "Our relationship has *cooled off* recently."

INTIMACY IS CLOSENESS
Subjective judgment: Intimacy
Sensory-motor domain: Physical closeness
Experiential basis: Being physically close to people you are intimate with
Examples: "We've been *close* for years." "Now we seem to be *drifting apart.*"

BAD IS STINKY
Subjective judgment: Evaluation
Sensory-motor domain: Smell
Experiential basis: Being repelled by foul-smelling objects and pleased by good-smelling things
Example: "This whole affair *stinks!*" "Something *smells fishy* with this contract."

MORE IS UP
Subjective judgment: Quantity increase or decrease
Sensory-motor domain: vertical orientation
Experiential basis: Observing the rise and fall of levels of piles and fluids
as more is added or taken away
Examples: "Prices are *sky-rocketing!*" "The number of crimes *rose* precipi-
tously this year."

ORGANIZATION IS PHYSICAL STRUCTURE
Subjective judgment: Abstract form or relationships
Sensory-motor domain: Perceiving and manipulating physical objects
Experiential basis: Interacting with physical objects and recognizing
their functional structure (correlation between observing part-whole
structures of physical objects and forming cognitive representations
of functional and logical relationships)
Examples: "The *pieces* of his theory don't fit together." "I can't see how
the premises are *connected to* the conclusion in your argument."

LINEAR SCALES ARE PATHS
Subjective judgment: Degree
Sensory-motor domain: Motion along a path
Experiential basis: Observing the amount of progress made by an object
in motion (correlation between motion and scalar notion of degree)
Example: "She's *way beyond* Bill in intelligence." "The temperature hasn't
moved very far over the past few minutes."

TEMPORAL CHANGE IS MOTION
Subjective judgment: Passage of time
Sensory-motor domain: Motion
Experiential basis: Experiencing the "passage" of time as one experi-
ences the motion of an object
Examples: "The time *is coming* when typewriters will all be in museums."
"Time *flies* when you're having fun."

PURPOSES ARE DESTINATIONS
Subjective judgment: Achieving a purpose
Sensory-motor domain: Reaching a destination
Experiential basis: Correlation of reaching a destination and thereby
achieving a purpose

Examples: "You've finally *arrived*, baby." "She's got *a long way to go* to the completion of her graduate degree."

KNOWING IS SEEING
Subjective judgment: Knowledge
Sensory-motor domain: Vision
Experiential basis: Gaining knowledge through visual perception
Examples: "I finally *see* the answer to our problem." "That's an *obscure* part of your theory."

Grady (1997) surveys a large number of such primary metaphors and argues that they are blended together to produce the more complex metaphors that form large systems in our abstract thinking. It is not always clear precisely how to decide what is and is not primary. For example, is the CATEGORIES ARE CONTAINERS metaphor discussed above primary or complex? While it appears to be primary (based on the correlation of bounded spaces or containers with kinds of objects located in a bounded space), it also might be viewed as a specification of the primary metaphor ORGANIZATION IS PHYSICAL STRUCTURE. According to this interpretation, the container is a specific type of physical structure that characterizes a source domain that is the basis for our understanding of categorization as a matter of perceiving abstract organization that defines a *kind*. However, even if the CATEGORIES ARE CONTAINERS metaphor is a specific instance of the ORGANIZATION IS PHYSICAL STRUCTURE metaphor, it is important to see that the specific logic of the metaphor for categories depends on the specific structure of containers and our experiences with them.

In spite of difficulties of this sort, the C. Johnson and Grady (1997) hypotheses together give us an account of how mostly unconscious correlations in our experience could be the basis for primary conceptual metaphors, which are then combined into complex metaphors. Their views are consistent with neural models of the sort developed by Srini Narayanan (1997) that can "learn" certain types of metaphors. To date, several of these primary metaphors have been modeled using constrained connectionist neural models (Lakoff and Narayanan 2017).

For many years, Raymond Gibbs has carried out a number of experiments to test for the existence of conceptual metaphors in our thinking and to probe the alleged bodily grounding of such metaphors. Gibbs's early work is summarized in his book *The Poetics of Mind* (1994), and he has continued to explore various experimental techniques to test hypotheses about the workings of conceptual metaphor (Gibbs, Lima, and Francuzo 2004; Gibbs 2008). One such study focuses on the bodily and experiential basis of conceptual metaphors for desire that underlie expressions in English and in Brazilian Portuguese (Gibbs, Lima, and Francuzo 2004; Gibbs 2003). Consider the question of whether there exists a bodily based conceptual metaphor DESIRE IS HUNGER. How could we show this using psychological testing methods? In the following passage, an American university student describes her romantic attraction to a boy she knew in high school. "Back in high school, I had this HUGE crush on this guy, James, who was a total hunk. He would flirt with me when we'd talk, but I didn't get a chance to know him very well, nevermind ever be alone with him. I was dying to get closer to him, and felt starved for his attention. I walked around for over five months feeling silly and empty because I wanted him so bad. I wanted to eat him alive! He was yummy!" (Gibbs 2003, 9).

Is this embodied way of talking about her desire as hunger merely a way of talking, or is it a conceptual metaphor grounded in her bodily experience of hunger? In other words, is DESIRE IS HUNGER a primary metaphor that underlies specific ways we conceptualize and talk about desire, or do we just sometimes coincidentally happen to use linguistic expressions about aspects of hunger when we talk about desire? An initial inspection of the language of desire in English and Brazilian Portuguese revealed that the concepts of hunger and thirst are used extensively in both languages to talk about a broad range of abstract desires. For instance, we can "hunger" or "thirst" for attention, promotion, righteousness, justice, power, revenge, or equality. But what evidence could there be that this is more than just *talk*—that it is *conceptual* and guides our *reasoning*?

What Gibbs and his colleagues did was first to determine how their American and Brazilian subjects understood hunger—or, one might say, what their cognitive model of hunger was. For example, both cultures associate hunger with *local symptoms* like a grumbling stomach, having one's mouth water (salivating), and a stomachache; with *general symptoms* like feeling discomfort, feeling weak, and becoming dizzy; and *behavior symptoms* like feeling anxious and feeling out of balance. Now, if such symptoms are strongly associated with hunger, and if they thus form a shared cultural model of hunger that is intimately tied to our shared bodily experiences, then these cognitive models should show up in manifestations of the DESIRE IS HUNGER metaphor, assuming, of course, that there really is such a conceptual mapping activated when we think about desire.

One way in which this hypothesis was tested was to formulate a number of linguistic expressions in the two languages concerning lust, love, and other desires. Some of these were constructed using the knowledge of the idealized cognitive model of hunger that was elicited in the earlier study. The other expressions were made up of a range of symptoms judged in the first study to be only weakly associated with hunger or not associated at all. Expressions of the following sort were used: "My whole body aches for you," "I have a strong headache for knowledge," "My hands are itching for you," "My knees ache for information about my ancestry." Participants read such statements, either in English or Portuguese, and were asked to rate how acceptable each of these ways of talking would be in their culture. As one would expect, if there actually exists a DESIRE IS HUNGER metaphor, then subjects would rate the sentences with expressions tied to the local, general, and behavioral symptoms of hunger (as specified in their cognitive models of hunger) much higher (as more appropriate) than those that conceptualized desire only with very weakly associated (or nonassociated) bodily experiences. Indeed, that is precisely what they found. Gibbs concludes that "the data demonstrate how knowing something about people's embodied experiences of hunger allows one to empirically predict which aspects of desire will, and will not, be thought of, and talked about, in terms of our complex embodied understandings of hunger. This evidence is generally consistent across two different languages and cultural communities. People use their embodied knowledge as the primary source of metaphorical meaning and understanding. In this way, the answer to the question "Where does metaphor come from?" is given by understanding how embodiment provides the foundation for more abstract concepts" (2003, 10). The "prediction" Gibbs refers to here is an experimental prediction about what expressions will be properly motivated by our shared embodied knowledge of hunger. He is not claiming that we can predict which primary metaphors will exist; rather, we can explain how various conceptual metaphors are grounded in bodily experience and motivated by it, and we can explain why we have the specific inferential structure in our conception of desire that we do.

What makes the theory of primary metaphor so potentially important is that it suggests answers to two crucial questions: (1) Why do we have the conceptual metaphors we do? (2) How can the meaning of abstract concepts be grounded in our bodies and our sensory-motor experience? The answer to the first question is that we have certain primary metaphors because of the way our brains, bodies, and environments are structured. Because of the specific kinds of cross-domain neural connections that we acquire through our mundane experience, we will naturally acquire a shared set of primary metaphors. The nature of our bodies and environments determines what precisely those metaphors will be. This explanation does not *predict* which metaphors will be activated for a particular person and thus show up in their symbolic interaction and expression; rather, it shows how the conceptual metaphors that we actually have in a given culture at a given time are *motivated by*, and make sense relative to, the kinds of cross-domain associations that are possible for creatures embodied like us.

The second crucial question that the theory of primary metaphor allows us to answer is how it might be possible for creatures embodied in the way we are to use their embodied meaning to develop abstract concepts and to reason with them. The key to all this imaginative activity is the coactivation of sensory-motor areas along with areas thought to be responsible for so-called "higher" cognitive functions. Primary metaphors are thus cross-domain mappings based on correlations between sensory-motor maps and structures in domains involved in judgment and reasoning about abstract domains. The strengthening of reentrant connections between these two domains establishes a pattern of understanding in which the source-domain structure and content are recruited for so-called abstract conceptualization and reasoning (Lakoff 2008). In other words, there is a directionality to the mapping—*from* the source domain *to* the target domain—and this is instantiated in the flow of activation *from* a sensory-motor area *to* a neural assembly responsible for what we regard as "higher" cognitive activity. Grady (1997) calls this second area a domain of "subjective judgment," but we really do not have a fully adequate account yet of how to describe these neural regions. The key point is that the inferences are actually performed in the sensory-motor areas and that these inferences are then carried over to the target domain via the cross-domain correlations that define the primary metaphors.

Metaphors Structuring Abstract Conceptual Systems

Once we have primary metaphors, we are off and running, so to speak. Through various types of blending and composition (Fauconnier and

Turner 2002), we develop vast coherent systems of metaphorically defined concepts. Detailed analyses have been performed of such complex metaphorical concepts for domains such as events, states, causes,
purposes, desire, thought, mind, emotion, reason, knowledge, values,
morality, and politics (Lakoff and Johnson, 1999; Kovecses 2010; Dancygier and Sweetser 2014). All our most impressive intellectual achievements—in physics, chemistry, biology, anthropology, sociology, mathematics, logic, philosophy, religion, and art—involve irreducible and
ineliminable conceptual metaphors. Detailed analyses of many of the
grounding metaphors have been carried out for mathematics and logic
(Lakoff and Núñez 2000), morality (M. Johnson 1993; Lakoff and Johnson 1999), law (Winter 2001; Bjerre 2005), politics (Lakoff 1996, 2006,
2008), theater performance (McConachie 2015), philosophy (M. Johnson 2008); science (Fernandez-Duque and Johnson 1999, 2002; Lakoff
and Johnson 1999), religion (Sanders 2016), advertising (Forceville
1996), multimodal media (Forceville and Urios-Aparisi 2009); literature (Lakoff and Turner 1989; Steen 1992), music (Spitzer 2004; Zbikowski 2002, 2008), and many other disciplines. In other words, all the key
concepts in all these disciplines are defined by multiple—often inconsistent—metaphors, and we reason using the internal logic of those metaphors.

As an example of the constitutive nature of conceptual metaphor in
science, Diego Fernandez-Duque and I (Fernandez-Duque and Johnson 1999, 2002) analyzed the metaphors used by cognitive psychologists
to define attention and to frame their experimental programs. What
we found—that the metaphors defined what phenomena count as part
of attention and also what counts as an adequate scientific explanation
of attention phenomena—appears to be characteristic of all fundamental metaphors in science. Consider, for example, the ATTENTION IS A
SPOTLIGHT metaphor that guides a great deal of scientific research. The
cross-domain mapping for the SPOTLIGHT metaphor is as follows:

The ATTENTION Is A SPOTLIGHT Metaphor

Source domain (spotlight)		*Target domain (attention)*
Spotlight	→	Mechanism Of Attention (attentional system)
Agent Who Controls Spotlight	→	Executive System
Agent Who Sees	→	Awareness System
Potential Field Of Vision	→	Representational Space
Area Illuminated By Spotlight	→	Attended Area

Notice how precisely the logic and knowledge structure of the source domain carries over into our understanding of, and reasoning about, the target domain. In the source domain:

(*a*) There is a field with (*b*) objects in it. (*c*) The spotlight sheds (*d*) light over some part of the field, thereby illuminating objects, (*e*) so that they can be seen by the person (*f*) who is looking.

This source-domain knowledge guides our understanding of the target domain as follows. In the target domain (attention) there is:

(*a′*) a mental field with (*b′*) unconscious ideas in it. (*c′*) The attentional system directs (*d′*) attention over the brain areas (or mental field), and this facilitates processing of certain ideas (or mental representations) in that part of the mental field, so that (*e′*) they are accessible by our awareness system (*f′*), and the idea becomes conscious.

What Fernandez-Duque and I showed, for the ATTENTION IS A SPOTLIGHT metaphor and for other key metaphors in the cognitive psychology of attention, is how tightly the details of the mapping control the empirical research that is done. For instance, visual spotlights have characteristics that determine the basic research problems for attention studies. Here are four cases:

1. Certain areas of the visual cortex have retinotopic maps of regions of the external world, such that objects adjacent to each other in the world activate adjacent areas in the visual cortex. Now, if attention "sheds light" over sensory areas, then cueing attention to a peripheral part of a visual field should increase blood flow in areas that map such a peripheral part of the visual field. Brefczynski and DeYoe (1999) tested this hypothesis and found empirical support for it.
2. In the source domain, the controlling agent is an entity distinct from the spotlight and from the field on which the light is directed. This logic dictates that there should be a distinct executive system that controls attentional focus and that is physically separate from the orienting system and from the sensory areas where attention is expressed. The concept of an executive system, as defined by the ATTENTION IS A SPOTLIGHT metaphor, led to the discovery of a network of cortical areas that participate in the control and movement of attention (Corbetta et al. 2000; Hopfinger, Buonocore, and Mangun 2000). What

is important here is that the ATTENTION IS A SPOTLIGHT metaphor entails an executive system; however, other metaphors (which are part of what is known as "effect" theories of attention) have no controller of the spotlight and hence no distinct executive for attention. In other words, the ontology of the phenomena is structured by the metaphor. It is not simply a fact that attention requires a control mechanism; rather, this is an entailment only for certain metaphors, and not others.

3. Since a spotlight moves in an analog fashion, the target-domain inference would be that attention would move in an analog fashion. Woodman and Luck (1999) confirmed that electrophysiological enhancement associated with the processing of attended stimuli does indeed move in an analog fashion.

4. It takes a finite period of time to move a spotlight from one location to another. Müller, Teder-Sälejärvi, and Hillyard (1998) interpreted the delay between a cue and the enhancement of the electrophysiological response at the cued location as an analog result of the time it takes the attentional spotlight to move to the cued location.

There is considerable (and growing) evidence that the central point here—that our theoretical concepts are defined by multiple metaphors that use various body-based source-domain knowledge and inference structures to generate target-domain knowledge—holds generally for our most basic theoretical concepts in all disciplines and fields of inquiry. The metaphors define what the relevant phenomena are, what counts as evidence, and what makes for an adequate explanatory framework. Moreover, it is the body-based character of such theory-defining metaphors that makes them understandable to us and gives them their internal logic.

As Lakoff and Núñez (2000) have shown, even logic and mathematics—the traditional bastions of allegedly pure, disembodied, universal reason—are thoroughly tied to embodied structures of meaning and are built up via body-based conceptual metaphors and other imaginative blending devices.

I cannot here survey the evidence for the pervasiveness of conceptual metaphor. However, there is a virtual cottage industry built around studying the role of conceptual metaphor in every area of human thought. Over the past thirty years research has come up with at least nine types of empirical evidence for the existence of conceptual metaphor in all aspects of our symbolic expression—evidence such as polysemy generalizations, inferential generalizations, extensions to novel cases, sign language, spontaneous gesture, psychological priming experiments, and discourse analysis (Lakoff and Johnson 1999).

The implications of the constitutive nature of conceptual metaphors are quite far reaching. We come to see that even our most abstract theories are webs of body-based metaphors. This discovery does not denigrate theoretical thinking. On the contrary, it humanizes it and shows us why it is even possible for us to understand a theory and to use it to organize our inquiries into experience. Such analyses give us new cognitive tools for exploring the internal logic of our theories, seeing how they are experientially grounded, and tracing out their insights and limitations. And, most important, this view gives us a way of understanding how embodied creatures like us can come to think what and how we do.

Tell Me Where Is Fancy Bred

The task of explaining how abstract conceptualization and reasoning are grounded in our embodiment is daunting. Perhaps it is helpful to end by reminding ourselves that we are not without plentiful resources as we set out to explore this new and dangerous territory. The territory is dangerous, I think, because what we are finding—and are likely to find—challenges many foundational assumptions of our received philosophical picture of how the mind works. It calls into doubt some of our inherited prejudgments about the universal, disembodied nature of mind and thought. It also challenges certain deeply rooted views about the origin of values. Yet, this territory is well worth the risks of exploration, insofar as it holds out the promise of revealing how we do what we do without the aid of disembodied spirit.

I want to conclude by suggesting that the picture of embodied mind, meaning, and symbolic expression that is emerging, and that remains to be extensively developed, will include at least the following dimensions of embodied meaning that are crucial for our ability to think abstractly and to come up with new ideas.

- *image schemas*: recurring patterns of sensory-motor experience that provide spatial and bodily logic and inferences that can become the basis of abstract inference
- *X-schemas*: executing schemas for motor programs that manifest the generic structure of events and actions known as "aspect"

- *force-dynamic structures*: structures of our bodily experience of force, such as forced motion, attraction, diversion from a path, speeding up and slowing down, and so on
- *primary metaphors*: unconscious cross-domain correlations based on coactivations of neural maps in different parts of the brain
- *complex conceptual metaphors*: large-scale systematic metaphors, built up from combinations of primary metaphors, that define our most important abstract concepts
- *grammatical constructions*: additional aspects of grammar based on our bodies and brains (e.g., agentive manipulation)
- *conceptual blendings*: there are a large number of forms of conceptual blendings (e.g., superimposition, combining two or more input spaces) by which we establish larger frames, scenarios, and narrative structures (Fauconnier and Turner 2002)

These are some of the more impressive resources available to those who are trying to frame a theory of embodied mind, meaning, and thought. To date, the most comprehensive marshaling of these and other resources of embodied cognitive science to outline a body-based, naturalistic, and nonreductive account of meaning, conceptualization, reasoning, and language is George Lakoff and Srini Narayanan's "The Neural Mind: What You Need to Know about Thought and Language" (2017). Obviously, we do not yet have fully adequate accounts of the bodily grounding of all these types of imaginative structure. We have but a small part of the neural side of this story. We have some phenomenological evidence for many of these structures. And we are developing a growing body of several types of converging experimental evidence, from recent work in the cognitive sciences. This is only the beginning — but if you contrast it with where we were thirty years ago, it looks like we are well on our way into the search for the meaning of the body in human thought.

CHAPTER 5

The Philosophical Significance of Image Schemas

The account of meaning, understanding, and reason that I have been developing in the previous chapters gives a central role to image-schematic structures that arise from the patterns of our bodily experience and can be recruited for abstract conceptualization and reasoning. In this chapter, I want to investigate more deeply the nature of image schemas and why they are so important for understanding the nature of philosophical and scientific perspectives.

The Problem Solved by Image Schemas

The term *image schema* first appeared simultaneously in 1987 in my book *The Body in the Mind* and in George Lakoff's *Women, Fire, and Dangerous Things*.[1] Our conception of an image schema was a key part of our explanation of the embodied origins of human meaning and thought. At that time, we were grappling (and still are) with a profound philosophical, psychological, and linguistic problem: What makes meaning and reason possible for creatures like us, whose cognitive operations are embodied? If the human mind is embodied—that is, if there is no fundamental ontological separation of "mind" and "body"—then how are we capable of abstract conceptualization and reasoning? In other words, how do meaning, imagination, and reason—the marks of human intelligence—emerge from our organic, bodily interactions with our environment?

If, as I do, you reject (on scientific, philosophical, and moral grounds) the notion of disembodied mind, then it is incumbent on you to explain

how all our marvelous feats of abstract thought are possible. Scientifically, there is a growing mountain of empirical evidence from the cognitive sciences that there can be no thought without a brain in a body in
an environment. Moreover, the natures of our brains, bodies, and environments constrain and shape what we can understand and how we are
able to reason about it. Philosophically, thinkers as diverse in their orientation as John Dewey ([1925] 1981), Maurice Merleau-Ponty (1962), and
Patricia Churchland (2002) have lambasted all the ontological and epistemological dualisms (such as mind/body, subject/object, cognition/
emotion, and knowledge/imagination) that characterize large parts of
Western philosophy of mind and language, and that underlie our dominant moral traditions. We thus need to replace disembodied accounts of
meaning, thought, reason, and value with an alternative general theory
of embodied cognition capable of explaining where our concepts come
from, and capable of explaining the syntax, semantics, and pragmatics
of natural languages. Obviously, this is not just a question about language. It is a question about the possibility of human cognition, and it
applies to all forms of symbolic human interaction and expression, such
as painting, sculpture, architecture, dance, music, spontaneous gesture,
ritual, and theatrical performance. It is a question about where meaning
comes from and how thought is possible.

The basic form of the answer to this embodiment problem appears to
be this: Structures of *perceiving* and *doing* must be appropriated to shape
our acts of *understanding* and *knowing*. Our sensory-motor capacities must
be recruited for abstract thinking. If you approach this problem at the
level of concepts, then you want to know where conceptual structure
comes from for both concrete concepts (e.g., *tree, house, on, in front of*)
and abstract concepts (e.g., *mind, ideas, knowledge, justice*) and how relations of concepts support inferences. Answering this question leads you
to focus on *structure*. That is, you must identify structures of sensory-
motor experience—image schemas—which can be used to understand
abstract concepts and to perform abstract reasoning.

Historically, Immanuel Kant was one of the first to deal extensively
with a similar problem, the problem of how concepts, which he thought
of as formal structures, could ever be applied to the "matter" of sensory
perception. In his *Critique of Pure Reason* (1781), in the famous chapter
"The Schematism of the Pure Concepts of Understanding," Kant tried
to find a connecting link, a "third thing," that would bind the concept,
which he thought of as *formal*, to the *matter* of sensation. That necessary
connecting link, he claimed, was the "schema" of a concept, by which he

meant a procedure of imagination for structuring images in accordance with concepts. Consider Kant's example of the schema for the concept *dog*. The schema is neither the *concept dog*, nor a particular *image* of a dog, nor the actual furry creature that wags its tail and looks cheerfully up at you. Instead, Kant asserted that the schema for *dog* is a procedure of imagination for constructing an image of a certain kind of four-footed furry animal, so that the image manifests all the features that are specified by the concept one has of a dog. To cite another of Kant's examples, the schema for the concept *triangle* would be a specific "rule of synthesis of the imagination, in respect to pure figures in space" (Kant [1781] 1968, A141/B180); in this case, it would be a rule of imagination for constructing an image of a three-sided closed plane figure.

The chief problem with Kant's account is his particular version of the form/content distinction. Form and content go together—but how is that possible? With respect to what Kant called "pure concepts of the understanding," he thought there could be "pure" form—form without empirical content—and his problem was to explain how this form could get connected to the material aspects of experience. He states the problem as follows: "But pure concepts of understanding being quite heterogeneous from empirical intuitions, and indeed from all sensible intuitions, can never be met with in any intuition. . . . How, then, is the *subsumption* of intuitions under pure concepts, the *application* of a category to appearances, possible?" (Kant [1781] 1968, A137–38/B176–77). Kant proceeds to explain that there must be some "third thing," something that is *both* formal *and* material, that bridges the alleged gap between the formal and the material aspects of cognition. Kant's candidate for this bridging function was imagination, which he thought of as a formal, structure-giving capacity to order material sensations into unified wholes of experience.

I have no interest in defending Kant's general metaphysical system, which seems to me to be too laden with a disastrous set of fundamental ontological and epistemological dichotomies, such as form versus matter, mental versus physical, pure versus empirical, a priori versus a posteriori, and cognition versus emotion. Once such dichotomies are assumed, they create absolute unbridgeable gaps that cannot capture the continuous and multidimensional character of our experience and understanding.

However, what *is* worth salvaging from Kant's account is his recognition of imagination as the locus of human meaning, thought, and judgment. Kant correctly recognized the schematizing, form-giving function of human imagination. Imagination is not an activity of pure understanding or reason; rather, it is an embodied process of human meaning-making that is responsible for the order, quality, and significance in terms of which we are able to make sense of our experience. Drawing on cognitive science research, I would argue that what Kant called the "faculty of imagination" is not a discrete *faculty*, but multiple processes for discerning and utilizing structure and qualitative differences within our experience.

We must not think of imagination as merely a subjective, idiosyncratic private "mental" operation to be contrasted with objective thought and reason. Imaginative activity occurs, instead, in the ongoing flow of our everyday experience that is neither merely mental nor merely bodily, neither exclusively cognitive nor emotional, and neither thought alone nor feeling alone. All these dimensions are inextricably tied together in the perceptual and motor patterns of organism-environment interaction, which provide the basis for our patterns of understanding and thought. What we identify as the "mental" and then contrast with the "bodily" dimensions of our experience are really just abstractions from the embodied patterns and activities that make up that experience. What we call "mind" and "body" are not separate things. Rather, we use these terms to make sense of various aspects of the flow of our experience. *Image schemas are some of the basic patterns of that flow.*

Where Do Image Schemas Come From?

The correct and highly important part of Kant's view is his understanding of the pervasive imaginative structuring of all experience. Unfortunately, because Kant believed in the existence of pure (nonempirical) autonomous reason, he did not recognize the crucial role of imagination (and feeling) in *all thought*. Subsequently, it took the nondualistic philosophies of people such as William James ([1890] 1950), John Dewey ([1925] 1981), and Maurice Merleau-Ponty (1962) — and, later, the burgeoning work of neonate cognitive science and neuroscience — to articulate a richer embodied view of imagination, meaning, and thought. James, Dewey, and Merleau-Ponty all shared the fundamental insight that mind and body are not two things or substances somehow yoked together, but rather that what we *call* "mind" and "body" are aspects of an ongoing sequence of organism-environment interactions that are at once both physical *and* mental. They recognized that what we call "mind" is embodied — that all our meaning, thought, values, actions, and symbolic expressions are grounded in patterns of perception, bodily movement, and organic biological processes.

George Lakoff and I coined the term "*image* schema" primarily to emphasize the bodily, sensory-motor nature of various structures of our conceptualization and reasoning. We wanted to stress that image schemas are not archetypes of some allegedly pure form-making capacity (as Kant ([1781] 1968) had held), nor are they merely abstract knowledge structures (such as Schank and Abelson's [1977] notion of a "script"). Instead, image schemas are the recurring patterns of our sensory-motor-affective experience by means of which we can make sense of that experience and reason about it, and they can also be recruited to structure abstract concepts and to carry out inferences about abstract domains of thought.

In the terms of contemporary cognitive neuroscience, we would say that image schemas are not the products of some (nonexistent) autonomous neural modules for producing form, but rather are patterns characterizing invariant structures within topological neural maps for various sensory and motor areas of the brain. In his book *The Human Semantic Potential* (1996), Terry Regier has developed what he calls "constrained connectionist" models that are able to compute the image-schematic structures of a range of selected spatial relations terms. The built-in constraints on such connectionist networks are intended to represent known neural architectures, such as motion detectors, spreading activation, orientation-sensitive cells, neural gating, and center-surround structures. These networks can learn to correctly apply terms for spatial relations and motions (such as *on, above, below, outside, to the right (left) of, across,* and *into*) to movies of static and moving objects.

In speaking of image schemas as relatively stable topological structures in various perceptual and motor maps, however, we must not think of image schemas as existing merely in the brain apart from the bodily perceptions, feelings, and actions in which that brain plays a central role. We must always remember that image schemas exist only for organisms that have certain kinds of brain architecture, operating within bodies of a particular physiological makeup, interacting with environments that offer very specific "affordances" (Gibson 1979) for creatures like us.[2]

Identifying Image Schemas

Since an image schema is a dynamic recurring pattern of organism-environment interactions, it will often reveal itself in the contours of our basic sensory-motor-affective experience. Consequently, one way to begin to survey the range of image schemas is via a phenomenological description of the most basic structural features of human bodily experience. When I speak of a phenomenological survey of image schemas, I do not mean the use of anything like a formal Husserlian method of "transcendental reduction,"[3] but rather only a reflective interrogation of recurring patterns of our embodied experience. Ask yourself what are the most fundamental structures of your perception, object manipulation, and bodily movement, and then ask how they arise from the way that human bodies share several quite specific sensory-motor capacities keyed to the size and constitution of our bodies and to the common characteristics of the different environments we inhabit. Certain obvious patterns immediately jump out at you. For example, given the relative bilateral symmetry of our bodies, we have an intimate acquaintance with right-left symmetry. As Mark Turner (1991) observes, if we were nonsymmetric creatures floating in a liquid medium with no up or down, no right or left, no front or back, the meaning of our bodily experience would be quite different from the ways we *actually* do make sense of things. Because of our particular embodiment, we project right and left, front and back, near and far, throughout the horizon of our perceptual interactions. In fact, the very concept *horizon* is image-schematic. Our perceptual fields have focal areas that fade off into a vague horizon of possible experiences that are not currently at the center of our conscious awareness, but are connected to what we are currently focusing on, and remain available for subsequent focal attention. Hence, it comes as no surprise that we have a CENTER/PERIPHERY image schema. Because of our ongoing bodily encounter with physical forces that push and pull us, we experience the image-schematic structures of COMPULSION, ATTRACTION, and BLOCKAGE OF MOVEMENT, to name but a few aspects of what Leonard Talmy (1983, 2000) calls "force dynamics." The bodily logic of such force schemas will involve inferences about speed of movement, the rhythmic flow of movement, whether a moving object starts and stops, and so on.

There are quite distinctive patterns and logics to these dimensions of our perception of moving objects and of our kinesthetic sense of our own motion. Because we exist within a gravitational field at the earth's surface, and due to our ability to stand erect, we give great significance to standing up, rising, and falling down. Our understanding of these bodily experiences is organized by a VERTICALITY schema. We experience and draw inferences about rectilinear motion (Cienki 1998) and draw different inferences about curved motions or deviating motions that have no obvious goal (relative to a SOURCE-PATH-GOAL schema). Because we must continually monitor our own changing bodily states, we are exquisitely attuned to changes in degree, intensity, and quality of feelings, which is the basis for our sense of scales of intensity of a quality (the SCALAR INTENSITY schema). Because we must constantly interact with containers of all shapes and sizes, we naturally learn the "logic" of containment (for the CONTAINER schema).

Through this type of informal phenomenological analysis of the structural dimensions of our sensory-motor experience, most of the basic image schemas will show themselves. However, we must keep in mind that phenomenological analysis alone is never enough, because image schemas typically operate beneath the level of conscious awareness. That is why we must go beyond phenomenology to employ standard explanatory methods of linguistics, psychology, and neuroscience that allow us to probe structures within our nonconscious thought processes. A great deal of our current knowledge of image schemas comes from linguistic analyses of their role in the semantics of spatial terms and bodily operations and of their role in conceptualizing and reasoning about abstract domains. Originally, Lakoff (1987) and I (M. Johnson 1987) hypothesized the existence of various image schemas in order to frame explanatory generalizations concerning syntactic, semantic, and pragmatic aspects of language and other forms of symbolic interaction. We argued that image schemas not only are products of language, but they structure the concepts and modes of thinking that underlie linguistic acts, as well as many other kinds of symbolic interaction. Over the past three decades, a burgeoning body of empirical linguistic research has explored the role of image-schematic structures in a vast array of syntactic and semantic phenomena in languages around the world. Raymond Gibbs (1994, 2003, 2006) has described the main types of empirical evidence currently available for image schemas. And there is considerable evidence concerning the role of image schemas in inference (Lakoff 1987; Lakoff and Johnson 1999, Lakoff and Núñez 2000). Hampe (2005) provides a survey of image schema research over the past three decades.

Alan Cienki (1997) has compiled a list of basic image schemas, although he recognizes that it is probably not exhaustive, and one could never be sure whether any list is completely adequate. Many complex image schemas are built up from the basic ones through processes of combination, superimposition, and further elaboration or specification.

Lakoff and Núñez (2000), for instance, have shown how the meanings of *into* and *out of* involve the superimposition of a SOURCE-PATH-GOAL image schema onto a CONTAINER schema. For example, *into* is based on a CONTAINER schema with the interior profiled and with the goal of the SOURCE-PATH-GOAL schema located within the interior of the container, thus capturing the motion of an object from a starting location outside the container to an endpoint within the container.

Three important aspects of image schemas can now be emphasized. First, image schemas are an important part of what makes it possible for our bodily experiences to have meaning for us. The meaning is that of the recurring structures and patterns of our sensory-motor experience, including its affective and value-laden dimensions. As such, it typically operates beneath the level of our conscious awareness, although it also plays a role in our discrimination of the contours of our bodily orientation and experience. Meaning structures of this sort are part of what Lakoff and I (1999) call the "cognitive unconscious." For example, based on pan-human experiences of things going up and coming down, rising and falling, humans will tend to develop some notion of VERTICALITY. They will learn the corporeal/spatial logic of vertical motion, such as "what goes up, must come down," and that if two identical objects are moving upward at different speeds, the faster-moving object will be *above* or *higher than* the slower-moving object at any given time. They learn—automatically, just by living and acting—that it takes more expenditure of energy to climb *up* as opposed to moving *downward*. This semantic and inferential information becomes sedimented in our unreflective understanding, just because, by virtue of the nature of our bodies, our brains, and our environments, we cannot help but experience the properties and patterns of effortful, forceful vertical motion.

Second, there is a *logic* of image-schematic structure. Consider a case in which you are moving along a linear path toward a destination and at time T_1 you are halfway to the destination. If you then travel farther along the path at time T_2, you will be closer to your destination at T_2 than you were at T_1. This is part of the spatial logic of the SOURCE-PATH-GOAL schema. Such apparently trivial spatial logic is *not* trivial. On the contrary, it is just such spatial and bodily logic that makes it possible for us to make sense of—and to act intelligently within—our ordinary experience.

The third moral is that image schemas are not to be understood either as merely "mental" or merely "bodily," but rather as contours of what Dewey ([1925] 1981) called the "body-mind." Dewey recognized the underlying continuity that connects our physical interactions in the world with our activities of imagining and thinking. He summarizes the body-mind continuity as follows: "Body-mind simply designates what actually takes place when a living body is implicated in situations of discourse, communication, and participation. In the hyphenated phrase body-mind, 'body' designates the continued and conserved, the registered and cumulative operation of factors continuous with the rest of nature, inanimate as well as animate; while 'mind' designates the characters and consequences which are differential, indicative of features which emerge when 'body' is engaged in a wider, more complex and interdependent situation" (ibid., 285).

If we could only disabuse ourselves of the mistaken idea that "thought" must somehow be a type of activity metaphysically different in nature from our other bodily engagements (such as seeing, hearing, holding things, and walking), then our entire understanding of the so-called mind-body problem would be transformed. Instead of interpreting the problem as how two completely different kinds of things (body and mind) can be united in interaction, we would rephrase the problem as being how patterns and qualities of our bodily (sensory-motor-affective) experience can be appropriated for understanding and reasoning about what we call abstract concepts. The former interpretation gives rise to an unsolvable problem, but the latter is solvable through empirical inquiry into how our bodies, brains, and environments are structured.

I am suggesting that the very possibility of abstract conceptualization and reasoning depends directly on the fact that "body" and "mind" are not two separate things, but only abstractions from our ongoing continuous interactive experience. Although Dewey did not have the benefit of the elaborate analyses from today's cognitive science showing how meaning and thought are based on patterns of sensory-motor experience, he understood that what we think of as "higher" cognitive activities are grounded in, and shaped by, activities of bodily perception and movement:

Just as when men start to talk they must use sounds and gestures antecedent to speech, and as when they begin to hunt animals, catch fish or make baskets, they must employ materials and processes that exist antecedently to these operations, so when men begin to observe and think they must use the nervous system and other organic structures which existed independently and antecedently. That the use reshapes the prior materials so as to adapt them more efficiently and freely to the uses to which they are put, is not a problem to be solved: it is an expression of the common fact that anything changes according to the interacting field it enters. ([1925] 1981, 285)

If you treat an image schema as merely an abstract, purely formal cognitive structure, then you leave out its embodied origin and its arena of operation. On the other hand, if you treat the image schema as nothing but a structure of a bodily (sensory-motor) process, you cannot explain abstract conceptualization and thought. Only when image schemas are seen as structures of sensory-motor experience that can be recruited for abstract conceptualization and reasoning does it become possible to answer the key question: How can meaning emerge from embodied experience to play a crucial role in the meaning of abstract concepts and in our reasoning with them, without calling on disembodied mind, autonomous language modules, or pure reason? Once we acknowledge the nondualistic mental-bodily reality of image schemas, we will then be able to utilize image-schematic structure and logic to explain abstract thought.

How Image Schemas Help Solve
the Embodied Meaning Problem

We are now in a position to address this problem of the bodily grounding of meaning and the nature of abstract thought. The principal philosophical reason why image schemas are important is that they make it possible for us to use the structure of sensory and motor operations (including their affective dimensions) to understand both concrete and abstract concepts and to draw inferences about them. The central idea is that image schemas, which arise recurrently in our perception and bodily movement, have their own logic, which can be recruited for conceptual understanding and reasoning. Image-schematic logic then serves as the basis for inferences about abstract entities and operations.[4] From a neural perspective, this means that certain connections to sensory-motor areas are inhibited while the image-schematic structure remains activated and is appropriated for abstract thinking. According to this view, we do not have two kinds of logic, one for spatial-bodily concepts and a wholly different one for abstract concepts. There is no disembodied logic at all. Instead, we recruit body-based image-schematic logic to perform abstract reasoning (Dodge and Lakoff 2005). In evolutionary theory, this appropriation of prior mechanisms for new tasks is called exaptation (Lakoff and Narayanan 2017).

Excellent examples of this use of image-schematic structure in abstract reasoning come from mathematics. In *Where Mathematics Comes From: How the Embodied Mind Brings Mathematics Into Being* (2000), George Lakoff and Rafael Núñez provide detailed analyses of scores of image schemas operating within conceptual metaphors that define the basic concepts and operations across a broad range of mathematical fields. To cite just a couple of elementary examples, consider two of the basic metaphors by which we understand the operations of arithmetic, such as addition, subtraction, multiplication, and division. Let's begin with the COLLECTION image schema, which involves the pattern of adding objects to a group or pile, or taking them away. We experience correlations between addition and the action of adding objects to a collection and between subtraction and taking objects away from a collection. Such correlations are the basis for a conceptual metaphor whose source domain is object collection and whose target domain is arithmetic. The metaphor ADDITION IS OBJECT COLLECTION is a mapping of entities and operations from the source domain (object collection) onto the target domain (mathematical addition).

The ADDITION IS OBJECT COLLECTION Metaphor

Source domain (object collection)		*Target domain (arithmetic)*
Collections Of Objects Of The Same Size	→	Numbers
The Size Of The Collection	→	The Size Of The Number
Bigger	→	Greater
Smaller	→	Less
The Smallest Collection	→	The Unit (One)
Putting Collections Together	→	Addition
Taking A Smaller Collection From A Larger Collection	→	Subtraction

Lakoff and Núñez show how several key entailments of this metaphor—which involves the COLLECTION schema—generate various laws of arithmetic:

Take the basic truths about collections of physical objects. Map them onto statements about numbers, using the metaphorical mapping. The result is a set of "truths" about natural numbers under the operations of addition and subtraction.

For example, suppose we have two collections, A and B, of physical objects with A bigger than B. Now suppose we add the same collection C to each. Then A plus C will be a bigger collection of physical objects than B plus C. This is a fact about collections of physical objects of the same size. Using the mapping Numbers Are Collections of Objects, this physical truth that we experience in grouping objects becomes a mathematical truth about numbers: If A is greater than B, then $A + C$ is greater than $B + C$. (2000, 56)

This simple analysis may seem pedestrian, but Lakoff and Núñez go on to show how the analysis explains many important properties of natural numbers, such as magnitude, stability results for addition and subtraction, inverse operations, uniform ontology, closure for addition, unlimited iteration for addition, limited iteration for subtraction, sequential operations, equality of result, preservation of equality, commutativity, associativity, and on and on.

A second fundamental metaphor for arithmetic is based on a SOURCE-PATH-GOAL schema. The SOURCE-PATH-GOAL schema underlies our understanding of bodily motion along a path, where there is a starting point (SOURCE), plus a continuous set of steps (PATH) taken toward the destination (GOAL). The SOURCE-PATH-GOAL schema is the foundation for our common understanding of arithmetical operations as motions along a linear path, according to the following mapping:

The ARITHMETIC IS MOTION ALONG A PATH Metaphor

Source domain (motion along a path)		Target domain (arithmetic operations)
Motions Along The Path	$\longrightarrow$	Arithmetic Operations
Point-Location On The Path	$\longrightarrow$	Result Of An Arithmetic Operation
Origin Point	$\longrightarrow$	Zero
A Point-Location	$\longrightarrow$	One
Further From The Origin Than	$\longrightarrow$	Greater Than
Closer To The Origin Than	$\longrightarrow$	Less Than
Moving From A Point-Location A Away From The Origin, A Distance That Is The Same As The Distance From The Origin To The Point-Location B	$\longrightarrow$	Addition Of B To A

Moving Toward The Origin From A, $\longrightarrow$ Subtraction Of B From A
A Distance That Is The Same As The
Distance From The Origin To B

Based on this important metaphor mapping, we thus utilize the structure of the SOURCE-PATH-GOAL schema plus our knowledge of the "logic" of motion along a path, in order to understand and to reason about arithmetical operations in abstract domains and fields. Lakoff and Núñez explore the pervasive use of this foundational metaphor to conceptualize iterative processes like multiplication and the calculation of fractions. They also provide an extensive analysis of the mathematics and geometry of the number line and of the Cartesian coordinate system, as it employs the SOURCE-PATH-GOAL schema.

Notice, importantly, that these two different metaphorical conceptions of arithmetic addition (and subtraction) are not just arbitrary, nor are they semantically and inferentially equal notions. It is easy to see this crucial point simply by observing that in the ADDITION IS OBJECT COLLECTION metaphor, there is *no notion of zero*, since there can be no zero collection (i.e., a collection requires objects collected). Nor is any notion of negative numbers possible in this metaphor, since there cannot be negative piles of collected objects. In contrast, via the ARITHMETIC IS MOTION ALONG A PATH metaphor, there can be a "number" *zero* (the origin point) and also *negative numbers* (as locations on a line "left" of the origin point). Therefore, each of these metaphors sanctions a different mathematical ontology!

In short, image schemas (operating within conceptual metaphors) make it possible for us to employ the ontology and logic of our sensory-motor experience to perform high-level cognitive operations for abstract entities and domains. The resources of our bodily experience are appropriated for abstract thinking. This process of image-schematic and metaphor-based understanding has been demonstrated for concepts in mathematics (Lakoff and Núñez 2000), law (Winter 2001; Bjerre 2005), morality (M. Johnson 1993), analogical problem solving (Craig, Nersessian, and Catrambone 2002), scientific causality (Lakoff and Johnson 1999), psychology (Gibbs 1994), and other areas of abstract reasoning and theorizing.

Putting Flesh on Image-Schematic Skeletons

However, there is a downside to our standard way of describing image schemas. The character of image-schematic analysis that has always worried me since its inception is its exclusive focus on recurring *structures* or *patterns* of organism-environment sensory-motor interactions. In short, if you attend only to *structure*, you necessarily ignore the nonstructural, more qualitative aspects of meaning and thought. You are left with a skeletal structure without the flesh and blood of embodied understanding. You lose—or at least overlook—the very thing that gives image schemas their life, motivating force, and relevance to human meaning, namely, *their embeddedness within affect-laden, value-laden, qualitative experience.* There may be no way around this problem, but we can at least recognize what is left out of our theory, without which image schemas could not play their crucial role in conceptualization and reasoning.

Before I address the depth of this problem, let me say unequivocally that the great value of image schema analysis, as mentioned above, is its contribution to a developing theory of the bodily basis of conceptualization and reasoning. The most striking and significant successes so far have come in the areas of lexical semantics and the theory of inference structure. Over the past years, a very large and rapidly growing number of outstanding studies have revealed the crucial role of image-schematic structure in a broad range of concepts, extending from spatial relations and motion concepts all the way up to our most abstract conceptualizations of reason, mind, knowledge, justice, rights, and values. These latter concepts draw on image-schematic structure in the source domains of conceptual metaphors. Image schema analysis gives us some of the most important *precise details* of the semantics of terms and expressions in natural languages, as well as the logic of our bodily experience. And, when coupled with metaphor analysis, it takes us a long way toward understanding inferential structure among abstract concepts.

This being granted, I still cannot shake off the nagging sense that the limitations of our exclusively structural analysis of image schemas leave out something of great importance. Conscious life is very much an affair of felt qualities of situations. The human experience of meaning concerns *both* structure *and* quality. However, beyond phenomenological description, we do not have very developed philosophical or scientific ways to talk adequately about the fundamental role of quality in *what* is meaningful and *how* things are meaningful. We can name the qualities, but we cannot even describe them adequately. When we describe the image-schematic structure alone, we never capture fully the qualities that are the flesh and blood of our experience.

This problem can be illustrated with an example of a SOURCE-PATH-GOAL image schema. When we experience motion along a path, there are always qualitative differences for different types of motion. There is a quality of rapid acceleration that differs markedly from gradually starting up. There is a particular quality of motion of the pulses one feels in a movement that consists of repeatedly starting and stopping a particular movement. There is a felt sense of completion as you gradually roll to a stop. Another example comes from numerous instantiations of the CONTAINER schema. There are felt qualities that you experience if you are held tightly, but nurturantly, in someone's arms, versus the feeling of being constrained within the confines of a small room or a cell. There are various ways it feels to leave a closed area and to enter an open expanse. Not only are there distinctive *qualities* for each of these experiences, but there are also possibly several layers of *values* and *norms* that characterize our interest and depth of engagement in these experiences. These values cannot be reduced to image-schematic structure. As a third example, consider any of the various manifestations of the SCALAR INTENSITY schema that populate our daily lives. There is the distinctive crescendo of a rush of adrenaline, of rapidly turning up the lights with a rheostat, of feeling a hot flash wash over your body, or thrilling at a spectacular musical crescendo. These are all "rushes," manifesting qualitative increase in intensity of some particular parameter (e.g., light, heat, or sound volume). There is much felt meaning here, but it cannot be reduced to discrete structural relations alone.

We are easily seduced into the habit of thinking only about the structural aspects of meaning and thought. This is not at all surprising, since it is principally the identification of discrete structures that allows us to discriminate features, to find meaningful gestalts, and to trace out relations among elements. But we must not mislead ourselves into thinking that this is the total content of meaning. Meaning is a matter concerning how we understand situations, people, things, and events, and this is as much a matter of values, felt qualities, and motivations as it is about structures of experience.

Eugene Gendlin has made a lifelong project of reminding us of the fundamental importance of this fact that there is much more to meaning than that which can be articulated via forms, patterns, and plans. He argues that "we can develop a new mode of language and thinking which enters, and speaks from, what is *more than* conceptual patterns (distinctions, differences, comparisons, similarities, generalities, schemes, figures, categories, cognitions, cultural and social forms . . .), although these are always inseparably at work as well. For example, 'more than' is a pattern, but here it says more than the pattern" (Gendlin 1997, 3). Gendlin's central point is that what we can formulate as articulate structure is always part of, and is interdependent with, *something more*—the felt experience of meaning that constitutes a dynamic process of organism-environment interaction. There are not two independent paths, one of symbolic structure and form and the other of felt qualities and tendencies of a situation. Rather, they are two dimensions of one process of experience and meaning-making. The structural, representational dimension cannot fully "represent" the nonformal, but the felt dimensions only achieve articulate form in and through the conceptual structural level of experience. As Gendlin says, that which exceeds the conceptual or proprositional structure is precisely the felt sense of that which carries meaning and thought forward within a situation, giving it relevance and direction. For example, as Dewey ([1925] 1981) observed, various grammatical constructions involve a felt sense of what should come next in a sentence. In "He heard the noise, just as the lights went out. His heart pounding, he slowly opened the door to the darkened basement," the passage sets up an anxious expectancy—an unsettling anticipation—of events to come. In "She seemed, to all appearances, supremely happy, but . . . ," we immediately *feel* a turn in the direction of the thought, from a sense of well-being and flourishing to an anticipation of some reversal or change of direction in our evaluation of the protagonist's life. William James ([1890] 1950) developed the notion of the "fringe" or "horizon" of meanings that surrounds any particular focal word or phrase. The fringe helps determine what is relevant in any particular act of thinking, but it cannot be adequately articulated in propositional terms, which necessarily remain highly selective and miss the feeling contours of our thought processes. Dewey describes the way the horizon of felt relations and connections guides our understanding: "Even our most highly intellectualized operations depend upon them (i.e., 'certain sensory qualities of which we are not cognitively aware') as a 'fringe' by which to guide our inferential movements. They give us our *sense* of rightness and wrongness, of what to select and emphasize and follow up, and what to drop, slur over and ignore, among the multitude of inchoate meanings that are presenting themselves" ([1925] 1981, 227).

Some psychologists, linguists, and philosophers might wish to restrict the term *meaning* only to that which can be structurally articulated. However useful this might be as a strategy for formalizing aspects of our thought and language, it is far too restrictive to capture the fully embodied expanse of human meaning. To consider only the image schema skeletons of understanding and thought is to miss the flesh-and-blood meaning and value that makes the skeleton into a living organism. I (M. Johnson 2007) have given an account of some of the more important nonlinguistic aspects of meaning, without which language itself would not exist, but which cannot be reduced to linguistic structure. This account includes images, image schemas, qualities, emotions, and feelings.

No method of linguistic or conceptual analysis focusing only on structural dimensions of experience and thought could ever adequately capture such deep qualitative aspects of meaning. I do not envision a different way of speaking about image schemas that would someday successfully incorporate their full qualitative dimensions. And yet, if image schemas play a central role in the way all meaning grows from bodily experience, then the qualitative and affective dimensions must surely be included. The least we can do is to keep in mind that image schemas are not abstract imagistic skeletons, but rather patterned, embodied interactions that are at once structural, dynamic, qualitative, and affective. The most promising direction for inquiring into such dimensions of meaning is today coming from neuroscience treatments of the role of emotions and feelings in conceptualization and reasoning (Damasio 1994, 1999, 2003, 2010; Tucker 1992, 2007, 2017).

William James and John Dewey famously tried to remedy this defect in our methods for explaining meaning, imagination, and thinking, but both were unsuccessful in convincing people to follow their lead. Neither of them could offer anything methodologically useful to linguists or psychologists. In his famous account of the "stream of thought" in *The Principles of Psychology* (1890), James reminds us that our inferences depend on the felt connections among our thoughts. These felt connections and transitions among thoughts are not merely formal structures, but are instead the contours of the flow of consciousness from one thought to another.

> If there be such things as feelings at all, *then so surely as relations between objects exist in rerum natura, so surely, and more surely, do feelings exist to which these relations are known.* There is not a conjunctions or a preposition, and hardly an adverbial phrase, syntactic form, or inflection of voice, in human speech, that does not express some shading or other of relation which we at some

moment actually feel to exist between the larger objects of our thought. If we speak objectively, it is the real relations that appear revealed; if we speak subjectively, it is the stream of consciousness that matches each of them by an inward coloring of its own. In either case the relations are numberless, and no existing language is capable of doing justice to all their relations. (James [1890] [1950], 1:245)

James offered no explicit account of anything like an image schema, but he did understand that thinking involves patterns of relation and connection, and he argued that we *feel* these patterns as transitions in our thinking: "The truth is that large tracts of human speech are nothing but *signs of direction* in thought, of which direction we nevertheless have an acutely discriminative sense, though no definite sensorial image plays any part in it whatsoever." ([1890] 1950, 1:252–53). James even went so far as to claim that we "feel" logical relations, such as those indicated by *if . . . then, and, but,* and *or* (ibid., 1:245). In spite of his remarkably rich account of the range of felt relations and qualities that populate our sentient experience, he never succeeded in convincing people to take seriously the role of feeling in thought. Only now, a century or more later, are cognitive neuroscientists returning to some of James's insights about the qualitative dimensions of thought and the role of emotion in reasoning (Damasio 1994, 1999, 2003; Tucker 1992, 2007).

The principal problem with this way of thinking about the nature of thinking is that it does not really seem to feed into syntactic or semantic explanations of the sort in which image schemas play a key role. We do not yet know how to account fully for the role of feeling in, and the qualitative dimensions of, image-schematic understanding. The chief issue is to determine whether feeling merely *accompanies* image-schematic structures, or whether it plays a more constitutive and constructive role in meaning. As I have suggested, the best arguments for the constitutive interpretation come from philosophers like James, Dewey, and Gendlin, and from cognitive neuroscientists like Damasio and Don Tucker. But neither they, nor I, pretend that such arguments are conclusive in any sense.

One might protest that I seem to be asking too much of image schema analysis — trying to make it responsible for all dimensions of meaning. Perhaps image schemas only play a role in some of the most basic structural aspects of meaning, and we then need to analyze various additional strata of meaning (such as the social and affective dimensions) to flesh out the full story of meaning and thought. This might be one possible strategy for at least identifying the full range of relevant phenomena for a theory of meaning and thought. However, I have suggested that the image schemas themselves have qualitative and normative dimensions. It strikes me that abstracting these dimensions is, at best, an artificial after-the-fact reflective move that fails to do justice to the ways we construct and experience meaning.

Perhaps there is no way to return this important qualitative flesh and blood to our image-schematic skeletons. But let us not forget that the truly significant philosophical work done by image schemas is tied to the fact that they are not merely skeletons or abstractions. They are recurring patterns of organism-environment interactions that exist in the felt qualities of our experience, understanding, and thought. Image schemas are the sort of structures that demarcate the basic contours of our experience as embodied creatures. They depend on how our brains work, what our physiology is like, and the kinds of environments we inhabit. As such, they come as close to being good candidates for universal meaning structures as we are likely to find, even though they are often incorporated into culturally different metaphors and other forms of imaginative meaning-making. They are one of the most basic means we have for discrimination, differentiation, and articulation within our experience, understanding, and reasoning. Exploring how they work allows us to overcome the ontological and epistemological dualisms—mind/body, inner/outer, thought/feeling, and so forth—that are deeply rooted in and continue to plague our shared cultural understanding. The key to overcoming such dualisms is to appreciate (1) the way image schemas arise from, and give structure and meaning to, our bodily engagement with our world, even as they (2) provide the form and content of our most basic forms of abstract conceptualization and reasoning, especially through metaphor. Their ultimate philosophical significance lies in the fact that although they do not supply the whole story of embodied cognition, they are an important basis for a nondualistic, embodied, affective, and value-based account of human meaning and thought.

CHAPTER 6

Action, Embodied Meaning, and Thought

Human perception, experience, consciousness, feeling, meaning, thought, and action all require a functioning human brain operating in and through a live body that is in ongoing engagement with environments that are at once physical, interpersonal, and cultural. This embodied perspective demands an explanation of how all the wondrous aspects of human mind—from our ability to have unified, intelligible experience all the way up to our most stunning achievements of theoretical understanding, imaginative thought, and artistic creativity—can emerge from our bodily capacities. In the previous chapter I explored some of the ways that meaning is grounded in our embodiment, especially the sensory, motor, and affective image-schematic dimensions of our experience. I now want to examine in greater depth how the intricate intertwining of perception and action provides the basis for our so-called "higher" acts of cognition and communication. In other words, I will investigate how important parts of our conceptualization and reasoning appropriate structures and processes of our most basic sensory-motor operations. Just as mind and body are not two distinct types of things, just as cognition and feeling are not radically independent processes, so also perception and action are not independent processes.

The proper starting point for an account of embodied meaning and thought is the acknowledgment that perception emerges in the context of action; that is, in the interaction of an organism with its environment. In an important early essay, "The Reflex Arc Concept in Psychology" (1896), John Dewey argued that perception—his example was visual perception—occurs as part of an *action* and not merely as a passive receptive event that later gives rise to responsive action:

> Upon analysis, we find that we begin not with a sensory stimulus, but with a sensorimotor co-ordination, the optical-ocular, and that in a certain sense it is the movement which is primary, and the sensation which is secondary, the movement of body, head and eye muscles determining the quality of what is experienced. In other words, the real beginning is with the act of seeing; it is looking, and not a sensation of light. The sensory quale gives the value of the act, just as the movement furnishes its mechanism and control, but both sensation and movement lie inside, not outside, the act. (1896, 359)

What in Dewey's day was a novel and disruptive claim is today probably a commonplace in perceptual psychology and cognitive neuroscience; namely, that we are active beings exploring our environment and that the character and directedness of our exploratory environmental interactions creates a circuit of action-perception coordination. Perception and action are not two independent functions, but rather are aspects of a series of ongoing organism-environment interactions. As Alva Noë argues, "According to this sensorimotor, enactive, or actionist approach, seeing is not something that happens in us. It is not something that happens to us or in our brains. It is something we do. It is an activity of exploring the world making use of our practical familiarity with the ways in which our own movement drives and modulates our sensory encounter with the world. Seeing is a kind of skillful activity" (2009, 60). This ongoing circuit of our skillful coping activity operates through energy transfer and transformation occurring between organism and environment. Vittorio Gallese describes this organic transformation process as follows:

> If we analyse at the *physical level of description* the relationship between biological agents and "the world outside," we will find living organisms processing the different epiphanies of energy they are exposed to: electromagnetic, mechanical, chemical energy. Energy interacts with living organisms. It is only by virtue of this interaction that energy can be specified in terms of the "stimuli" (visual, auditory, somatosensory, etc.) to which every organism is exposed. The result of the interaction between energy and living

organisms is that the energy, now "stimulus," is translated, or better, transduced into a *common information code.* The receptors of the different sensory modalities are the agents of the transduction process: they convert the different types of energies resulting from organisms–world interactions into the common code of action potentials. Action potentials express the electro-chemical excitability of cells, and constitute the code used by the billions of neurons that comprise the central nervous system to "communicate" with each other. (2003, 1232)

Here we have the elementary basis for the organic transformations we know as cognition:

1. Perception arises in the context of an organism's action—that is, its directed engagement with aspects of its environment.
2. This engagement is an interaction of energies (of the organism and its environment).
3. For the organism, the energy it receives is a "stimulus" that gets transduced into action potentials for the firing of nerve cells.
4. For the most part, there is no language-like structure involved here, but only the "code" of action potentials by which systems of neuronal assemblies "communicate" with one another.

However obvious this embodied cognition orientation might perhaps be for most cognitive neuroscientists, its implications for contemporary philosophy of mind and language strike me as far reaching and profound, because (1) it ties perception inextricably to directed action within an organism-environment process, (2) it grounds meaning in sensory-motor processes (or so I shall argue), and (3) it challenges the representational theory of mind. By a "representational theory" I mean the idea that human thought consists of a series of functional computational operations on language-like symbols "in the mind" that can be used to represent external states (Fodor 1975, 1987). As Fodor puts it: "Mental representations (including, paradigmatically, thinking) are computations, that is, they are operations defined on the syntax of mental representations, and they are reliably truth preserving in indefinitely many cases" (2000, 19). These mental representations are supposedly given meaning to the extent that they can be connected with mind-independent objects, actions, and events (Fodor 1987). I will argue that the representational theory of mind is not just unnecessary to account for human meaning and thought; rather, it is also false and misleading, insofar as it asserts that "the mind" thinks in a language of thought with quasi-linguistic symbols, as Fodor (1975) claims.

It is *not* my primary purpose in this chapter to mount a direct sustained critique of the representational theory of mind. My chief concern is to sketch the outline of an alternative view of meaning and concepts as being grounded in our bodily transactions with our world. I would only note that Lakoff and I (Lakoff and Johnson 1999) have analyzed the THOUGHT IS LANGUAGE metaphor to show its fateful influence on early cognitive science and much of contemporary philosophy of mind and language. We then show how it leads us to overlook all the embodied processes that go into human meaning-making and thought processes that are not intrinsically language-like, even though some of our highest achievements of thought often employ language. (For extended critiques of the representational view, see, for example, Barsalou 1999; Patricia Churchland 1986, 2002; M. Johnson 2007; Horst 2016.)

The chief alternative to various discredited representational theories of mind would be some view of meaning and concepts as embodied. The version of embodied cognition I want to explore here is what Gallese and Lakoff (2005) have called an interactionist, multimodal, simulation theory of meaning and thought. The interactionist perspective focuses on "the information processing carried out by the brain of an organism in the larger frame of the interactions between the organism and the environment it is acting upon. . . . The brain, a brain wired to a body that constantly interacts with the world is, at the same time, the vehicle of information *and* part of its content, the latter being conceived as a way to model organism-environment interactions" (Gallese 2003, 1233). A theory of this sort has a teleological dimension insofar it recognizes that the locus of human meaning and thought is the directed activity of an embodied creature whose surroundings supply various "affordances" (Gibson 1979) for present and future engagement with its world: "The energetic signals resulting from the organism-environment interactions are transduced and processed in the way they are, in respect of their content, because of the *relevance* (see Sperber 2000) of this content for the possibility of establishing appropriate links between animal behavior and environment" (Gallese 2003, 1233). On this view, then, meaning and cognition are situated, embodied, and shaped by values that emerge for an organism with a certain type of body that orients and moves itself within specific types of environments.

Multimodal Neuronal Clusters

From this interactional/enactive perspective (Varela, Thompson, and Rosch 1991), I want to focus primarily on the controversial claim that sensory-motor systems are multimodal, instead of being only a set of modular units connected by supramodal links. To explain and illustrate the multimodal character of sensory-motor systems, Gallese and Lakoff (2005) have used recent research on the perception, performance, and understanding of acts of grasping. The most detailed studies have so far been done with monkeys, but Gallese and Lakoff argue that there are strong parallels between sensory-motor processing in monkeys and humans—enough to support a strong analogy between the monkey and human brain regions under examination. More recent studies with humans are beginning to confirm the presence of similar structures and processes in our bodies and brains.

To explain the notion of multimodality, consider what goes on in an act of grasping some small object in peri-personal space (that is, in the area of space that can be reached by your body parts, such as your head, hands, arms, and feet). In any act of grasping, perception and motor activity have to be intricately coordinated within a physical setting. A number of motor synergies—such as the ability to straighten each finger on the grasping hand and then to bend each finger around the object grasped—have to be sequenced into a coordinated, smooth motor action of closing the hand in just the right way and with just the right amount of force applied to some object located in peri-personal space. Grasping a baseball bat with the whole hand and palm is distinctively different from picking up a coin with your thumb and forefinger. The different types of grasping and gripping actions can thus be defined by identifying sets of action *parameters* and then giving specific values to those parameters. Typical parameters would be based on functional neural clusters such as the action performed (grasping a small object), its direction (movement toward object), its amplitude (the "size" of the motion), its force (strength of motion), and so on. A specific type of grasping action—say, grasping an egg versus grasping a softball—gets defined by specifying the values of the relevant parameters of the action, such as which parts of the hand need to be activated, in which direction the hand must move, and how much force is required in the gripping action. Grasping, of course, is not just an action of the hand, so further parameterizations are required for prior positioning of the trunk of your body, proper bending and twisting of the arm, and the eye-hand coordination that guides the hand to the location of the ball. The entire story of this sequencing of motor synergies is a small wonder that involves a grand orchestration of bodily perception and action. Each of the motor synergies must happen in just the right manner, at just the right moment of time. Too much force applied in grasping the egg and you crush it, too little force and you drop it. Although these parameterizations of neuronal clusters operate automatically (mostly beneath the level of consciousness), we are sometimes consciously aware of specific parameters, such as when we feel the force with which we are gripping a ball or are proprioceptively aware how wide we have opened our hand in reaching for the ball.

To say that an action, such as grasping an egg, is *multimodal* is to say that "(1) it is neurally enacted using neural substrates used for both action and perception, and (2) that the modalities of action and perception are integrated at the level of the sensory-motor system itself and not via higher association areas" (Gallese and Lakoff 2005, 459). Multimodality is contrasted with the idea of "supramodality," according to which an action such as grasping would be seen as requiring an association area in the brain that is independent of any sensory or motor areas but which is capable of integrating outputs from both the perceptual and motor systems. This is not to deny the existence of some supramodal areas, but only to argue that much of our sensory-motor activity is done via multimodal structures.

Philosophically, there is a great deal at stake in the debate between supramodal and multimodal accounts. The supramodal view is compatible with a disembodied view of concepts that claims widespread modularity of systems and posits conceptual structure computed in brain areas other than those responsible for sensory-motor processing. The *multimodal view*, by contrast, argues that our conceptual knowledge is embodied through and through, because the multimodal sensory-motor system actually supplies the semantic content *and* the inferential structure of our concepts. *In other words, the very same sensory-motor structures that make possible our perceptions and actions are the basis for our capacity to conceptualize those processes.* Multimodal structures are an example of what Goldman and de Vignemont call "bodily formats," in which "mental representations in various bodily formats or codes have an important causal role in cognition" (2009, 156); however, Goldman and de Vignemont do not embrace the strong Gallese-Lakoff claim that multimodal neural clusters are the basis for all our perceptual concepts.

I am not denying the existence of supramodal systems. Indeed, I will identity some, especially Damasio's (2010) account of what he calls "convergence zones," which are higher-level association structures. However, I am claiming that the existence of multimodal systems is sufficient to undermine strong versions of the representational theory of mind.

Support for the multimodality hypothesis comes from studies of perception and action in monkeys and humans. It has been shown that sensory-motor processing is carried out via certain *functional clusters* of neurons, each of which constitutes a specific cortical network organized so as to carry off a specific function for the organism. Gallese and Lakoff describe three major types of functional clusters in three parietal premotor cortical networks in monkeys:

1. *Spatial position locators*: The F4-VIP neural cluster makes it possible for the monkey to be consciously aware of, and to interact purposively with, objects in peri-personal space. Neurons in this cluster are activated, for instance, when the monkey is aware of the spatial location of an object that it is about to reach for. Consequently, the visual presentation of an object within reach, or of a sound associated with that object in the same spatial location, appears to trigger an *action simulation* for interacting with that object. At the human level, we have hundreds or thousands of these action simulation plans that permit us to go about our daily business of living. Moreover, these plans can be activated even when we don't actually perform an action, in which case we are said to be *simulating* that specific action, such as imagining ourselves reaching out toward a ball 30 degrees to the right of center and within our grasping range.

2. *Canonical neurons*: The F5ab-AIP cluster plays a key role in actual and simulated action. When you see an object before you that you want to pick up and ingest, you automatically and nonconsciously prepare yourself for the requisite motor program for engaging that object. Gallese and his colleagues at Parma found that area F5 contains what they call "canonical neurons" (Rizzolatti and Fadiga 1998) that fire not just when a monkey grasps an object, but also when the monkey merely sees an object that it might grasp in a certain way. The neural "representation" is not merely a visual experience, but rather a visuomotor activation: "Because most grasping actions are executed under visual guidance, a relationship has to be established between the features of 3D visual objects and the specific motor specifications they might engender *if* the animal is aiming at them. The appearance of a graspable object in the visual space will retrieve immediately

the appropriate 'motor representation' of the intended type of hand-object relation" (Gallese 2003, 1236). Whereas the functional cluster described in (1) above focuses on the *location* of an object, canonical neuron clusters focus on the *shape* of an object as that relates to the capacity to grasp and manipulate that particular object.

3. *Mirror neurons*: The third and most widely celebrated type of evidence for multimodality comes from the so-called mirror neurons. These are neurons in the F5c-PF cluster that fire both in the performance of a purposeful, goal-directed activity (such as grasping or manipulating an object) and also when the monkey merely sees another individual perform the same type of motor action. Mirror neurons are highly specific: they fire only relative to purposeful, goal-directed activity. They fire when a specific grasping action is either performed or observed, but they do not fire when merely observing the use of a tool, instead of the hand, to perform the action. The excitement over mirror neurons and their importance for neural simulation has engendered numerous studies of their operation in humans, whereby it has been shown that analogous clusters operate when humans perform specific actions, see them performed by others, imagine performing them, and dream about performing them. Over the past few years, some of the more exaggerated claims about mirror neurons have come under critical scrutiny, but I would suggest that there is nonetheless substantial converging experimental evidence for mirror neuron systems in humans.

For our purposes, these three types of functional clusters are important because they support the multimodality hypothesis, and because they give evidence for a simulation theory of meaning and conceptual understanding. The first type of neuronal cluster ties perception of spatial location to possible action plans. Canonical neurons, the second type, are clearly multimodal, because they fire both when the individual interacts with an object (e.g., grasps it) and when he or she sees the object that could be interacted with (e.g., grasped). The third type, mirror neurons, reveal perceptual and motor multimodality as well as the existence of simulation. You see someone reach for and grasp a banana and you automatically understand that action as it is simulated via mirror neurons, as though you were reaching for and grasping that banana. All three of these systems make possible the simulation of a purposive action without actually carrying that action out.

The moral here is an important one: "Within the operational logic of such neural networks, a series of physical entities, 3D objects, are identified, differentiated and conceptualized, not in relation to their mere physical appearance, but in relation to the effect of the interaction with an acting agent" (Gallese 2003, 1236).

Embodied Concepts

The most promising and potentially revolutionary aspect of the *interactionist, multimodal, simulation view* is the way it provides an account of concepts as truly embodied. According to the traditional representationalist view, all concepts are essentially disembodied, in the sense that concepts are alleged to be modality-neutral representations that are processed in different brain areas than those responsible for perception and bodily movement. Even though our present neuroscience cannot definitively disprove the disembodied view of concepts, it is at least possible to suggest the general outline of an alternative embodied, multimodal, neural theory of concepts. The Gallese-Lakoff thesis is a bold one—namely, that "*the job done by what have been called 'concepts' can be accomplished by schemas characterized by parameters and their values.* Such a schema, from a neural perspective, consists of a network of functional clusters" (Gallese and Lakoff 2005, 466).

What is most radical about this embodied view of concepts is that it eliminates the need to postulate a vast set of neuronal clusters that are alleged to be above, beyond, and utterly independent of sensory-motor networks, and that are supposed to do the work of conceptualization and reasoning. Instead, our concrete concepts are computed via sensory-motor functional clusters. If it is true, this model is elegant and parsimonious from an evolutionary perspective, because it piggybacks conception onto sensory-motor processes. It sees "higher level" cognitive processes as exaptations of evolutionarily prior sensory, motor, and affective processes.

An Embodied Concept: The Grasp Schema

My discussion so far has been highly theoretical and somewhat abstract. It is useful to give a concrete example of what it might mean—from an interactionist, multimodal, simulation perspective—to say that we have a concrete concept such as *grasp*. What is given below is a cognitive model for *grasp* that uses the notion of parameters and their values to specify the dimensions of a progressive action that moves purposively from an initial condition, through a series of intermediate stages, to a final state. This GRASP schema is symbolically described in terms of names for functional neuronal clusters. Though the schema is represented conceptually and propositionally, the schema itself is a complex cluster of neuronal networks, and there is nothing symbolic, in the traditional sense, about it. Crudely put, this schema presents our concept of *grasp*, and the key idea is that this concept is executed neurally using our multimodal sensory-motor systems. This example, adapted from Gallese and Lakoff (2005), is meant to give the general idea of how one might begin to go about explaining concrete concepts of bodily perception and action.

The grasp schema.
1. The role parameters: agent, object, object location, and the action itself.
2. The phase parameters: initial condition, starting phase, central phase, purpose condition, ending phase, final state.
3. The manner parameter.
4. The parameter values (and constraints on them).

The various parameters can be described as follows.

Agent: An individual.
Object: A physical entity with parameters: size, shape, mass, degree of fragility, and so on.
Initial condition::[1] Object Location: Within peri-personal space.
Starting phase:: Reaching, with direction: Toward object location; opening effector.
Central phase:: Closing effector, with force: A function of fragility and mass.
Purpose condition:: Effector encloses object, with manner (a grip determined by parameter values and situational conditions).
Final state:: Agent in-control-of-object.

(Gallese and Lakoff 2005, 467)

Although this description of the GRASP schema may seem simplistic and overly abstract, each part of it is meant to be neurally realizable, both via computational neural models and by actual human neural systems. In the central phase and purpose condition, for instance, closing an effector in a certain way and with a certain force is meant to be accomplished by coordinated and sequenced motor synergies.

Another important fact about this concepts-as-schemas notion is that schemas are not typically defined by necessary and sufficient conditions in the way assumed by classical theories of concepts. Functional clusters can be activated to various degrees, rather than in an all-or-nothing fashion. They can be activated with various dimensions or phases left out. And, as we will see shortly, they can be extended metaphorically in the constitution of abstract concepts.

What I am suggesting about the analysis of the concept *grasp* is that it can be generalized as a way of explaining *all* our concrete concepts of physical objects and physical actions. I have presented some evidence of the multimodal nature of our sensory-motor system, which consists of connected functional neuronal clusters. I then used the *grasp* example to show how a sensory-motor *system* for grasping can actually characterize a sensory-motor *concept* of grasping. Understanding a sensory-motor concept is a process of sensory-motor *simulation*. The elegance and parsimony of this account consists in the way it eliminates the need to posit two entirely independent systems, one for sensory-motor processing and a different one for forming sensory-motor concepts. The work of conceptualization is carried out via a simulation within neuronal clusters for perception and bodily movement.

On the Way to Abstract Concepts

The embodied, multimodal, simulation story might seem to make sense for concrete concepts; that is, for concepts of discrete physical objects and events, sense perceptions, and bodily movements. But what about our vast panoply of abstract concepts? How are we to explain them as embodied? Obviously, this is going to be a complex process, but I can at least sketch three of the components that are necessary for such an account: image schemas, cogs, and conceptual metaphors.

Image Schemas

My key hypothesis is that abstract conceptualization and reasoning operate via the recruitment of the meaning and inferential structures of our bodily experience. Although I have not argued this point so far, it can be shown that our sensory-motor schemas have their own internal logics. There are simple corporeal and spatial logics of various bodily actions. Consider, for example, the image-schematic structure of the motion of some object along a path from a starting point to a destination. The structure of this motion is what is known as the SOURCE-PATH-

GOAL image schema (M. Johnson 1987; Lakoff 1987; Lakoff and Johnson, 1999), and it includes at least the following:

- a starting point (source)
- an ending point (destination or goal)
- an object that moves (the trajector)
- a path connecting the starting point to the destination
- the speed with which the object moves
- possible obstacles or hindrances to motion
- the location of the moving object at a given time
- the manner of motion of the object (e.g., smooth, jerky, bouncy)

Simply by virtue of the fact that we have bodies with certain specific perceptual and motor capacities, along with the fact that we interact routinely with certain types of structured environments, each of us will automatically acquire the ability to experience and enact scores of such image-schematic patterns, such as VERTICALITY, BALANCE, ITERATION, LEFT/RIGHT, CENTER/PERIPHERY, COMPULSIVE FORCE, CONTAINMENT, DEGREE OF INTENSITY (SCALARITY), and on and on (Cienki 1997; Gibbs 2006; Hampe 2005; M. Johnson 1987).

Each specific image schema has its own internal bodily or spatial logic, which we learn automatically from interacting with objects and moving our bodies in space. Within a situation structured by the SOURCE-PATH-GOAL schema, for instance, we are able to make inferences of the following sort, based on the logic of the schema:

- Two objects starting from a source point and moving at the same speed along the same path will reach the goal simultaneously.
- If two objects start out from the same source point and move along the same path toward a destination, and if one of them moves faster than the other, then the faster object will arrive at the destination before the slower one.
- If an object has moved along a path to the halfway point toward the goal, then it has covered the intermediate points along the path up to that point.

Such logical relations are so simple as perhaps to seem trivial, but they are logical relations nonetheless, and we reason (make inferences) with them about our perceptual and motor experience all the time.

The structure of typical image schemas and their internal logics has been studied for cultures and languages around the world (Hampe 2005), and I cannot pursue this further here. However, it should be noted that the neural basis of image schemas is beginning to be explored, and structured connectionist neural models have been constructed that can process certain image-schematic structures (Dodge and Lakoff 2005; Regier 1996; Lakoff and Narayanan 2017).

Cogs

Srini Narayanan (1997) has developed structured connectionist neural models of motor actions and our concepts of those actions. He has modeled premotor systems, motor systems, and premotor-motor connections in which the premotor system coordinates and sequences the specific motor synergies. Narayanan's models recognize the various possible stages or phases of motor actions: (1) initial state, (2) starting phase transition, (3) precentral state, (4) central phase transition (instantaneous, prolonged, or ongoing), (5) postcentral state, (6) ending phase transition, and (7) final state. His model also has structures for assessing progress to goal, reiterating an action sequence, deciding to terminate the action, and so forth. The model can sequence actions, run them in parallel, or embed one action within another. Narayanan gave the name "executing schemas" (*X-schemas*) to these premotor structures of actions.

One of the more important features of Narayanan's model is that it is capable of representing what linguists call the "aspect" of an action—the temporal manner in which an action is done (e.g., one time only, repeatedly, prolonged over a span of time). All languages the world over must have ways of representing the necessary aspectual temporal dimensions of actions. Although in retrospect this may seem obvious, Narayanan saw that, since his models of sensory-motor actions could represent all the key features of aspect, it follows that his model might be able to represent the structure of *any* action, whether a spatial motion, a general change of state, or an abstract mental process. In other words, once again, the sensory-motor system manifests all the pattern and inferential structure necessary for any kind of action, even a "nonphysical" or "mental" action.

The premotor cortex is a *secondary (supramodal) area* of sorts, since it structures information going to both sensors and effectors, even though it does not have direct connections to sensory-motor areas. Think of *action structure* as an abstract concept, which Narayanan, Feldman, Lakoff, and others have called a "cog." Cog structures can be characterized as follows (Gallese and Lakoff 2005):

- They are simulated in secondary neural areas that are not directly connected to primary sensory or motor areas.
- If the connections to primary areas are inhibited, then the simulation can be run "abstractly," without any specific motor action resulting.
- The simulation involves inferences that are computed based on the structure of the cog.
- Such simulations can characterize concepts in the grammar of a natural language.
- These concepts apply generally, and not just to sensory-motor events, so they can be used for abstract conceptualization and reasoning.
- Cogs will typically have image-schematic structure as part of their logic.

The cogs hypothesis is important insofar as it gives us a way of accounting for certain abstract structures that are necessary in natural languages around the world. The neural modeling is only beginning, but there have been promising developments over the past decades. Feldman (2006) provides a general introduction to some of this computational neural modelling, and Lakoff and Narayanan (2017) employ multiple perspectives and methods (e.g., cognitive linguistics, neuroscience, neural modeling, and other cognitive science approaches) to provide a massive, remarkably comprehensive attempt to explain the neural processes that give rise to meaning, concepts, understanding, and reason.

Conceptual Metaphor

A third important piece of the puzzle about abstract concepts is the notion of conceptual metaphor. Metaphor draws on, and blends with, all the elements of embodied meaning we have surveyed so far: multimodal sensory-motor concepts, image schemas, executing schemas for action structures, and other cogs for the structure of grammatical constructions. A conceptual metaphor is a cross-domain conceptual mapping. The mapping is asymmetrical and directional, typically (but not always) from a sensory-motor source domain onto a nonphysical or abstract domain. For example, consider the basic metaphor PURPOSES ARE DESTINATIONS. The source domain is motion in physical space and the target domain is any form of purposeful action. The mapping is as follows:

The Purposes Are Destinations Metaphor

Source domain (motion in space)		Target domain (purposive action)
Starting Location S	→	Initial State (Having A Purpose)
Ending Location E	→	Final State (Purpose Achieved)
Destination	→	Purpose
Movement From S To E	→	Progress Toward Achievement Of Purpose
Distance Moved At Time T	→	Stage Of Progress Toward Purpose
Obstacles To Motion	→	Impediments To Action
Lack Of Direction	→	Lack Of Purpose

Although for notational purposes we give the metaphor a propositional name (in this case, Purposes Are Destinations), the metaphor is the underlying conceptual mapping, and that mapping is realized neurally as a complex neural binding, typically from sensory-motor areas of the brain to areas responsible for understanding and reasoning about nonphysical or abstract objects or processes. We are lulled into believing the classical view that metaphor is linguistic—a mere matter of words—primarily because the conceptual mapping gives rise to polysemous linguistic expressions that have meanings pertaining both to physical, sensory-motor experiences and also to abstract notions. For instance, the polysemous term *arrived* in "She has finally arrived" could have both a spatial sense (as in "Sally finally arrived at her destination after a long bus trip") or a metaphorical sense (as in "Sally finally arrived at her goal of gaining the respect of her coworkers").Thus, the Purposes Are Destinations metaphor shows up in English in expressions such as "She *started out* to get her doctoral degree," "She *wandered off the track* along the way," "He *stood in the way* of her progress," "Her friends helped her *get moving again along the right path*," "She was able to refocus on *where she was going* and *how to get there*," "She finally *reached her original destination*—she got her PhD." Notice that the conceptual metaphor is revealed not just in language, but in all types of symbolic expressions. For example, we often represent progress to some abstract goal visually as a point moving along a line toward a destination. We might diagram progress as an arrow point that gets progressively closer and closer to some destination-goal. Or, you might hold up your thumb and forefinger a quarter of an inch or so apart to indicate that you were *soooooo* close to winning the championship. David McNeill (1992, 2005) has pioneered the empirical study of metaphor in spontaneous gestures, and his methods have been used for cross-cultural studies (e.g., Cienki 1998; Kovecses 2010).

Another important aspect of conceptual metaphor is its role in reasoning and inference. We utilize our knowledge of the source domain, which is typically structured via image schemas, to reason about the target. As we just noted above, the spatially closer you are to your destination, the sooner you will arrive there. Applied metaphorically, via the conceptual mapping above, to progress toward any abstract goal, the "closer" you are to it, the sooner you will achieve it. We know that if someone blocks our path to our destination, it will frustrate our journey. So, if "The North Koreans *put a roadblock* in the peace-talk process," they are frustrating efforts to achieve nuclear nonproliferation. This reasoning may seem simple—almost trivial—but it is not, because it shows how the image-schematic logic of the source domain can be utilized in drawing target-domain inferences, via the mapping.

Joseph Grady (1997) has studied the experiential origins of basic conceptual metaphors in our mundane bodily experience, pursuing the hypothesis that these metaphors are learned simply because we have bodies of a certain makeup that routinely interact with environments in structured ways. Grady incorporated Christopher Johnson's (1997) research on the acquisition of metaphorical competence in children, which revealed three stages of development that lead to the understanding and use of metaphors. In the first stage, a child uses a perceptual term like *see* only in its "literal" visual sense. In other words, that term is used only in the source domain (here, the domain of visual experience). In the second stage (the *conflation stage*), the term is used in cases where both the source and target domains are active together, such as using *see* when there is visual experience (source domain) that is also correlated with knowing something (target domain), as in "See, Mommy's home." In this case the child uses a source-domain term with a meaning that is also appropriate to the target-domain semantics and grammar. In the third stage (the *differentiation stage*), the term is used metaphorically, such as when there is no actual visual experience (e.g., "I *see* your point").

Building on Johnson's theory of the development of metaphoric competence, Grady hypothesized that an ordinary person interacting with his or her environment would acquire scores of metaphors simply through experiential correlations; that is, cases in which there are two conceptual domains coactivated. In neural terms, there are two functional clusters firing together, and, via the Hebbian neurons-that-fire-together-wire-together rule, these clusters are neurally coactivated and longer-term connections (potentiations) are established between them. Grady (2007) called these bindings across different domains (or functional neuronal clusters) "primary metaphors." In the case of the PURPOSES ARE DESTINATIONS primary metaphor, every child and adult has many experiences each day in which some object's motion along a path is correlated with the progressive achievement of a purpose. For instance, the baby sees its coveted pacifier on the floor under the table. Its crawling motion toward the pacifier is correlated with progress toward the baby's satisfaction of its intended goal of getting that pacifier in his mouth and sucking. Later, this experiential correlation (realized as a neural coactivation with neural simulation of progress toward goal) is reactivated in the use of the language of motion in a context of purposive action in general, even for cases where there is no actual physical motion involved.

Grady thus hypothesized that in this mundane way, without conscious reflection and based principally on bodily engagement with our environment, we learn large numbers of experientially grounded primary metaphors, each with its own inference patterns. The TEMPORAL CHANGE IS PHYSICAL MOTION metaphor is grounded in our experience of seeing the movement of an object through space as correlated with our sense of the passing of time, giving rise to expressions such as "The hours *flew by*," "The time *is approaching* when there will be no clean water," and "The time *has arrived* to take action." The STATES ARE LOCATIONS metaphor is based on the experienced correlation of being at some location and being in a certain condition tied to that location, as in "She's really *in* trouble now," "The water *went from* hot *to* cold," and "We're *out of* danger now."

The large-scale systematic mappings that Lakoff and I (1980, 1999) have called conceptual metaphors are defined by sets of submappings, each of which is either a primary metaphor or else has primary metaphors as part of its submapping. For example, the vast systematic LOCATION EVENT-STRUCTURE metaphor has as submappings such primary metaphors as STATES ARE LOCATIONS, CHANGE OF STATE IS MOTION, CAUSATION IS FORCED MOTION, CAUSES ARE FORCES, HINDRANCES ARE OBSTACLES TO MOTION, ACTIONS ARE SELF-PROPELLED MOTIONS, PURPOSES ARE DESTINATIONS, and several others. There is a large and growing literature analyzing the workings of conventional conceptual metaphors in language groups and cultures around the world (see, for example, any issue of the journal *Metaphor and Symbol*). There is also an emerging field of attention on what Charles Forceville has called "multimodal" metaphors, in which the source and target domains are in two different perceptual or experiential modes (Forceville and Urios-Aparisi 2009). For example, Forceville analyzes a commercial in which a French green bean and a mini corncob "stand" together in front of a frozen vegetable pouch while we hear the strains of Mendelssohn's "Wedding March" playing in the background. Such cases provide excellent evidence for the reality of metaphor as conceptual—as constitutive of our thinking—and not just matters of words.

In the context of my present focus in this chapter on perception and action, I want to conclude with some examples of cases where our conception of mind and thought is metaphorically understood in terms of processes of perception and bodily movement or manipulation of objects. Lakoff and I (1999) analyzed five of the major metaphors for thinking that appear in English. In each case, the source domains are drawn—as we would predict—from types of bodily action: perceiving (especially seeing), object manipulation, moving one's body through space, eating, and reproducing. What follows are partial mappings for some of the metaphors we found that have source domains tied to acts of perception and bodily movement, followed by the kinds of expressions that arise from each of these cross-domain mappings. What we found so striking was the vast polysemy evidence for the existence of these metaphors and the manner in which the details of the mapping generate a distinctive logic for thinking about the nature and operations of thinking itself. Here are four major metaphors, selected parts of their constitutive mappings, and examples of the polysemy in each of these metaphorical conceptions of thinking.

The THINKING IS MOVING Metaphor
The Mind Is A Body
Thinking Is Moving
Ideas Are Locations
Reason Is A Force
Rational Thought Is Motion (that is, direct, deliberate, step-by-step, and
   in accord with the force of reason)
Being Unable To Think Is Being Unable To Move
A Line Of Thought Is A Path
Thinking About X Is Moving In The Area Around X

Communicating Is Guiding (along a path)
Understanding Is Following
Rethinking Is Going Over The Path Again

Examples: My mind *strayed from* the topic. Sarah's mind *wandered* all over the place. He's always *going off on flights of fancy*. Show me how you *reached that conclusion*. Take me *step by step* through your argument. I don't see *how to move from* that assumption *to* this conclusion. I'm *stuck*! I can't *go any further in this line of reasoning*. Don't *skip any steps* in your proof. Mike's *going in circles* and never *gets to* his point. *Slow down!* You're *going too fast* for me. I can't *keep up with* you. Could you *run over (go over)* that again? *Where are* you *going* with this?

The THINKING IS PERCEIVING Metaphor (Vision Version)
The Mind Is A Body
Thinking Is Perceiving (Seeing)
Ideas Are Things Perceived (Seen)
Knowing Is Seeing
Communication Is Showing
Becoming Aware Is Noticing
An Aid To Knowing Is A Light Source
Capacity To Know Is Being Able To See
Impediments To Knowledge Are Impediments To Vision
Knowing From A "Perspective" Is Seeing From A Point of View
Explaining In Detail Is Drawing A Picture
Directing Attention Is Pointing
Paying Attention Is Looking At

Examples: I *see* what you're saying. I *see* your point. The politician attempted to *cover up* the facts. He *pulled the wool over* their *eyes*. He *put up a smokescreen* with his arguments. Your explanation is *unclear/murky/opaque*. Jayne was *looking for* a solution, but she only *discovered* more problems. We were left *in the dark*, hunting around *blindly*. That was the most *enlightening* account of relativity theory I've ever heard. New facts have *come to light*. You'd *see* the truth if you didn't *have blinders on*—it's as *clear/plain* as the nose on your face. He *pointed out* the best solution. Do I have to *draw* you *a picture*? We couldn't *see* the forest for the trees.

Note: There are obviously other systematic metaphors based on the other sensory modes of perception (touching, hearing, tasting) that would be subcases of the generic THINKING IS PERCEIVING metaphor.

The THINKING IS OBJECT MANIPULATION Metaphor
The Mind Is A Body
Ideas Are Objects
Thinking Is Object Manipulation
Communication Is Sending
Understanding Is Grasping
Memory Is A Storehouse
Remembering Is Retrieval (Recall)
The Structure Of An Idea Is The Structure Of An Object
Analyzing Ideas Is Taking Apart Objects
Examples: It's a hard idea *to grasp*. Let's *play with* that idea awhile — *toss it around* a bit. I've got the argument *firmly in mind*. I *get it*. She *gave* me the best idea for a paper topic. The negotiators *exchanged* ideas throughout the night. His idea *came across* to me. Our teacher's always trying to *cram* our heads *full of* ideas. He's *putting* dangerous ideas *into* their young minds. His theories *sail way over* my *head*. That's a *slippery* concept. The speaker was *throwing* too many ideas *at* me all at once. What Sophia revealed *threw me a curve*. Let's *take apart* his *theory* and *break it into* its key components. Complex ideas have to be carefully *crafted, shaped*, and *reshaped*. Jack *turned the idea over* in his mind, *examining* every aspect. He *held up* my ideas to scrutiny, *putting* every one of them *under the microscope*.

The THINKING IS PREPARING AND EATING FOOD Metaphor
A Well-Functioning Mind Is A Healthy Body
Ideas Are Food
Acquiring Ideas Is Eating
Interest In Ideas Is Appetite For Food
Good Ideas Are Healthy Foods
Helpful Ideas Are Nutritious Foods
Bad Ideas Are Harmful Foods
Disturbing Ideas Are Disgusting Food
Interesting Ideas Are Appetizing Food
Uninteresting Ideas Are Flavorless Foods
Testing An Idea Is Smelling Or Tasting
Considering Is Chewing
Accepting Is Swallowing
Fully Comprehending Is Digesting
Preparing Ideas To Be Understood Is Food Preparation
Communication Is Feeding

Substantial Ideas Are Meat

Examples: Derek has a real *thirst* for knowledge, a *huge appetite* for learning, and an *insatiable* curiosity. You don't expect me to *swallow* that
garbage, do you? I'll have to *chew on that* for a bit. The whole idea
smells fishy. He's known for putting out a bunch of *raw facts, half-baked
ideas*, and *warmed-over theories*. Let's *put that on the back burner* for a while
and *let it simmer*. What've you *cooked up* for me now? What a *rotten*
idea—*disgusting*, *unsavory*, and enough to *make you puke*, if you have
any intelligence at all. That's pure *bullshit*. You're not *shittin'* me, are
you? We're gonna have to *sugar-coat it* to *make it palatable* to her, or
even *force it down her throat*. Do you ever feel like you have to *spoon-feed*
your students? His scheme *left a bad taste in my mouth*. There's *too much*
here for me *to digest*. Where's *the beef* in your theory? The really *meaty*
issue is sustainability. Let's just *chew the fat*. Finally, something you can
really *sink your teeth into*! Now that's *food for thought*! Our philosophy
teacher just wants us to *regurgitate* what she gives us in lecture—just
spit it back to her.

There are other major metaphors for thinking, such as the planting,
tending, and harvesting of plants, or the insemination, gestation, and
giving birth to ideas. All of them are grounded in bodily source domains of human action that supply the semantics and logical inferences
enacted in the target domain. It is no accident that the source domains
are bodily, physical acts of perception and movement. We recruit the
meaning and structure of our bodily experience for the purposes of abstract conceptualization and reasoning. George Lakoff and I (1999) have
proposed that virtually all our abstract concepts are defined by systematic conceptual metaphors composed from primary metaphors. Examine any abstract concept from any field of human activity and you do not
have to look far to find metaphors—built up from primary metaphors—
defining the way we think and reason with that concept. We appropriate
the logic of our source-domain reasoning for our reasoning in the target domain. You may have some vague and highly abstract literal sense
of the meaning of a concept, but the details of the semantics and the
specific inferences are generated by the metaphors that characterize the
concept, not by some abstract literal core of meaning. The metaphorical constitution of our key concepts has been studied in nearly every
field and discipline you can imagine, such as causal theories (Lakoff and
Johnson 1999), metaphysics (M. Johnson 2008), logic and mathematics
(Lakoff and Núñez 2000), theory of knowledge (Lakoff and Johnson

1999), morality (M. Johnson 1993; Lakoff and Johnson 1999), law (Winter 2001; Bjerre 2005), science (Magnani and Nersessian 2002), psychology (Gibbs 2006; Fernandez-Duque and Johnson 1999; Kovecses 2000), music (Zbikowski 2002, 2008; Spitzer 2004), advertising (Forceville 1996), and on and on.

The metaphorical constitution of our most important abstract concepts—the ones that lie at the heart of our most significant ways of understanding and making sense of our world—is not a shortcoming to be bemoaned. Rather, it is a fact about how creatures like us are able to use the resources of our bodily encounters with our world in order to make sense of things and to gain insight.

If the experiential grounding of conceptual metaphor is a correct hypothesis, then one would expect that semantic priming of a specific source domain would facilitate the processing of a metaphor with that source domain, insofar as the priming would activate a simulation of source-domain structure and inferences. There is now ample evidence of such priming effects (see Gibbs 1994, 2006). For example, Boroditsky and Ramscar (2002) studied the priming effects of two different conceptual metaphors for temporal change. According to the MOVING TIMES or TIMES ARE MOVING OBJECTS metaphor, times are objects moving with various speeds toward and then past a stationary observer. Thus we say things like "The day is *fast approaching* when we will leave for China," "The time for action *has arrived*," "That sordid event is *past us* now," "Tuesday *follows* Monday, but it *comes before* Wednesday." The second spatial motion metaphor for temporal change is the MOVING OBSERVER metaphor, in which times are locations on a landscape and the observer moves toward and beyond various time-locations. This second metaphor gives rise to expressions like "We're *fast approaching* Thanksgiving," "We're *coming up on* Christmas," "It's a *long way to* Memorial Day," "What's *up ahead* for us?" and so on. Lakoff and I noticed that an expression like "Let's *move* the meeting *ahead* two days" can have two different meanings, and can generate two different outcomes, depending on whether one is understanding it via the MOVING TIMES or the MOVING OBSERVER metaphor. If the original meeting was scheduled for Wednesday, then according to the MOVING TIMES metaphor, the meeting is moved *ahead* (earlier) to Monday, while with the MOVING OBSERVER metaphor, the meeting would be moved *ahead* (later) to Friday. Lera Boroditsky (2011) hypothesized that she could predict which interpretation would be favored based on which source-domain structure (hence, which metaphor) was primed. So, if the subject saw a video of a person seated in an office chair pulling a second chair toward her with a rope, the subject was more likely to interpret (via the MOVING TIMES metaphor) "move the meeting *ahead* two days" to mean move it to Monday, while a subject who saw the person seated in the chair pull herself across the floor by a rope tied to a fixed object was more likely to select the move-to-Friday interpretation via priming of the MOVING OBSERVER metaphor. These and other similar experiments have given evidence of priming effects for conceptual metaphors, based on the experiential structure of the source domains for the metaphors.

Conclusion: Embodied, Multimodal Meaning

I have been pursuing the pragmatist "enactivist" hypothesis that all perception occurs in relation to ongoing action with and within an environment, and I have argued that large parts of human meaning and thought are based on this perception-action connection, and that we recruit sensory and motor structures for abstract conceptualization and reasoning. The interanimation of perception and action is evidenced by the multimodal character of both our perceptual experience and our perceptual concepts. Following Gallese and Lakoff (2005), we saw that a good portion of our conceptual knowledge is embodied via sensory-motor structures. In other words, our sensory-motor system not only makes it possible for us to act in the world, but it also provides both the content and structure for concrete concepts, based on perceptual and motor simulations. Jerome Feldman (2006) and Benjamin Bergen (2012) have provided extensive neuroimaging evidence for what they call "simulation semantics," showing how our hearing or reading about various scenes activates the appropriate sensory and motor regions responsible for having the perceptual experiences and performing the actions we are currently reading or hearing about.

The sensory-motor system of the brain appears to be multimodal rather than strictly modular, and language exploits this multimodality. Image schemas, cogs, and conceptual metaphors are three of the chief dimensions of our conceptual system by which we can recruit aspects of sensory-motor processing for "higher-level" cognition, thereby moving from concrete to abstract concepts. At these levels of semantic and inferential structure, supramodal neural systems can come into play.

If the general outlines of the picture of conceptualization that I have sketched are cognitively realistic, this would be an evolutionarily elegant and neurally parsimonious picture of the appropriation of bodily experience and meaning for the highest reaches of human thought. Dewey put this well in *Experience and Nature* (1925) when he wrote:

> Since mind cannot evolve except where there is an organized process in which the fulfillments of the past are conserved and employed, it is not surprising that mind when it evolves should be mindful of the past and future, and that it should use the structures which are biological adaptations of organism and environment as its own and its only organs. In ultimate analysis the mystery that mind should use a body, or that a body should have a mind, is like the mystery that a man cultivating plants should use the soil; or that the soil which grows plants at all should grow those adapted to its own physico-chemical properties and relations. ([1925] 1981, 277)

And Dewey then concludes that "since both the inanimate and the human environment are involved in the functions of life, it is inevitable, if these functions evolve to the point of thinking and if thinking is naturally serial with biological functions, that it will have as the material of thought, even of its erratic imaginings, the events and connections of this environment" (ibid., 279). Thinking is a form of human activity that changes the patterns of our ongoing, developing experience by changing the structure of our brains. Thinking is in and of the world. As a highly complex mode of action, it is grounded in and recruits our capacities for perceiving and acting, which are themselves profoundly intertwined.

CHAPTER 7

Knowing through the Body

The common theme running through the previous chapters is that all our meaning and thought emerges from our ongoing bodily and social engagement with our environments, which are at once physical, interpersonal, and cultural. As we saw in the last chapter, action in an environment is the source of these processes of meaning-making. It should be no surprise, then, that when Pragmatists turn their attention to accounts of knowledge, action remains the basis for all knowing. Consequently, the emphasis falls on *knowing* as an experiential activity, rather than on *knowledge* as the finished product of certain types of cognition.

The approach to knowledge that I am developing is mostly at odds with mainstream epistemology, which focuses primarily on *knowledge that* something is the case, and then tries to state the necessary and sufficient conditions for someone (person S) to know that some proposition (P) is true. Peruse any recent text on analytic epistemology and you will encounter the following type of analysis: The "proper" or exemplary notion of knowledge is *knowing that* something is the case, although we can also recognize other forms of knowing, such as knowledge by acquaintance, knowing how, knowing a person, or knowing a place. Having acknowledged these other forms of knowing, they are often then conveniently set aside in favor of an exclusive focus on propositional knowledge and the conditions under which it is true to say that "S knows that P." For a representative example of this strategy, consider the first paragraph of the "Analysis of Knowledge" entry of the *Stanford Encyclopedia of Philosophy*:

The objective of the analysis of knowledge is to state conditions that are individually necessary and jointly sufficient for propositional knowledge. Propositional knowledge should be distinguished from knowledge of "acquaintance," as obtains when Susan knows Alyssa. The relation between propositional knowledge and the knowledge at issue in other "knowledge" locutions in English, such as knowledge-where ("Susan knows where she is") and especially knowledge-how ("Susan knows how to ride a bicycle") is subject to some debate. The propositional knowledge that is the analysandum of the analysis of knowledge literature is paradigmatically expressed in English by sentences of the form "S knows that p," where "S" refers to the knowing subject, and "p" to the proposition that is known. A proposed analysis consists of a statement of the following form: S knows that p if and only if j, where j indicates the analysans: paradigmatically, a list of conditions that are individually necessary and jointly sufficient for S to have knowledge that p. The objective of the analysis of knowledge is to state conditions that are individually necessary and jointly sufficient for propositional knowledge. (Ichikawa and Steup 2012)

In the context of this sort of "S knows that P" epistemology, my emphasis on the body will strike many philosophers as doubly problematic. First, in focusing on knowing activity, my account rejects any radical distinction between *knowing that* and *knowing how*. Second, it stresses the role of human embodiment, quite in contrast to sentential approaches that focus either on the relation of sentences to supposedly mind-independent states of affairs in the world, or else on social practices of justification that are alleged to have little or nothing to do with our bodies.

I am going to argue that recent epistemology has been trapped in an unproductive debate that pits foundationalism against relativism, and that the key to moving us beyond this impasse is attention to "*knowing* through the *body*." A deeper understanding of the structures of our embodied experience can provide an alternative view of knowledge without absolute foundations that is nevertheless grounded in our experience and therefore free from the specter of an "anything goes" relativism that sees all knowledge as conventional and socially constructed. The key is to overcome our deeply rooted attachment to the idea of knowledge as fixed, complete, propositional, and sentential. Yes, there is propositional knowledge, but it must be understood in relation to other important forms of knowing.

The Problem with Foundationalist Epistemology:
Rorty's Deconstruction

Contemporary epistemology has left us in a miasma. If we take seriously the devastating critiques of both essentialism and foundationalism mounted repeatedly over the last several decades, it might seem as though we are left with an unavoidably irrational relativism. If neither the mind (reason within us) nor the external world (objects outside us) have any fixed and complete essences, then it might seem that the only constraints on what we take as knowledge are arbitrary social conventions subject to change at any moment according to contingent social practices. We are left with the skeptical and cynical view that knowledge is merely whatever those in power (within certain communities of inquiry) say it is. Yet we must take these critiques seriously, lest we mistake some particular community's privileged claims to "truth" for objective prescriptions.

To see how we got into this skeptical mess, let us consider Richard Rorty's influential sociology of knowledge. In his *Philosophy and the Mirror of Nature* (1979), Rorty shows us how mainstream Western epistemology has been trapped by the MIND'S EYE and MIRROR OF NATURE metaphors for knowledge. These metaphors, however, provide their own deconstruction, for they lead inescapably to skeptical arguments irrefutable on their own terms: The mind is regarded as a GLASSY ESSENCE that forms images or representations of the external world. But the mind sees (by the mind's eye) only what is reflected in it, that is, its own internal representations and their relations. So, if the mind knows only its own "internal" ideas and thought, then there is no way for the mind to be certain that any internal representation (i.e., image, concept, idea, proposition) in fact corresponds to or correctly mirrors the objective, mind-independent external reality it purports to represent. Rorty surveys the many failed attempts (based on unuseful metaphors for the knowledge relation) to guarantee the correspondence of internal representations to external states of affairs. He urges us to give up the whole project of trying to identify absolute conditions for knowledge. We need to abandon these powerful metaphors for mind (as mirroring reality) and truth-as-correspondence, along with the assumption that we can find absolute knowledge foundations in some a priori structure of human rationality, in a logical grammar of language, or in uninterpreted "raw" sense givens.

What we need, says Rorty, is to supplant these outworn, no-longer-useful metaphors with new ones that better serve our purpose in coping with our world. However, it is not so clear what these new metaphors might be. The key is supposed to be recognition of a distinction between the "logical space of causal explanations" and the "logical space of reasons" (Rorty 1979, 161). Rorty claims that the fundamental mistake of Enlightenment epistemology was to think, as Locke did, that having a causal explanation of how one comes to have certain ideas has any bearing at all on the issue of what counts as knowledge, that is, what counts as epistemic justification. Knowledge, says Rorty, is a matter of justification, of giving reasons for one's claims. This is a *social* practice that depends solely on what a community of inquirers will permit you to count as a reason in support of an epistemic claim. In other words, it is a question of what some particular community chooses to recognize as a condition of knowledge. Having a causal account of how one came to have a candidate knowledge claim is thus taken to be irrelevant to these epistemic social practices of reason-giving and justification.

Once epistemology has been removed from the "space of causal explanation" and narrowed in scope to considerations of the "logical space of reasons," it becomes a discussion of the socially imposed constraints on practices of justification. The nature of epistemic justification is thus supposedly determined solely by those whose beliefs and values are dominant at a given historical moment, within a communally validated sphere of reason-giving activity. In Rorty's terms, what counts as knowledge will depend on whose "vocabulary" of knowledge is in place guiding the discussion. It becomes a matter of who gets to define the "language game" of epistemic justification within a particular community.

At this point the recalcitrant antirelativist will insist that, even if knowledge does ultimately depend on our dominant vocabulary—such as our metaphors for mind, cognition, and judgment—at least some vocabularies and language games are not merely optional and are not random, irrational, unmotivated, arbitrary beliefs unconstrained by the world. But it is precisely Rorty's claim, in *Contingency, Irony, and Solidarity* (1989) that the shift of epistemic vocabularies from one view of knowledge to another is just such a historically contingent shift of fundamental metaphors, all of which are entirely optional (i.e., none of which are necessary).

According to Rorty, metaphors are merely indicia of a move from one "vocabulary" or "language game" to another and, thereby, potentially from one conception of epistemic justification to a different conception. Rorty sees the creation of a new metaphor as something that just happens, a result of mere historical contingencies that end up changing our view of what counts as knowledge. On this view, as Rorty is keen to point out, a metaphor is not regarded as a semantic phenomenon—not part of meaning—but is rather a nonsemantic means for breaking away from one vocabulary or language game and supplanting it by another. Rorty thus claims to be adopting Donald Davidson's (1978) view that there is no such thing as a distinct metaphorical meaning. Instead, according to Davidson, there is only the literal interpretation of the expression, which we then *use*, as a pragmatic device, to influence our interlocutor. That literal interpretation can have truth conditions within a language game; but the metaphor cannot, because it has no sense or meaning, since it is merely a pragmatic, not a semantic, function! According to Davidson (1978, 970), metaphors "intimate," or "suggest," or "get us to notice" things, and none of this involves grasping propositions that have semantic content. The key to Davidson's view is to "give up the idea that a metaphor carries a message, that it has a content or meaning (except, of course, its literal meaning)" (ibid., 95). Following Davidson, Rorty claims that metaphors are simply nonsemantic linguistic flares we send up to catch and redirect someone's attention:

> Tossing a metaphor into a conversation is like suddenly breaking off the conversation long enough to make a face, or pulling a photograph out of your pocket and displaying it, or pointing at a feature of the surroundings, or slapping your interlocutor's face, or kissing him. Tossing a metaphor into a text is like using italics, or illustrations, or odd punctuation or formats.
>
> All these are ways of producing effects on your interlocutor or your reader, but not ways of conveying a message. (1989, 18)

In short, we are left with a deflationary conception of metaphor as a nonsemantic rupture within a vocabulary or language game that suggests a new possible vocabulary. How this pragmatic tool accomplishes this vocabulary shift Rorty never explains. He merely asserts that the metaphor becomes the vehicle that motivates us imaginatively to construct a new language game within which the metaphor then becomes literal (i.e., familiar). When this process is complete, the original metaphor ceases to be a metaphor and is transformed into a literal expression or term that, miraculously, *does* have a meaning and truth conditions within the new language game. In other words, the metaphor somehow shifts — though Rorty cannot explain how — from being nonsemantic to being semantic (i.e., to having meaning and truth conditions).

The point I want to stress is that such a view of metaphor entails a view of semantic change, theory change, and the growth of knowledge that makes the whole process a nonrational result of sheer contingencies. There is no rationality to such change according to Rorty's Davidsonian view. The metaphors, as such, have no special meaning and no truth conditions. This leaves us with an extreme relativism because, ultimately, the very conditions that make the practices of epistemic justification possible are themselves supposedly mere matters of which metaphorically framed vocabulary we happen to prefer in a given context, at a given point in history.

It should therefore not be surprising that Rorty's particular brand of what today has come to be known as "linguistic" or "analytic" pragmatism strenuously tries to avoid any mention of "experience" as a basis for knowledge (see M. Johnson 2014a for a critique of this orientation). In an essay entitled "Dewey's Metaphysics," while approving Dewey's antidualistic and antifoundationalist tendencies, Rorty (1982) argued that Dewey violated these critical insights when he continued to insist on a notion of *experience* as the basis for meaning, thought, and knowledge. Reference to "experience," he suggests, is just one more failed attempt to find an absolute grounding for knowledge and truth. To the contrary, Rorty claims that all meaning, understanding, and knowing are dependent on language (i.e., specific vocabularies and language games), and therefore, we only have knowing access to our world through language. He eschews any talk of experiential grounding, on the grounds that it would be merely another mistaken attempt to establish metaphysical and epistemic foundations.

Bringing the Body Back into Knowing

Now, how did we get ourselves into such a relativistic mess? Rorty's logic is impeccable. He saw why foundationalist theories of knowledge cannot be defended, and so he rejects the whole foundationalist project, in favor of a sociology of communities of inquiry. However, the chief problem is that Rorty has an inadequate view of meaning and metaphor that misses the way semantic structure and sematic change have a grounding in patterns within our bodily experience. When he assumes that the "logical space of causal explanation" is irrelevant to social practices of reason-giving and justification, he dismisses any account of how meaning arises from our bodily engagement with our surroundings and thereby constrains what can count as knowledge.

As we have seen repeatedly in earlier chapters, more than thirty years of extensive research within conceptual metaphor theory reveals that, far from being a nonsemantic shift from one vocabulary to another, metaphor is an experientially motivated meaning-making process that is a fundamental and indispensable part of our cognition.[1] Given the extensive account of conceptual metaphor developed in the previous chapters, it should be clear why I regard Rorty's theory of metaphor as a "pragmatic" nonsemantic device to be profoundly mistaken. But to see where Rorty goes wrong, why metaphor is part of meaning, why the emergence of new metaphorical systems is highly motivated by structures of our bodily experience, and why, therefore, we need not embrace his extreme relativism, we must go back to the beginning. The problem is Rorty's fundamental assumption that all knowledge of the "knowing that" variety is sentential and propositional. We need to start again; but this time from the phrase "knowing through the body."

First, let us focus on know*ing* (as an activity) as opposed to knowledge (as a state or product). It is Dewey (one of Rorty's heroes) who sets us on the right track by urging a view of knowledge as a mode of activity, a means of change, rather than as a fixed or static thing: "If things undergo change without thereby ceasing to be real, there can be no *formal* bar to knowing being one specific kind of change in things, nor to its test being found in the successful carrying into effect of the kind of change intended" ([1908] 1973, 211).

Instead of viewing knowledge as a subject's being justified in believing that a particular proposition is true (i.e., that a certain correspondence relation exists between a proposition and a state of affairs in the world), Dewey urges us to think of knowledge as an ongoing interactive process between organism and environment. This brings into play the crucial role of an organism's embodiment in its interaction with, and knowing of, the world. This kind of knowing is a use of intelligence to work out solutions to problematic situations, and much of the time, this process has nothing to do with framing propositions. It is Dewey, once again, who sees the crucial connection between the structures of our bodily interactions and the nature of our "higher" cognitive functions:

> The parts and members of the organism are certainly not there primarily for pure intellect or for theoretic contemplation. The brain, the last

physical organ of thought, is a part of the same practical machinery for bringing about adaptation of the environment to the life requirements of the organism, to which belong legs and hand and eye. . . . And even if we try to believe that the cognitive function has supervened as a different operation, it is difficult to believe that the transfiguration has been so radical that knowing has lost all traces of its connection with vital impulse. ([1908] 1973, 127–28)

The continuity of our bodily interactions and knowing with our more abstractive modes of thought is the key to a unified view of knowledge as a means of transforming our experience. Dewey's emphasis on the bodily basis of knowing cannot be dismissed as an arcane product of an outdated biology or psychology. Indeed, within current cognitive science, and with reference to our best neuroscience, Patricia Churchland has recently proposed a similar focus on the central importance of sensorimotor processes for our understanding of so-called "higher" rational processes:

It seems to me quite possible that some capacities hitherto considered strictly cognitive may be discovered to share fundamental elements with paradigmatic motor skills. . . . (Patricia Churchland, 1986, 449)

Higher functions are surely not discontinuous with lower functions; they are not a sphere unto themselves. . . . If we want to understand the fundamental principles of cognition, we may need to understand the emergence in evolution of those paradigmatically cognitive processes, and hence we may need to understand their origins in sensorimotor control. (441)

Churchland is certainly no closet Deweyite, but they both share a rejection of wholly sentential and overly intellectualized approaches to knowledge,[2] and they both suggest the relevance of structures of sensorimotor activity for any account of higher cognitive functions.

Knowing as Activity and Process

Dewey insists on a conception of knowledge focused on know*ing* as an organism-environment interaction. He urges us to think of knowing as an *activity* by means of which an organism transforms a relatively problematic situation into one that is clarified and made more determinate in accordance with the organism's needs and ends. This is an *interpretive* activity—which is to say, a way of probing the meaning of our world and the possibilities for realizing certain values and modes of action. Much of this interpretive assessment goes on well below the level of conscious cognition, but occasionally we subject it to conscious evaluation and criticism. Every organism is continually trying to "get on" in its world, mostly through acquired habits of valuing, desiring, and acting. The organism realizes certain potentialities of the situation in light of its evolved cognitive capacities, past experience, purposes, interests, and ends-in-view, as it acts in its world. The ends and values in play are not just fixed and pre-given. They are also subject to ongoing critique and reconstruction. Most of the time it is only in and through the interaction of organism and environment that ends become definite and the nature of the situation becomes clearer. Knowing thus constitutes a way of being-at-home-in-one's-environment, an at-home-ness that reveals an intimate bodily involvement in one's surroundings, which are both physical and cultural.

As Rorty saw, Dewey's view challenges the metaphor MIND IS A MIRROR OF NATURE, within which knowledge consists of a fixed relation between either a mental *state* (i.e., a representation) or a descriptive *state*ment and a corresponding fixed *state* of affairs in the world. Such a static view of knowledge leads one to focus exclusively on questions of statement-world correspondence and of epistemic justification—that is, questions of the conditions under which a person is justified in asserting certain propositional statements. This in turn often leads to a quest for unshakeable, objective foundations for knowledge and requires an attendant method of inquiry that would guarantee the production of justified statements.

But what if, following Dewey, we were to give up the static and foundationalist conception of knowledge embodied in the MIND IS A MIRROR OF NATURE metaphor? What if we were to give up our self-concept of the *human* as located in and defined by some transcendent, disembodied rational ego that stands over against the external world? Then we could entertain *a more ecologically sound conception of ourselves as continuous with, and growing from, our surroundings, and this would support a conception of knowledge (or, rather, knowing) as an active transforming of problematic situations that helps us better understand ourselves and our world and thereby helps us pursue our mutual interests and ends.* This is what I mean when I say that knowing concerns our ways of "being at home in" our world.

We are not inherently separated and alienated from some allegedly pre-given, fixed, and completed environment, forever doomed to try-ing (impossibly) to bridge the unbridgeable gap between supposedly subjective "inner" representations and some objective "outer" reality. Rather, we exist only insofar as we are to a certain extent "in touch" with our world—which is to say, continuously engaged with our sur-roundings in an ongoing process of mutual interaction, adjustment, and transformation. Both environments and organisms are what they are at a given moment only in relation to each other and only as the result of a continual process of constructive interaction. "Inner" and "outer" are thus only dimensions of an integrated process of organism-engaging-its-environment. Knowing is just one way of developing this ongoing process of experience that jointly shapes ourselves and our surroundings.

According to this view, knowing is one mode of experience by which we inhabit a world, together with other organisms—a world we can make some sense of and act more or less fluidly in. We evaluate our knowledge communally in the context of how well or how poorly it allows us to function and to flourish within an ever-changing environ-ment that both resists some of our attempts to understand and act within it, even as it supports other ways of acting. Reality does not "hide" be-hind experience, in such a way that we need a knowledge judgment to reveal what is real and what is mere appearance. In other words, reality is not a *Ding an sich* lurking, unseen, forever behind an opaque veil of rep-resentations that prevents us from gaining any access to the way things "really are" outside our skins and skulls. There is not and never has been an autonomous reality from which we are inescapably divorced, for we have *always* existed only in and through our relations with our evolving environment, as we experience it. We could not continue to exist if we were not more or less in touch with our surroundings in the most inti-mate fashion. We are what we are at this instant, and our world is what it is at this instant, only because of our embodied interactions with our surroundings.

In short, reality is what we experience, and knowing is just *one of many* possible modes of experience. Dewey explained this radical con-ception of reality in his important 1905 essay "The Postulate of Immedi-ate Empiricism." The postulate states that "things are . . . what they are experienced to be." Dewey thus had a rather deflationary attitude toward the term *reality*, which he feared was too often held up as the "test" of any knowledge claim or theory—as if there were things-in-themselves against which our concepts and truth claims might be measured. Instead, what we experience is "real"; but such experience does not automatically amount to a knowing experience. Rather, knowing is only one particular mode of experiencing:

> By our postulate, things are what they are experienced to be; and, unless knowing is the sole and only genuine mode of experiencing, it is fallacious to say that Reality is just and exclusively what it is or would be to an all-competent knower; or even that it *is*, relatively and piecemeal, what it is to a finite and partial knower. Or, put more positively, knowing is one mode of experiencing. . . . To assume that, because from the *standpoint of the knowledge experience* things are what they are known to be, therefore, metaphysically, absolutely, without qualification . . . is . . . if not the root of all philosophic evil, at least one of its main roots. For this leaves out of account what the knowledge standpoint is itself *experienced as*. (Dewey 1905, 116)

Consequently, what is experienced is "real" for the person experiencing it, but that does not necessarily or inevitably constitute knowledge. We start from experienced reals, and then we must "decide" (not always a conscious act) which reals to reinforce and carry forward as the basis for future experience and action. There are technical, moral, aesthetic, and other cultural values operating that set tentative limits to what we will count as a *knowing* experience. "Knowledge" is a term of praise we use for habits of inquiry, understandings of situations, and proposals of actions that turn out to allow us to function fluidly in our surroundings. So, saying that something is "real" is not the end of the matter with respect to knowledge, but instead it is only the beginning of our attempts to test out various proposals for how to act and function well in the world. "Reality" reveals itself as what is experienced, but which of the "reals" of experience we develop and carry forward will depend on our physical makeup, our interpersonal relations, our cultural values and practices, and our imaginative capacities. Rorty saw the cultural dimensions of this knowing process, but, focusing exclusively on those social constraints, he overlooked the other experiential dimensions stemming from the body-based aesthetics of how we engage our world. In his attempt to avoid any mention of "experience," he failed to appreciate the very experiential processes that are so crucial to our knowledge practices.

There are thus constraints—real experienced constraints—on what is meaningful to us, on what we can know, and on how we can know it. These are not just matters of what other people will allow us to say or do (although that is part of the story). These are also matters of the nature of our brains, our bodies, our motivational systems, and our varied and plural values. Let us consider, then, some of these bodily constraints that play a basic role in our knowings.

Image-Schematic Structures of Cognition as One Source of Constrained Knowing

Once we entertain this nonstatic, process view of knowing, our attention turns away from questions of absolute justification towards questions about the nature of the structures of our knowing interactions with our world. And the obvious place to begin an exploration of those structures is just where Dewey and Patricia Churchland alike say it is: in the patterns that emerge through our sensorimotor activity as we orient ourselves spatially and temporally, direct our perceptual focus for various purposes, move our bodies as functional unities, and manipulate objects to pursue certain ends and realize certain values. In short, the place to begin is with our embodiment, which is the locus of our experience.

As an example of sensorimotor structures, I would like to explore briefly one of the most pervasive and constantly recurring image-schematic structures (already described in considerable detail in chap. 4) that is central to our embodied knowing—namely, the SOURCE-PATH-GOAL schema. As infants, as we begin to develop our ability to focus our eyes, first only on close objects but eventually at greater distances, we also begin to track forms (and later, objects) as they move through our visual field. Even at the most primitive and unrefined levels there is already a recurring structure to such experiences: some visual form or object which was previously only on our perceptual horizon becomes an object of attention, is tracked across some part of our visual field, and then either stops at some temporary resting point within that field or else passes off beyond our perceptual horizon again. No doubt, every particular experience of tracking a trajectory from one point *A* to another point *B* is different from every other experience of this kind, yet there is a recurring pattern manifested in each of these tracking experiences. The recurring structure is what we may call the SOURCE-PATH-GOAL schema.

$$A \longrightarrow B$$

SOURCE-PATH-GOAL schema

To be accurate we would need to qualify this generic or prototypical diagram in many ways. First, it will hardly ever be the case that there are definite, atomic, pre-given starting and ending points *A* and *B*. More likely, there will be a fuzzy region in our perceptual horizon within which, over a period of time, we are becoming ever more selectively attentive to some one thing as a perceivable form or object. Second, we must remember that the image schema is the pattern of a *process*, the pattern of an interaction, rather than a static gestalt structure. Third, the pattern will emerge within (and may be modified or transformed by) our ongoing experience, so that it is a generic structure capable of many different instantiations in many different experiences. Fourth, this is an embodied schema that exists across multiple sensory modalities. So, for example, the SOURCE-PATH-GOAL schema will be exhibited as we run our hand over an object from one end to another, whereas the same image schema may be projected to organize our perception of a melody as moving from a starting point through intermediate phrases to some melodic culmination.

To illustrate these points—and to warn against mistaking the visual diagram or verbal description for the actual image schema—we need consider only a few of the variety of experiences of perceptual tracking. Visually, either the starting point *A*, the endpoint *B*, or the object moving between them may be more or less well defined or perceptually distinct. The path itself may take any of an indefinite number of shapes; and it may be continuous, interrupted and partial, or even just imagined as a possible path. Any number of objects can fill the role of trajector, and the path may exist in any of several media (water, air, earth, etc.). Also, the same image schema will exist as an embodied imaginative structure capable of supporting correlations across different sensory modes (such as when we both see and feel via a SOURCE-PATH-GOAL schema in one and the same experience; for example, watching carefully as we simultaneously draw out a route on a road map).

As our perceptual tracking skills develop, so also does our ability to manipulate objects. The infant moves the rattle from the crib to its mouth, later it reaches for the bottle to satisfy its hunger, and much later it crawls after a prized toy. In each of these cases of causal efficacy there is a budding experience of intentional action. Soon there emerges a complex mapping and coordination of image-schematic structure across different modes of perception and actions, such as between vision, bodily motion through space, and bodily manipulations of arms, hands, and fingers. The toddler visually tracks the ball as it rolls across the floor (vision), moves her body toward a projected point of contact with the rolling ball (bodily motion), and finally reaches her hands to grasp it (bodily manipulations).

Emerging image-schematic structures of this sort exhibit the development of form, order, and relative determinateness in our experience of a world that we are able to interact with more or less reliably. But there are ways in which these attempts at knowing can go wrong and can fail to give us an understanding adequate to our tasks, projects, and communal needs. There are greater and lesser successes in realizing potentialities of a particular situation, based on one's skill, resources, experience, imagination, and creativity. Michael Jordan and Mikhail Baryshnikov know ways of moving from point *A* to point *B* that I can only dream about, and we can say correctly that they know the world in ways that I never could.

So far, we have focused exclusively on sensorimotor skills as involving such image schemas as SOURCE-PATH-GOAL. A critic might insist that we are dealing only with what Oxford philosophers have taught us to call disparagingly "knowing *how*," as opposed to "knowing *that*." But this is a misleading distinction. It cannot carry the epistemic weight put on it by those who think that only *knowing that* is knowing in the eminent or privileged mode and that it is essentially sentential and propositional. There is no route, they will claim, from nonpropositional schemas like SOURCE-PATH-GOAL in our bodily skills to propositional knowledge in the "true" sense of the term, such that it is rationally assessable with respect of truth value.

This static and propositional view of knowledge is inadequate in at least three major respects. First, it mocks itself in its very expression of the alleged objection to image schemas operating in abstract thinking. Notice how the argument of the last sentence of the previous paragraph is *itself* entirely dependent on the SOURCE-PATH-GOAL schema, as in "There is no *route from* . . . nonpropositional schemas . . . *to* propositional knowledge." Second, it fails to see that even our "bodily" skills are exercises of our intelligence and are one basis for our knowing experience of the world we inhabit. Such embodied intelligence is central to our ability to understand and transform our world. Third, it begs the question at issue here by overintellectualizing knowledge, as though there could be no connection between our bodily understanding and alleged "higher" cognitive functions. In other words, the standard objectivist view misses the fact that knowledge is always a matter of the character of the interaction of organisms and their environments, and, as such, must necessarily depend on embodied experience as its locus.

The pragmatist emphasis on action may make it seem as though we must reject entirely any attempt to distinguish between "knowing that" and "knowing how," but the correct moral is, rather, that we simply need to remember that this is never an absolute distinction, and that *knowing that* and *knowing how* actually represent relative poles on a continuum of *action*. Some of our knowledge judgments are mostly descriptive acts, while others emphasize the way inquiry permits us to reconstruct experience through action in the world. However, as Dewey explained in impressive detail in his 1938 book *Logic: The Theory of Inquiry*, "knowing that" something is the case is really simply a way of stating that certain beliefs are likely to "test out" through active inquiry in our experience, to the extent that those beliefs guide us to expect certain experiences and observed behaviors that we may be able to encounter in future situations. In other words, all knowledge judgments are practical, in the sense that to claim that one knows something is to be able to forecast how certain situations will or would play out in practice; that is, in our ongoing interactions with our surroundings. In Dewey's words, "All controlled inquiry and all institution of grounded assertion necessarily contains a *practical factor*; an activity of doing and making which reshapes antecedent existential material which sets the problem of inquiry" ([1938] 1991, 162).

William James expresses this active, constructive dimension of knowing in a similar way when he says that we can say we know something (some fact, some person, some situation, some skill) just insofar as we are able to function successfully on the basis of the meanings we attribute to a given situation we find ourselves in: "Knowledge of sensible realities thus comes to life inside the tissue of experience. It is *made*; and made by relations that unroll themselves in time" (1904, 201). He gives an illustrative example: Stating that I know where Emerson Hall is amounts to saying that I could navigate my way through my surroundings and arrive at Emerson Hall (the "object" of my knowledge), given appropriate circumstances and resources. Or, I could direct you to Emerson Hall. In short, from a pragmatist perspective, all knowing really is a knowing how, even though we sometimes may not need to take any particular actions in order to know "that" something is the case. However, absent the possibility of acting successfully on the meaning we ascribe to a situation, we could not be said to know something.

What we "know" is the meaning of a situation, which involves an understanding of the various ways that situation might possibly be transformed and developed into the future. This in turn requires grasping the many relations that exist between objects, persons, and events, which determine the ways in which that particular situation can be carried forward, so to speak.

Projections of Image-Schematic Structure in Abstract Domains

A number of studies over the past several years have focused on some of the ways in which our embodied, imaginative organism-environment interactions involve image-schematic structures that work their way up into more abstract domains of understanding and reasoning.[3] I have described some of these processes in previous chapters. As an example, let us carry on our exploration of the SOURCE-PATH-GOAL schema to see how it comes to play a role in our "higher" cognitive functions. As noted in chapter 4, over and over each day, we experience, without conscious reflection, our moving of our bodies as correlated with the achievement of some purpose. Children gradually come to know their world through knowing interactions in which their bodily movement through space is the means for accomplishing some end, as when the toddler makes her way from one place to another in order to satisfy her hunger by picking up her bottle, or when she engages in a more general exploration of her surroundings. In such cases where there is a directed purpose—such as reaching a certain location to grasp the bottle for feeding—that is satisfied by moving our bodies from starting point A, through an intermediate sequence of spatial locations, to the endpoint B. In the domain of intentions there is an initial situation where the intention is not satisfied, a sequence of intermediate actions directed toward realizing that intention, leading to a final situation (though only temporarily final) in which the intention is (if we are successful) satisfied.[4] There arises, then, a connection in our experience between structure in the domain of physical actions and structure in the domain of intentions, as follows:

initial situation = location A
final (desired) situation = location B
action sequence = movement from A to B

This experiential correlation between moving and achieving a purpose is the basis for a pervasive metaphorical system by which we structure a large part of our understanding of purposive activity. We can name this system of experiential connections the PURPOSES ARE DES-TINATIONS metaphor, so long as we remember that the metaphorical system is an imaginative projection in the structuring of our experience and is *not* merely the verbal propositional structure we use as a short-hand to name it. In the PURPOSES ARE DESTINATIONS metaphor, we use structure from the source domain (directed physical movement) to organize our understanding of the target domain (purposive activity in general). Both domains are structured by a SOURCE-PATH-GOAL schema, but in the target domain there need not be any overt physi-cal activity involved in achieving a purpose, although there often is. Consequently, we come to understand and reason about our intentional action—whether it involves bodily movement or is only mental—as in-volving a SOURCE-PATH-GOAL structure.

This metaphorical understanding is so pervasive and so deeply con-stitutive of our intentional interactions within our environment that we are virtually unaware either of its existence or of its metaphorical character. But the fact is that, as our common experience and culture have developed in the West, the PURPOSES ARE DESTINATIONS meta-phor and its underlying SOURCE-PATH-GOAL schema are very nearly definitive of our understanding of intentional action (see Lakoff and Johnson 1999, chap. 11). Our language is filled with expressions that are systematically related in terms of this underlying conceptual metaphor. Thus, we *start off* to get our PhD, but *along the way* we get *sidetracked*, are *led astray* and are *diverted* from our original purpose. We try to *get back on the right path* and to *keep our end in view* as we *move along*. If we are lucky and determined enough, even though we originally *had a long way to go* to get the degree, we finally *reach our goal* and can *look back over the long course* of our studies with great satisfaction. It is important to notice that it is not just how we speak that is systematically structured by the PURPOSES ARE DESTINATIONS metaphor, but rather that our very understanding of intentional action itself—including reversals and problems we must interpret and try to resolve—is constituted by the metaphorical system.

Our understanding of intentions is but one of the many domains structured by the SOURCE-PATH-GOAL schema. Any process or activity can take on such structure, principally because of the deep-rootedness in our culture of metaphorical systems that spatialize time, such as that of the metaphors TIMES ARE MOVING OBJECTS, TIMES ARE LOCATIONS, and TEMPORAL CHANGE IS CYCLICAL MOTION.[5] George Lakoff and I (1999) have provided an extensive analysis of the chief metaphors by which we conceptualize temporal change, and the most influential one features the passage of time as relative motion in space. The TIME IS AN ARROW metaphor is a specification of the SOURCE-PATH-GOAL schema that can thus provide a way of understanding certain temporal processes as unidirectional movements from one time point to another. Thus, we would expect to find the SOURCE-PATH-GOAL schema in our understanding of temporal acts of reasoning, such as following out in one's head the steps of a logical argument, which covers a certain amount of time. In analyzing an argument, for example, we can see how certain assumptions *lead the way* to certain intermediate *steps* in an argument, which *point toward* a conclusion, the *end point* of the argument. We can *follow a line* of argument, in order to see *where we got off track*. Here the underlying metaphorical conception is ARGUMENT IS A JOURNEY, which is based on the SOURCE-PATH-GOAL schema as it is realized in our experience and understanding of journeying.

Moreover, the SOURCE-PATH-GOAL structuring of temporal processes is also extended to include what are commonly considered to be atemporal patterns. I am thinking here particularly of the way in which temporal processes of reasoning and the drawing of inferences are correlated with their corresponding products; namely, logical argument structures (which are thought of as timeless forms). Some of our language of rational argument (e.g., "*following* an argument") will be ambiguous, in that either it can be used to refer to the temporal process of reasoning to a conclusion, or else it can refer to the abstract logical structure of that argument. So, when I say that assumptions A and B *lead to* conclusion C, I might just as easily mean the logical form of the argument (as a universal atemporal structure) as I might mean the temporal process of reasoning from A and B to C.

Image-Schematic Structure in Reasoning

I am arguing that human understanding is image-schematic through and through, from the most primitive and mundane unreflective acts of perception and motor activity, all the way up to abstract reasoning and argument. Consequently, all this body-based meaning, understanding, and value serves as a basis for, and constraint on, what we can know and how we know it. Therefore, contra Rorty, I am saying that in addition to the linguistic constraints established by particular communities who share a vocabulary, there are also experiential constraints on knowing. What we "know" is the meaning of a situation, and that meaning is structured by image schemas, conceptual metaphors, and other forms of embodied understanding. The meaning of any particular object, person, or event is the range of related experiences (past, present, and future) that it affords us, and such affordances are grounded, in part, in sensory, motor, and affective dimensions of our experience.

In this continuum from image schemas structuring experiences of physical objects and events all the way up to the same image schemas structuring our thinking about abstract entities and mental processes, there is no discrete point where we can absolutely draw a clear line of demarcation between the physical and the mental, or between knowing *how* and knowing *that*.

The example of the SOURCE-PATH-GOAL schema on which I focused is but one of many image schemas that structure much of our understanding of both bodily experiences and movements and of what we regard as abstract thought. Among the dozens of more prominent image schemas that are indispensable to any account of understanding and knowledge would be: OBJECT, FIGURE/GROUND, CONTAINER, CYCLE, COMPELLING FORCE, ATTRACTION, POTENTIALITY, COUNTERFORCE, BALANCE, SCALAR INTENSITY, ITERATION, and CENTER/PERIPHERY.[6] Image schemas of this sort allow us to have meaningful experiences that we make sense of and reason about. The same image schemas so crucial to our sensory-motor activity are equally crucial to our more abstractive modes of cognition that involve language proper. Patterns of conceptual significance, symbolic import, and logical relations are thus prefigured in the imaginative patternings of our bodily experience.[7] From a neuroscientific perspective, this would translate into the claim that our brains recruit prior existing sensory, motor, and affective structures and processes to perform abstract conceptualization and reasoning (Feldman 2006; Lakoff and Núñez 2017).

To give an elementary example of the way in which image-schematic structure rooted in bodily activity comes to order logical relations and patterns of inference, let us briefly return to our earlier analysis of the CONTAINER schema, with its minimal structure of boundary, interior, and exterior. As we saw in chapter 4, the CONTAINER schema structures and provides experiential motivation for the law of the excluded middle: experientially, any given thing is either within a container or outside it (or transitioning between interior and exterior). When categories are understood metaphorically as containers, we then get the logical relation, "Any given thing is either *P* (i.e., is *in* the category-container *P*) or else it must be not-*P* (i.e., it is *outside* the category-container *P*)." In this way, "either P or not-P" (the law of noncontradiction) has an intuitive grounding in our daily experience of containment, since nothing can be both within a container and outside it at the same time.

Consider now the case where you are lying *in* your bed, which is located *in* your room, which is *in* your house, and so on. Now ask the question: If you are *in* your bed, are you then *in* your house? The answer is obvious and easy via your experience of the transitivity of containment: if container A is within container B, and B is within C, then A is within C. Once again, the logical relation of transitivity is a projection of the transitivity of containment.

Along similar lines, George Lakoff (1987, 456–58; also Lakoff and Núñez 2000) has provided an outline of the way in which the Boolean logic of classes can be understood using only CONTAINER schemas, PART/WHOLE schemas, and metaphorical mappings as follows:

- CONTAINER schemas are mapped into classes.
- PART/WHOLE schemas, where both parts and wholes are themselves CONTAINER schemas, are mapped into subclass relations.
- Entities inside a CONTAINER schema are mapped into members of the class corresponding to that schema.
- The exterior of the CONTAINER schema is mapped into the complement of the corresponding class.

On the basis of metaphorical mappings of this sort, it is easy to see how one could define such fundamental notions as class, proper subclass, member of a class, complement of a class, set union, and set intersection. For example, a member of a class is some entity (physical or abstract) *contained within* a particular category-container. Of course, this is only a preliminary sketch of a small sampling of image-schematic bases for logical relations and patterns of reasoning. Nobody, to my knowledge, has yet worked out such a program for logic and reasoning in any comprehensive way. However, Gilles Fauconnier (1985) has explored some of the implications of this general orientation for such issues as scope, presupposition, counterfactuals, anaphora, and referential opacity (see also Fauconnier and Turner 2002). Lakoff and Núñez (2000) have provided extensive analyses of the workings of image schemas, conceptual metaphors, and conceptual metonymies in various types of mathematics and logic.

The point is that image schemas have sufficient internal structure to support various sorts of logical relations and inferential patterns within our reasoning. Instead of viewing reason as dropping down a priori from some transcendental heaven, it is possible to conceive of an experiential grounding and motivation for what we normally think as "higher" acts of reasoning and logical form. It is image-schematic and metaphoric structures of this sort that constitute the basis of our capacity to know something about our world. Contrary to Rorty, who thought that no account of the sources of meaning in experience could have any relevance for what counts as knowledge, I am claiming that it is precisely just such body-based meaning that makes possible and constrains what counts as knowledge, in ways that go beyond any constraints established by particular linguistic communities.

What a Theory of Knowledge Might Be

We are now in a position to contrast sharply this theory of embodied knowing with the conventional objectivist account of knowledge. The objectivist view assumes a rigid distinction between *knowing that* and *knowing how*. *Knowing that* is regarded as a theoretical judgment about states of affairs existing in the world, while *knowing how* is taken to be a form of practical, value-laden activity manifested in actions that achieve desired states of affairs. *Knowing how* may presuppose some theoretical understanding, but this form of knowing has traditionally been considered less philosophically interesting, insofar as it lacks the required propositional form capable of corresponding to preexisting states of affairs in the world. No continuity is recognized as existing between these two allegedly different types of knowing. Knowledge is then viewed as a finished product, the result of cognitive judgments that adhere to certain forms of logical inference employing concepts that correspond objectively to a mind-independent reality. The central issues of epistemology become those of reference, correspondence, and rational warrant, all of which center on the question of determining under what conditions one can justifiably assert that person S knows that *P* (a proposition).

Although Rorty correctly mounts a major critique of the foundationalist aspect of this objectivist conception of knowledge, he does not doubt that knowledge should take the form of propositional statements about how the world is. His claim, instead, is that (1) the truth claims would be formulated within some particular metaphor-based vocabulary, and (2) the criteria for truth would be established only within particular communities of inquirers who share some particular vocabulary.

Consequently, questions about truth are settled in the "logical space of reasons" (Rorty 1979, 161), relative to what a community allows to count as justified belief. What Rorty denies, as we saw above, is that any account of the "causes" of our ideas and explanatory frames would ever be relevant to what counts as truth within a community of inquirers. We are left with a set of social practices of justification, or reason-giving, couched in vocabularies that have no "grounding" in the world. Rorty's claim is that there is nothing philosophically important to say about experiential grounding, especially in the form of causal explanations of our ideas. It is, rather, merely a matter of the sociology of knowledge — a question about what counts as knowledge, evidence, and justification within a particular vocabulary and language game that is preferred within a historically situated community.

There is much of value in Rorty's critique of the quest for absolute epistemic foundations and ultimate methods. He is also correct in stressing the importance of metaphor in structuring our communally sanctioned conceptions of knowledge. However, I have argued that Rorty's erroneous conception of metaphor (and language, for that matter) leads him to miss the ways that knowledge can be grounded in experience, though not in some foundational or absolute manner. Contrary to Rorty, we are not left merely with sociological reflections on the conditions under which certain communities will count certain kinds of reason-giving and justification as acceptable.

Instead, a constructive, nonfoundationalist theory of knowing is possible. It would be a theory of knowing as activity — as the way a world emerges and is transformed as organism and environment interact. For us, this world is relatively orderly in the sense that we can pursue our interests and purposes with varying degrees of success. What counts as success, more or less, in our attempts to understand and transform our organism-environment interactions is, as Rorty sees, very much a matter of our purposes, interests, and values. So it *is* correct to say that knowledge must be relativized (contextualized) in this way. There is no God's-eye view of things-in-themselves.

It does not follow, however, that we are left only with arbitrary, historically contingent, and utterly blind changes in what a community will count as knowledge. Rorty makes such a misguided claim primarily, as we have seen, because he thinks (correctly) that all knowledge is relativized to extended metaphorical systems, but he then adopts the seriously mistaken view of metaphor as meaningless sounds, and of metaphor change as a nonrational, nonsemantic, discontinuous rupture within an established vocabulary that moves us radically from one language game or vocabulary to a new or different one.

Against this view, I have argued that image schemas and conceptual metaphor systems are at the heart of meaning, insofar as they underlie and organize extensive networks of concepts and their corresponding expressions in natural languages (and, I would add, all other forms of symbolic expression, such as the arts, music, dance, theater, architecture, and ritual). We have seen, very briefly, how such metaphorical systems are constrained by image-schematic structure in the source and target domains in our experience. There is extensive experimental evidence to show that semantic change is often guided systematically by conceptual metaphors, contrary to Rorty's view.[8]

Having abandoned foundationalism, we are not thrown over into an extreme linguistic relativism of communal reason-giving and justification, as Rorty would have us believe. Explanations—causal or otherwise—of how our concepts and values emerge from the structures of our brains and bodies, as they interact with the material and social worlds they are continually engaging, reveal where our knowledge comes from and why it can appropriately serve as a guide for our actions. Our knowing interactions are constrained in certain ways, such as by image-schematic patterns which have their own internal logic and connections, as well as by conceptual metaphors rooted in experiential correlations between the source and target domains. For example, the PURPOSES ARE DESTINATIONS metaphor places very definite (though open-ended) constraints on the way we conceive purposive, intentional activity of all sorts, both physical and mental. A theory of knowledge can explore what these basic image-schematic patterns are, how they can be metaphorically and metonymically extended or elaborated, and how they thereby constrain our reasoning. There is nothing foundationalist about this, because there is imaginative leeway with respect to how we elaborate and extend image-schematic structure. Yet, theorizing about such processes can give us insight into the way we "have a world," the way we understand, and even what kinds of strategies have proved better and worse for various purposes.

What could such a theory of knowledge consist in, if it is not a theory of justification? It would be a theory of how our embodied understanding shapes our abilities to function in the environments we inhabit— environments that are at once physical, interpersonal, and cultural. It would be a theory of the components and structures of our understanding and knowing interactions that constitute our experience of our world. It must go beyond mere armchair theorizing about the social basis of epistemic justification within a community; instead, it will have to take into account the best ongoing work in the cognitive sciences concerning brain and body functions, perception, motor skills, concept formation, reasoning, language, emotion, values, and so forth.

In other words, we need, contra Rorty, to recognize a role for causal (and other) forms of explanation of how meaning is developed, how our concepts are formed, and how understanding and reasoning work. Knowing about the neural, interpersonal, and cultural conditions of meaning and thought can tell us a great deal about how we are able to "get on"—knowingly—in our world. This insight into the cognitive processes of the brain-in-a-body-interacting-with-a-structured-environment helps us understand how and why certain patterns are meaningful to us and afford us constructive possibilities for acting in, and being at home in, our world. After all, being at home in our world, and the well-being and flourishing that accompanies this, is the chief reason for prizing knowledge.

So, where have propositions and truth-as-correspondence gone? The answer is that, at least since Dewey—and surely since Quine—we ought to have learned that there is nothing to be gained from trying to say how it is that sentences map onto a mind-independent "world."[9] If, as the history of logical empiricism shows, we cannot give a one-to-one mapping of cognitively meaningful sentences onto states of affairs existing objectively in the world as it is in itself, then Rorty is right that we ought to quit pursuing theories of objective truth and reference. We cannot get such theories, and we don't need them. What we can do is to apply what we are learning about how structures of embodied cognition—such as image schemas and conceptual metaphors—play a key role in every aspect of our understanding and reasoning. Then we will better understand how human organisms negotiate their feeble way through the ongoing transformative process of constructing a relatively orderly experience that permits them to realize some of their purposes, that is, to know (and to be at home in) their world in certain tentative and highly fallible ways.

CHAPTER 8

Embodied Realism and Truth Incarnate

Do We Need a Theory of Truth?

If knowing is construed as a process for transforming experience in a way that resolves indeterminacies that arise in our lives, thereby helping us function in our world, then what becomes of truth? In the previous chapter, we focused on *knowing* as a reconstructive activity, rather than on *knowledge* as a fixed product. We are said to "know what we're doing" when we achieve an understanding of our situation that allows us to move forward in a way that releases our energies, enhances and deepens meaning, and reveals relations among aspects of our experience. In this sense, knowing is a process, not a finality. It is always tentative and subject to revision in light of new circumstances. This means that we need to give up the mistaken notion of knowledge as an objective relation between a sentence or proposition and some mind-independent state of affairs. Knowing is a *doing*—a way of acting intelligently and realistically in the world so that we are more or less "at home" in our world.

What holds for knowing holds also for truth. Truth ceases to be an absolute fixed relation between a proposition and some aspect of a mind-independent world, as most philosophers have traditionally conceived it. Instead, to say that something we believe or propose is "true" is to say that it represents a well-supported workable hypothesis for guiding our action in the world. Holding something as true generates anticipations about what to expect as our experience unfolds. Truth is just that part of an intelligent inquiry that signals our degree of confidence in the understanding of experience on which we are currently acting. And, just as knowing is always perspectival and context dependent, so also is truth. This pragmatist conception does not make truth arbitrary or whimsical, but it does keep us ever mindful that what we currently take to be true might someday come under scrutiny and possible criticism as we learn more.

This may seem to some to be a rather deflationary view of truth, insofar as it denies the usefulness of trying to specify the *reference relation* that supposedly makes possible objective, universal knowledge and truth. Although there is an aspect of my view that recalls Richard Rorty's highly influential critique of the idea that we should, or even could, construct a general theory of the truth, I will argue that Rorty goes too far when he concludes that there is nothing much philosophically interesting or significant to say about truth.

Over a period of many years, in books ranging from *Philosophy and the Mirror of Nature* (1979) to *Consequences of Pragmatism* (1982), to *Contingency, Irony, and Solidarity* (1989), Rorty mounted an impressive sustained criticism of the many ways that philosophers throughout history have tried to erect foundational theories of knowledge and truth—ways that seek to secure strong metaphysical realism and notions of truth for all times and places. Over and over again, he shows how the classical correspondence theory of truth collapses in on itself when we investigate the claims made about "things-in-themselves," "pure concepts," "observation terms and sentences," "raw sense perceptions," "pure reason," "reference," and other such notions that are meant to guarantee objective truth. Rorty, therefore, urged philosophers encamped for the purpose of explaining truth relations as a way of justifying absolute knowledge claims, to pack up their tents and go home to their daily lives, where "truths" are just permissible moves in various language games, each with its particular internal logic, constitutive rules, and underlying values. The idea of a general theory of truth is to be replaced by an investigation of how "is true" operates within particular language games that people find themselves engaged in.

Rorty thought that William James more or less got it right when he said that "is true" is just a term of praise we employ for beliefs that cohere with other beliefs we are fond of: "The question is precisely whether 'the true' is more than what William James defined it as: 'the name of whatever proves itself to be good in the way of belief, and good, too, for definite, assignable reasons.' On James's view, 'true' resembles 'good' or 'rational' in being a normative notion, a compliment paid to sentences that seem to be paying their way and that fit in with other sentences which are doing so" (1982, xxv).

However, despite some significant similarities, James is a different kind of pragmatist than Rorty. James thought that "better" beliefs—beliefs we tend to call "true"—were those that help us be somewhat more "at home" in our world and to function better within it, whereas Rorty wants to abandon any appeal to terms like "the world" as a way of sorting better from worse beliefs. Rorty (1982, 3–18) rejected talk of "the world," as if it were some kind of grounding metaphysical notion, in favor of the view that truth is defined relative to a given language game that some community happens to find useful.

Rorty's argument against correspondence theories of truth is therefore also, as he sees it, an argument against metaphysical realism, which is the view that our world consists of mind- and language-independent objects, properties, and relations that we have experiential and epistemic access to. The classical correspondence theory of truth defines a true sentence as one that maps onto, or corresponds directly to, some mind- and language-independent state of affairs in the world. Rorty argues, to the contrary, that the only way we have of making sense of something called "the world" is through a *linguistic description* of some part of that world. Therefore, it would seem that we can never break out of language when we try to describe the "world" to which our truth claims supposedly correspond. This, Rorty claims, empties the notion of "the world" of any significant metaphysical or epistemic import. He concludes: "One cannot see language-as-a-whole in relation to something else to which it applies, or for which it is a means to an end" (Rorty 1982, xix). The reason for this is that all our world descriptions are articulated linguistically, and so we cannot, Rorty insists, extricate ourselves from our language games or vocabularies to see how aspects of our world correspond (or not) to our linguistic utterances. In Rorty's terms, truth cannot be "out there" in the world:

> To say that truth is not out there is simply to say that where there are no sentences there is no truth, that sentences are elements of human languages, and that human languages are human creations.
>
> Truth cannot be out there—cannot exist independently of the human mind—because sentences cannot so exist, or be out there. The world is out there, but descriptions of the world are not. Only descriptions of the world can be true or false. The world on its own—unaided by the describing activities of human beings—cannot. (1989, 5)

Rorty is not denying that there is a world outside our minds. Indeed, he cheerfully admits the commonplace that most things "out there" in space and time "are the effects of causes which do not include human mental states" (1989, 5). What he is denying is that we could have a direct knowing access to things "out there" that doesn't involve some particular vocabulary. When it comes to knowledge and truth, therefore, we must forever dwell in the house of language. Hence, for Rorty, any reference to something called "experience" that might exist beyond some particular language game or vocabulary is a nonstarter.

Rorty's critique of correspondence theories of truth is thus part of his general attack on any notion of "experience" that might be used to ground claims about knowledge or truth. He insists that we only have "a world" under some description—relative to some language game we find ourselves within. Therefore, we cannot compare a given language game or vocabulary against reality "out there," because any descriptive account of reality "out there" would involve *some* particular language game or vocabulary.

So, is a useful philosophical theory of truth even possible? Rorty did not seem to think so, other than to explore how terms for truth and knowledge appear to function within specific language games and vocabularies.

While I agree with Rorty's dismissal of any foundational epistemology that might be proposed to ground a classical correspondence theory of truth, I am going to challenge Rorty's claim that once we give up the impossible project of absolutely grounding our language in a mind-independent world, there is then nothing more to be said. Instead, I am going to argue that there are some significant things we can say about human understanding and reasoning that bear directly on how we think of truth. None of these insights support a foundational notion of truth; in fact, they undermine such a view. However, neither do any of these insights support Rorty's linguistic relativism. An inquiry into how our embodiment shapes our understanding turns out to show us how we make sense of our world and what we count as better and worse in the way of knowing, along with what it means to say that something is true.

Truth as an Empirical Issue

The nature of truth is an empirical issue. By this I mean that it is a question that can be answered only by the proper empirical study of mind, thought, and language. The reason why truth must be approached from an empirical perspective is that the nature of truth depends on the nature of concepts, the nature of the mind, and the nature of human experience; and the study of these things requires experimental investigation from the cognitive sciences. I am going to argue that only by investigating the nature of meaning and where our concepts come from can we understand how they both constrain and enable our knowing and what we count as true. Contrary to Rorty's linguistic view, truth is more than just "choosing" a certain vocabulary that we prefer.

Rorty thought that no scientific account of embodied cognition could be relevant to an understanding of truth, because he believed that such an account could have nothing to say about what justifies our knowledge and truth claims. He selects John Locke as a good representative of the attempt to give a causal account of where our concepts come from, and he selects Hegel as the representative of the idea that what counts as knowledge—and hence what counts as a justification of a truth claim—depends on the historically contingent language game you are playing within a particular community of inquirers. In *Philosophy and the Mirror of Nature*, Rorty distinguished the "logical space of causal explanation" (the Lockean project) from the "logical space of reasons or justifications" (the Hegelian project). Each project has its uses, but Rorty thinks we cannot derive a normative theory of what counts as justified knowing or true belief from a causal account of how we acquire our conceptual system. In *Consequences of Pragmatism*, Rorty concludes: "Dewey wanted to be as naturalistic as Locke and as historicist as Hegel. This can indeed be done. One can say with Locke that the causal processes that go on in the human organism suffice, without the intrusion of anything non-natural, to explain the acquisition of knowledge (moral, mathematical, empirical, and political). One can say, with Hegel, that rational criticism of knowledge-claims is always in terms of the problems that human beings face at a particular epoch. These two lines of thought neither intersect nor conflict" (1982, 82).

Rorty is saying that the logical space of reasons is sufficient to tell us everything we need to know about what a particular group of inquirers counts as knowledge and truth. He thinks that explaining where our concepts come from does not add to our account of justification within a language game (or communal framework of inquiry). In short, there is no legitimate move from the logical space of causal explanation to the logical space of justification.

This is a shrewd and nuanced deflationary move on Rorty's part, insofar as it seeks to keep the factual (i.e., causal explanation) utterly separate from the normative (i.e., justificatory explanation). It holds steadfastly to a mistaken fact/value dichotomy. Still, even if one were to accept (as I do not) this bifurcation of explanatory functions (i.e., causal versus justificatory), there nevertheless remains something significant to extract from a naturalistic scientific account of concept formation, as it bears on our notions of knowledge and truth. For one thing, an embodied cognition account of the origins of our conceptual systems can show us why knowledge is not just a matter of selecting language games or vocabularies at will, as if we were merely picking a desired view of justification from a smorgasbord of linguistic and epistemic practices.

However, as we saw in the previous chapter on knowing, Rorty's account of language games and selection of "vocabularies" does not adequately explain how our systems of meaning and our knowledge practices actually work. I argued there that, contrary to Rorty's view of language change, we typically do not "choose" our metaphors; rather, they emerge for us as primary metaphors acquired unreflectively and automatically from deep experiential correlations of the source and target domains, which are realized neurally as cross-domain coactivations of functional neuronal clusters. It would be far more accurate to say that we are "chosen" by our primary metaphors than it would be to say that we "choose" them along with a systematic "vocabulary" spawned by the underlying metaphor.

What embodied cognition theory and conceptual metaphor theory can show us, therefore, is how our knowledge practices and ideas about truth are shaped by our embodiment, as well as what the constraints are on the conceptual systems by which we organize our knowing understanding of the world. Admittedly, this will not provide us with some new theory of truth, but it will help us see how our knowing activities are rooted in our bodily and social nature, which is the source of any knowledge and truth possible for us.

Toward an Account of Truth as Embodied

The classical Correspondence Theory of Truth has traditionally been interpreted in a way that is at once literalist, disembodied, and objectivist. In its simplest form, the correspondence theory can be stated as follows: "A statement is true when it fits the way things are in the world. It is false when it fails to fit the way things are in the world." On the face of it, what could be more obvious and correct? It is true that it's sunny out when the sun is out. It's true that my shoes are brown when my shoes are brown. It's true that my dog, Lucy, has four legs, if and only if she has four legs. In short, if what you say fits some aspect of the mind-independent world, then what you've asserted is, well, *true*. Nobody seems to have any problems with using "true" in these garden-variety situations.

However, as soon as this ordinary commonsense understanding of truth is elevated to the level of an expert theory within analytic philosophy, it becomes highly problematic, or even downright false. What typically happens is that the objectivist and literalist views of meaning that are built into our common understanding and are carried over into analytic philosophy of language run afoul of our scientific understanding of how cognition works. There are two related parts of the classical correspondence theory that require empirical scrutiny:

1. A Disembodied Metaphysical Realism

    The world consists of entities that have certain definite properties and that, at a given time, stand in certain relation to one another. This world is mind-independent. The truths that can be stated depend only on the relation of linguistic signs (or the propositions expressed by those sentence-like structures) to states of affairs in the world. Therefore, truth is not dependent on the nature of human embodiment. It is simply a correspondence between propositions and objective aspects of the world.

2. The Literalist Theory of Truth

    There is only one way the world is at any given time. Truths about this world are given by propositions that consist of literal concepts that can refer to, or map onto, states of affairs in the world. The "correspondence" of statements to states of affairs depends on the existence of literal concepts that can fit the way things are in the world.

Although these two theories are logically independent, they go together comfortably in traditional correspondence theories, because they both support the view of univocal literal propositions mapping onto mind-independent states of affairs in the world.

Both of these theories are mistaken, and their inadequacy can be seen by simply recalling some of the empirical research on the nature of mind, meaning, thought, and language explored in the preceding chapters. We have focused on the way our concepts arise from our sensory,

motor, and affective experiences, based on our ongoing bodily interactions with our environment. We also saw how this sensory–motor,
body-based meaning and conceptual structure can be recruited to provide the source domains of conceptual metaphors that shape our abstract conceptualization and reasoning. This account of meaning and
thought reveals that *truth depends on the nature of our embodied understanding* and that *many of our most important truths depend on systems of inconsistent metaphorically defined abstract concepts.* In short, it turns out that truth
is both *embodied* and, when it pertains to abstract concepts, *metaphorical.*
Therefore, truth cannot be explained with either a disembodied metaphysics or a literalist and objectivist account of meaning. Correspondence needs to be reconceptualized as being dependent on the nature of
our understanding (of experiences and language) that emerges from and
is rooted in our bodily capacities for sense-making. The question of the
nature of truth becomes an empirical question that reaches down into
the depths of human understanding in the neural pathways within our
brains and bodies. In what follows I want to muster empirical research
from the cognitive sciences to show why the disembodied and literalist
theories of truth are mistaken and to point the way to a more empirically adequate conception of embodied, metaphoric truth.

The alternative view of truth is suggested by this research is what
Lakoff and I (1999) called an "experientialist theory of truth." The experientialist view starts by observing that sentences do not simply "fit"
the world in some mind-independent way. Rather, if there is any "fit"
involved, it would have to be between our *understanding* of a sentence
and our *understanding* of a given situation, and that understanding is embodied. The experientialist view makes the following claims:

1. Truth is relative to human understanding (and not to language as
   such).
2. Human understanding is embodied; that is, grounded in our sensory,
   motor, and affective capacities and organism-environment interactions.
3. There are multiple, ontologically distinct levels or dimensions of embodiment.
4. Moreover, each of these spatial or bodily logics gives rise to metaphors that define virtually all our abstract concepts. Typically, these
   conceptual metaphors are not consistent with one another, because
   their source domains have different ontologies built in.

5. Therefore, there are multiple inconsistent truths about many domains of experience, which support multiple, incompatible ontologies and inferences.
6. So, we must have an embodied, pluralistic view of truth.
7. Nonetheless, in spite of this pluralism, truth is neither arbitrary nor radically subjective, since it is tied to organism-environment interactions that involve shared perceptual and cognitive structures as well as shared environments.

A crucial part of the argument for an experientialist account of truth is the claim that whether a statement is true or not will often depend on which level of embodiment one is focusing on. In *The Meaning of the Body* (2007), I listed five different levels of embodiment, from our neural systems and our interpersonal transactions, all the way up to the ways our culture inflects our embodiment. For our purposes here, however, we need only consider two levels—the phenomenological and the neural—using, as a representative example, an examination how truth claims about color depend on which of these two levels of embodiment we are interested in.

The phenomenological level consists of our felt, qualitative experience of color. When I look out my office window, I see the green grass of winter in Oregon and I perceive the *greenness* as being "in" the *objects* that are "colored." At this level, there are common, obvious truths: new grass is green, the sky on a clear day is blue, blood is red. *Green, blue,* and *red* are one-place predicates holding of *grass, the sky,* and *blood.* At this phenomenological level the correspondence theory says the following about sentences like "The grass is green": the word *grass* names things (or stuff) in the world. The word *green* names a property that inheres in certain things in the world. If the green-property inheres in the grass-things, then the sentence "Grass is green" is true.

This is a phenomenology-first account of truth, because it implicitly privileges that level of embodiment over other levels, such as scientific accounts of the neural processes of vision. The science of color is irrelevant in this context, if we are judging based only on the phenomenological character of our experience. The word *green* has a meaning that reflects our conscious experience of colors as properties inhering in objects themselves. That is, the meaning of *green* is a one-place predicate denoting a physical property in the world.

But what if we now give priority to our neurophysiological embodiment and the neural account of color vision that it entails? At this level of embodied experience, from the perspective of the science of color, we know that colors do not inhere in objects themselves. Color perception depends on at least *four* components: the color cones in our retina, the neural circuitry that connects those cones to areas in the visual cortex (and perhaps to other areas as well), wavelengths of light reflected off surfaces, and ambient lighting conditions. In terms of our neural level of embodiment, then, color is conceived as a complex interactional property between reflected light, the structure of our eyes, ambient light, and the visual processing areas of the brain. Color does not exist in any one of these components, but only in all four of them together. At this neurophysiological level, then, it is false to say that "the grass is green" because the greenness does not inhere in objects or stuff existing in the mind-independent world; nor can it be reduced merely to reflectances of objects.

In short, *at the neural level, green is a multi-place interactional property, while at the phenomenological level, green is a one-place predicate characterizing a property that inheres in an object.* So we are faced with a dilemma: a scientific truth claim based on knowledge about the neural level is contradicting a truth claim at the phenomenological level. Which is true?

The answer is that they are both true, but only relative to two different levels of embodiment. Truth is thus tied to embodied understanding, and there is no one level of embodied understanding that always takes precedence over all other levels. Which level one appropriates at a particular historical moment will depend on one's deepest values, one's context, and one's purposes and interests. What counts as correspondence will depend on which level one assumes, and there is no consistent unified ontology that is neutral across all levels of embodied experience. To see this, you need only to realize that color-as-a-one-place predicate locates color's reality as a property of things in the world, whereas color-as-multi-place predicate locates the color in the conjoint transactions of at least four parts of our world (i.e., eyes, visual processing regions of the brain, reflectances, and ambient light).

There are contexts in which the phenomenological level is the one we need, along with its truths, and there are contexts where various scientific accounts are what we need, along with their truths. From the point of view of such an embodied realism, there is not any one way the world is, in itself; and there is no single notion of correspondence that works for all cases. Truth is relative to embodied understanding, and that embodied understanding is shaped relative to our bodies, our brains, the structured energies in our environment, and our cultural embeddedness.

One important upshot of this is that we must recognize the need to replace the commonsense version of the correspondence theory of truth given above with an embodied correspondence view of truth. There is no truth-in-itself, but only truth as shaped by our embodied understanding. What emerges is an experientialist/embodied view of truth:

> A person takes a sentence as "true" of a situation if what he or she understands the sentence as expressing accords with what he or she understands the situation to be. *Accordance* is not merely some abstract stand-in for the "fit" of a sentence to a situation; rather, it signals that taking something as true means that he or she expects certain experiences to follow if he or she acts on that truth assumption, and also that "is true" indicates confidence that certain experiences are likely to be forthcoming and also that certain actions are entailed by taking a particular understanding to be true.

The phenomenological and neural levels provide different body-based modes of understanding, each drawing on a different sense of embodiment. The first treats understanding from the perspective of everyday conscious experience, while the second draws on the neurophysiology of perception.

The standard response to such a relativizing of truth to embodied understanding is to claim that it leads to an unacceptable arbitrariness and radical relativism. To avoid such relativism, we supposedly need to assert the primacy of one level of embodied understanding over others (such as when a scientist privileges her "scientific" over the everyday, commonsense, phenomenological view). But this leads to false hopes, because it overlooks the fact that there are multiple scientific perspectives, each involving different modes of embodied understanding, and each serving different interests and values we have on different occasions. There is, therefore, no way to fix any one account as "The Truth," once and for all time.

Rorty saw this point, but he mistakenly concluded from it that there is therefore really nothing interesting or useful to say about the nature of truth. He would say, "Pick a language game (or be picked by one) and simply run with its attendant notion of truth conditions as defined by a specific community of inquirers. In some other context, perhaps another language game (with *its* particular notion of truth-claim justification) will seem more useful to you, and then you go with that one. But there is nothing much to say about truth in a general sense." He summarizes his deflationary view of truth by saying that "our purposes would be served best by ceasing to see truth as a deep matter, as a topic of philosophical interest, or 'true' as a term which repays 'analysis'" (Rorty 1989, 8).

Rorty gets James's pluralism (both epistemological and metaphysical) right, and he therefore sees truth as plural in nature. But he draws the inference that there are no better or worse ways of describing things and stating truths than are found in the various language games we inhabit. This places all our candidate language games and practices (each with their own internal values) on a par with respect to correctness. Denying any general notion of correctness, Rorty thus wants to replace "correctness" with "usefulness" for various purposes. Consequently, according to his view, "is true" is either an empty notion or a routine move within a particular language game or vocabulary. With respect to my example of green grass, Rorty would agree that whether "the grass is green" is true depends on whether we select what he might call the phenomenological commonsense vocabulary or the neuroscience vocabulary, and he sees that there is no value-neutral way to decide which language game is appropriate.

The principal difference, then, between Rorty's *linguistic relativist* view of truth and my *embodied, experientialist* view of truth is this: Rorty argues that truth is relative to particular contingent *vocabularies*, whereas I am arguing that truth is relative to different embodied *understandings*, and I do not regard understanding as merely a linguistic phenomenon. Embodied understanding may include language, but it reaches beyond and beneath language proper, down into the embodied structures and processes by which we meaningfully inhabit, make sense of, and act within our world.

Is there anything more to be said on this subject? Rorty doubts that there is, but I submit that investigating the embodiment of human understanding, conceptualization, and reasoning gives us important insights about knowledge and truth claims that we would not otherwise have access to. In short, I will suggest that, besides knowing that something is true or false within some particular language game, if we investigate how our concepts have emerged from bodily transactions with our environments, we will better understand the logics of knowing and truth operating at the various levels of our embodiment. This is something more—and more important—than merely saying that we pick a language game and whatever conception of truth comes with it. For one thing, the idea that we just "pick" or "choose" a certain language game is misleading and does not capture what is actually involved in understanding a situation. For another, embodied understanding is more than language alone.

Embodied Truth: Multiple, Inconsistent Metaphors of Causation

In order to see how truth depends on embodied understanding at different levels, I propose to examine just some of the many embodied conceptions of causation that operate usefully both in our everyday commonsense and in various theoretical and practical sciences of our day. It is hard to imagine a more basic and important concept than *causation*, and yet it turns out to be anything but the clear, literal, unified concept we have been led to believe in. There is no single literal concept of causation that could possibly serve to express all the causal truths we claim to know. Instead, just like all our abstract concepts, causation turns out to be defined by multiple, sometimes mutually inconsistent, conceptual metaphors. Causation is what Lakoff (1987) calls a "radial category." Our causal knowledge and causal reasoning depends on the entailments of the various metaphors we employ for these very different notions of causation, and no notion can be singled out to cover all cases of scientific explanation. Rorty could perhaps observe that we operate with multiple inconsistent vocabularies of causation, but he never offered a workable, empirically grounded account of meaning, concepts, and reason that could back up such a claim. I will be suggesting that, were he to do so, he would have to go beyond his linguistic relativism to a richer account of embodied understanding.

Let us start with some of the familiar causal logics that are used to state truths about causation in various social sciences:

- *Causal paths and trees*: Change depends on other changes. (Paul David—economic history; Sid Verba—comparative politics; Stephen Krasner—international relations)
- *The domino effect*: Once one country falls to communism, then the next will, and the next . . . until force is applied to keep one from falling (e.g., Vietnam War rhetoric).

- *Thresholds*: For a while there is a buildup with no effect, but once change starts, it becomes uncontrollable.
- *The plate tectonic theory of international relations*: When causal force is applied to something large, the effect lags after the action of the cause but then occurs in a massive fashion. (Stephen Krasner; John Lewis Gaddis)

These are metaphorical causal models. Each has its own logic, taken from some specific domain of physical causation and then applied, via a cross-domain mapping, to international relations. These metaphorical models of causation are not merely arbitrary ways of conceptualizing change; rather, they have profound implications for peoples' lives. How many civilians and soldiers died, on both sides of the Vietnam War, because of the domino-effect logic used by the Kennedy, Johnson, and Nixon administrations? How much money and other resources are pumped into foreign aid with the idea of tipping the political balance (as a threshold effect) in some "third world" country?

These are but four of the numerous causal metaphors. Consider the following examples (individual words, idioms, and grammatical constructions) of just a small portion of causal expressions in English, and ask what concepts of causation might underlie them.

The noise *gave* me a headache.
The aspirin *took* it away.
The Democrats *blocked* the balanced budget amendment in the senate.
FDR's leadership *brought* the country out of the Depression.
The home run *threw* the crowd into a frenzy.
He *pulled* me out of my depression.
That experience *pushed* him over the edge.
The trial *thrust* O. J.'s attorneys into the limelight.
They *handed* me the job.
The Republicans are trying to *derail* the Democrats' legislative agenda.
The alchemist wanted to *turn* lead into gold.
Her political views were *shaped* by the Depression.
The earthquake *held up* the project.
A rise in pressure *accompanies* a rise in temperature.
Smoking *leads to* cancer.
Cancer has been *linked to* smoking.
Russia *replaced* one government with another.

He *carried* the project to completion by himself.
They *closed the door on* a settlement.
She died *from* pneumonia.
Pressure goes up *with* temperature.

The following words express causation in these sentences: *give, take, block, bring, throw, drive, pull, push, thrust, hand, derail, turn, shape, hold up, accompany, lead to, linked to, replace, carry, close the door on, from, with.*

Why do these words—which differ greatly from one another in their most basic senses—express causation? Cognitive linguistics research reveals that each of these lexical items is understood relative to some particular underlying metaphorical frame for causation.

I cannot analyze all these metaphors for causation here (for a fuller treatment of these and other important causal metaphors, see Lakoff and Johnson 1999, chap. 11). Instead, I will focus on two major systematic metaphors that provide a representative account of how causation is understood via multiple, typically inconsistent, metaphors.

The Underpinnings of Causal Metaphors

Causation is part of the structure of events, and events are generally understood via some very basic systematic conceptual metaphors. Therefore, to understand the range of metaphorical conceptions of causation, we have to look at causation in the context of event structure in general; that is, we have to look at metaphorical conceptions of states, changes, purposes, means, difficulties, actions, activities, and so on. Only then does the metaphor system for causation become clear. Here is one of the two most important metaphors for events, with its mapping from the source domain (motion through space) to the target domain (events).

The EVENT STRUCTURE Metaphor (Location Branch)

States Are Locations (Bounded Regions In Space)
Changes Are Movements (Into Or Out Of Bounded Regions)
Causes Are Forces
Causation Is Forced Movement
Actions Are Self-Propelled Movements
Difficulties Are Impediments To Motion
Purposes Are Destinations
Means Are Paths (To Destinations)

Projects Are Routes
External Events Are Large, Moving Objects

Each of these specific cross-domain mappings provides the conceptual basis for a range of related linguistic expressions for causation. Even more important, the mappings give rise to the specific causal logic and causal inferences that are used in our causal reasoning. In other words, the ways we understand and reason about causation in various fields are structured by the specific conceptual metaphors that define the key concepts. Our ability to state causal truths depends on the various conceptual metaphors that define our notion of events. This can be seen by looking more closely at a few of the submappings of the location branch of the EVENT STRUCTURE metaphor.

STATES ARE LOCATIONS (BOUNDED REGIONS IN SPACE)

I'm *in* love. He's *out of* his depression. He's *deep in* a depression. He's *on the edge of* senility. He's *close to* insanity. We're *far from* safety.

> *Inference Patterns Mapped*
> If you're *in* a bounded region, you're not *out* of that bounded region.
> If you're *in* a state, you're not *out* of that state.
> If you're *out* of a bounded region, you're not *in* that bounded region.
> If you're *out* of a state, you're not *in* that state.
> If you're *deep in* a bounded region, you are *far from* being *out of* that bounded region.
> If you're *deep in* a state, you are *far from* being *out of* that state.
> If you are *on the edge of* a bounded region, then you are *close to* being *in* that bounded region.
> If you are *on the edge of* a state, then you are *close* to being *in* that state.

The first member of each of these pairs gives some spatial logic of the source domain (physical motion in space). The second member shows that same logic mapped onto the target domain (change of state). In other words, the metaphorically based logic of change of state is grounded in the inference patterns of our embodied sensory-motor experience of movement in space.

CHANGES ARE MOVEMENTS (INTO OR OUT OF BOUNDED REGIONS)
I *came out of* my depression. He *went* crazy. He *went over the edge.* She
  entered a state of euphoria. He *fell into* a depression. He *went deeper*
  into his depression. In the sun, the clothes *went from* wet *to* dry in an
  hour. The clothes are *somewhere between* wet *and* dry.

> *Inference Patterns Mapped*
> If something *moves from location A to location B,* it is first *in A* and
>   later *in B.*
> If something *changes from state A to state B,* it is first *in A* and
>   later *in B.*
> If something *moves* from *location A to location B* over a period of
>   time, there is a *point* at which it is *between A* and *B.*
> If something *changes from state A to state B* over a period of time,
>   there is *point* at which it is *between A* and *B.*

CAUSES ARE FORCES

The rain *forced* us to retreat to the tent. His speech *moved* me to tears.
  She was *struck by* what he said. The election results *impacted me* in a
  devastating way. I was *compelled* to do what he ordered.

Although one might think that causes are, literally, physical forces,
the metaphorical character of this conception becomes evident with
cases in which the causation is not just physical force applied to an object, but also emotional, psychological, economic, political, and other
types of forces.

CAUSATION IS FORCED MOVEMENT

FDR's leadership *brought* the country out of the Depression. The home
  run *threw* the crowd into a frenzy. He *drove* her crazy. She *pulled* me
  out of my depression. That experience *pushed* him *over the edge.* His
  speech *moved* the crowd to rage. The stock market crash *propelled* the
  country into a depression. The trial *thrust* O. J.'s attorneys into the
  limelight.

Notice here that the causal logic of "bringing" water to a boil is quite
different from the logic of "throwing" a crowd into a frenzy. *Bring* requires continuous contact to move something. For example, to *bring*
someone a glass of water, we have to apply continuous force to carry
the glass to that person. This logic carries over into the metaphorical
concept of bringing water to a boil, since that requires the continuous
application of heat to the water to change its state. By contrast, *throwing*

involves an initial strong force applied to propel an object through the air. Thus, to *throw* a crowd into a frenzy entails a sudden strong metaphorical force (here, the event of the home run).

ACTIONS ARE SELF-PROPELLED MOTIONS

She got herself *going* again. He's *moving toward* making a decision. After the recession, I've had to *jumpstart* my career. Eileen *ran with the ball* on the new project. She's *moving* right along in finishing up her dissertation.

According to this metaphor, we would then expect that anything about the nature of actions—what enables or aids them, the manner in which they are performed, and how obstacles affect them—would generate further submappings of the following sort:

Aids To Action Are Aids To Motion
Manner Of Action Is Manner Of Motion
Careful Action Is Careful Motion
Speed Of Action Is Speed Of Motion
Difficulties Are Impediments To Motion
Making Progress Is Forward Movement
Amount Of Progress Is Distance Moved
Achieving A Purpose Is Reaching The End Of A Path
Means Are Paths

AIDS TO ACTION ARE AIDS TO MOTION
It is *smooth sailing* from here on in. It's all *downhill* from here. There's *nothing in our way*. The *path* to democracy is *wide open*.

MANNER OF ACTION IS MANNER OF MOTION
He *stumbled through* life. She *fell right into* the new job. Otto got *tripped up* on the final question. Jenny just *drifted along* without any clear direction.

CAREFUL ACTION IS CAREFUL MOTION
I'm *walking on eggshells*. He is *treading on thin ice*. He is *walking a fine line*. They *tiptoed around* that problematic issue.

SPEED OF ACTION IS SPEED OF MOTION
He *flew* through his work. She is progressing *by leaps and bounds*. I am moving *at a snail's pace*. The construction project is *creeping along*.

DIFFICULTIES ARE IMPEDIMENTS TO MOTION

Blockages

He got *over* his divorce. He's trying to get *around* the regulations. She went *through* the trial. We ran into a *brick wall*. We've got him *boxed into a corner*.

Features of the terrain

He's *between a rock and a hard place*. It's been *uphill* all the way. We've been *bogged down*. We've been *hacking our way through a jungle* of regulations.

Burdens

He's *carrying* quite *a load*. He's *weighed down* by lot of assignments. He's been trying to *shoulder* all the responsibility. Get *off my back*!

Counterforces

Quit *pushing* me *around*. She's *leading* him *around by the nose*. He's *holding* her *back*.

Lack of an energy source

I'm *out of gas*. They're *running on fumes*. We're *running out of steam*.

MAKING PROGRESS IS FORWARD MOVEMENT

We are *moving ahead*. Let's *forge ahead*. Let's keep *moving forward*. We made lots of *forward* progress.

AMOUNT OF PROGRESS IS DISTANCE MOVED

We've *come a long way*. We've *covered lots of ground*. We've *made it this far*. No more *backsliding* from now on!

ACHIEVING A PURPOSE IS REACHING THE END OF THE PATH

We've *reached the end*. We are *seeing the light at the end of the tunnel*. We only have *a short way to go*. The *end is in sight*. The *end is a long way off*. We're *far from* finished.

MEANS ARE PATHS

Do it *this way*. She did it the *other way*. Do it *any way* you can. However you want to *go about it* is fine with me.

Ontological Duality in the Metaphorical Logic of Causation

So far, I have surveyed some of the more prominent aspects of just one branch of the EVENT STRUCTURE metaphor, with its attendant metaphors for causation. I have tried to show that the causal truths we express in certain domains depend on the logic and knowledge structure of metaphors like these. One of the most monumental consequences of this analysis is that the various metaphors often do not share a consistent logic—and they may not even share a compatible ontology! In order to see this most clearly, we need to very briefly consider the second major branch of the EVENT STRUCTURE metaphor, known as the OBJECT-EVENT STRUCTURE metaphor, which is involved in expressions like the following:

- I *have* a headache. (The headache is a possession.)
- I *got* a headache. (Change is acquisition—motion to.)
- My headache *went away*. (Change is loss—motion from.)
- The noise *gave me* a headache. (Causation is giving—motion to.)
- The aspirin *took away* my headache. (Causation is taking—motion from.)

According to this object branch of the EVENT STRUCTURE metaphor, attributes are possessions that can be given or taken, lost, found, shared, and transferred in various ways. Thus, a lecture can *give* you a headache, but then aspirin can *take it away*.

We can now give a very abbreviated summary of the two different branches of the EVENT STRUCTURE metaphor, with some of the key submappings that show the two different conceptions of causation operating in the two different metaphors for event structure.

EVENT STRUCTURE (Object Branch)
Attributes Are Possessions
Changes Are Movements Of Possessions (Acquisitions or Losses)
Causes Are Forces
Causation Is Transfer Of Possessions (Giving Or Taking)
Purposes Are Desired Objects

EVENT STRUCTURE (Location Branch)
States Are Locations
Changes Are Movements (To Or From Locations)
Causes Are Forces
Causation Is Forced Movement
Purposes Are Desired Locations (Destinations)

Incompatible Causal Logics

The key point in all of this is that the object and location branches of the EVENT STRUCTURE metaphor have different, incompatible ontologies. In the object branch, a state is a possessable and transferable object and causation is forced transfer of that object, while in the location branch, a state is a spatial location and causation is movement from one state-location to another. Moreover, these two different branches are figure/ground reversals of each other. In the location branch, the figure is the *affected entity* and the ground is the *effect* (as in "I went from happy to sad in no time"), while in the object branch, the figure is the *effect* and the ground is the *affected entity* (as in "The loud music gave me a headache").

Implications of Conceptual Metaphor for Truth

In this chapter, I have only presented a small number of the nearly twenty causal metaphors that Lakoff and I analyzed in *Philosophy in the Flesh*. Nonetheless, however partial this sampling is, it provides us ample evidence to support three conclusions. First, *analyses of these underlying causal metaphors provides the only way to explain the semantics and inference patterns of causation, which are the bases of the causal truths we can state.* Without the metaphors, we can make no sense of why we use words like *hold back, propel, bring, take, start out, slow down, move toward,* and so on, to conceptualize causation; nor can we explain our causal reasoning, or what counts as a causal truth in some domain. Consequently, any adequate account of causal truths will depend on working out the mappings of the metaphors and learning how their source domain logics come out of our sensory-motor experience and are projected to structure our understanding of causation in abstract domains.

The second highly significant conclusion is that *these systems of causal metaphor are based primarily on the structure of the sensory and motor capacities possessed by humans.* This means that there are very substantial constraints that determine which causal metaphors a community will have access to, and it fundamentally shapes how that community will reason about causal relations. Moreover, the structure of the source domains for the metaphors of causation is not merely the result of language. It depends to a considerable extent on the nature of our bodies, our brains, our social relations, and the types of environments we inhabit. This is the primary basis for my claim that embodied understanding, rather than language alone, is the locus of our grasp of causation.

These two conclusions should already be startling news, because they undermine the literalist theory of truth and the disembodiment theory of truth. However, there is an equally important third point that is even more startling. As we have just seen, *different metaphors for causation may operate with different underlying incompatible ontologies.* In both the location and the object duals of the EVENT STRUCTURE metaphors, CAUSES ARE FORCES. However, in the location dual, STATES ARE LOCATIONS, and the causal force moves the object of the causation into that state-location, whereas in the object dual, STATES ARE POSSESSIONS that are moved by forces from one individual to another. Are states LOCATIONS or are they POSSESSIONS? Are causes physical forces that move objects to new state-locations, or are they forces that allow us to transfer possessions? Well, the answer depends on which EVENT STRUCTURE metaphor system we are using, and we cannot express the relevant truth claims without using the appropriate metaphors.

Is There a Single Literal Concept of Causation?

The literalist view of truth requires a literal concept of causation that would be shared by all the many metaphorical conceptions. Is there such a literal core for the fifteen to twenty metaphorical concepts we have discovered so far (see Lakoff and Johnson 1999, chap. 11)? The answer is yes, but this does not save the literalist view of causation. The reason why is that the literal skeletal concept (which is that *a cause is a determining factor*) is so underspecified that it cannot give rise to any of the actual causal inferences that permit us to state causal truths in various fields and disciplines. The causal truths that we can state depend on the causal metaphors that frame them. If a literalist asks you whether it is true that *A caused B*, you will be quite justified if you answer by asking, "Which of the fifteen or twenty basic metaphors for causation that we have discovered so far are you talking about? Do you mean one of the several versions of the location branch of the EVENT STRUCTURE metaphor, one of the versions of the object branch, or other metaphorical notions such as the plate tectonic theory of causation?" Until you specify which metaphorically defined concept of causation is relevant to which context, there is no way to answer causal truth claim questions.

The Metaphysics of Metaphorical Truth

Philosophers of an objectivist persuasion will protest that, according to the form of empirical analysis I've been employing, there would be no such thing as a cause! But this, of course, is palpably ridiculous.

The answer, as we can now see, is that of course there are causes. In fact, there are many different notions of causation, most of which are defined by body-based metaphors. *Causation* thus becomes a very complex radial category, with prototypical cases of physical force causation at the center of the category and many noncentral metaphorical concepts branching off from the prototypical cases according to various metaphorical principles of extension (Lakoff and Johnson 1999).

What *does not* exist is any single entity called "a cause." Causation is complex, often systematic (involving multiple levels of event interactions), and seldom simply singular and linear. You can only state causal truths relative to some level of embodied understanding, and since there are multiple, sometimes inconsistent ontologies for these various levels of embodiment, we cannot specify the truth or falsity of causal claims *überhaupt*.

Rorty seems to have understood the fact that so many of our most important scientific, philosophical, and moral concepts are defined by metaphors, so one might think that analyses of the sort just given do nothing but reinforce Rorty's claim that we merely select the metaphors that seem most useful to us. This is a serious misunderstanding of what conceptual metaphor theory shows about our causal concepts. Rorty's claim is that there is no deep explanation to be had of why we have the metaphors we do. Instead, he says, we simply find that one metaphor replaces another, because some language community finds it "more useful" than the previous metaphor, which they now discard. Rorty explains that "the world does not provide us with any criterion of choice between alternative metaphors, [so] that we can only compare languages or metaphors with one another, not with something beyond language called 'fact'" (1989, 20). In other words, there is no place to stand from which to show how one metaphor fits a situation better than another, for our description of any situation is already framed by one or another metaphor within a particular vocabulary. This is the same we-can-never-get-outside-language argument explained earlier, but here taken down to the level of metaphor. And when it comes to competing metaphors, there is really no way, Rorty insists, to absolutely justify adopting one metaphor over another. Rorty urges us to "see language, as we now see evolution, as new forms of life constantly killing off old forms—not to accomplish a higher purpose, but blindly" (ibid., 19). Choosing a certain metaphor is "having hit upon a tool which happened to work better for certain purposes than any previous tool" (ibid.).

The account of meaning, understanding, and reasoning that I have developed in the previous chapters reveals what is missing in Rorty's account of metaphor change—namely, loose body-based constraints. Rorty's theory of metaphor as a nonsemantic pragmatic effect is not based on any empirical research from linguistics or psychology about how metaphors actually function, why we have the metaphorical concepts we do, and why they "work" for us in different contexts. He thinks that there is nothing philosophically interesting to say about such issues, because his erroneous theory of metaphor (and of language generally) has no resources to answer such questions. For Rorty, metaphors are just irrational, highly contingent ruptures in our received conceptual system (which he calls our inherited vocabulary).

On the contrary, I have been presenting evidence that our metaphors arise from our sensory-motor engagement with our environments and that the metaphors we find useful are grounded in the nature of our bodies and the affordances offered us by the environments we inhabit. *Since truth is relative to understanding, understanding is embodied, and our abstract concepts are metaphorically structured by recruitment of embodied meaning processes, there are constraints and limits to what can count as true for creatures embodied in the ways we are.* Our embodiment provides our engagement with the world in a way that both constrains our understanding and opens up a range of affordances for our future action. There are only certain kinds of causal truths, and these depend directly on the nature of our bodies, our brains, our perceptual and motor systems, the kinds of environments we inhabit, the situations we encounter, our purposes, interests, desires, goals, and needs.

This is the view that Lakoff and I (1999) called "embodied realism," which we claimed was necessary for an adequate understanding of truth. We argued that a plausible realism makes three claims: (1) There is a world independent of our understanding of it. (2) We are in constant interaction with that world through our bodily engagement with our environment. (3) This engagement provides a basis for a stable knowing relation to dimensions of that world. In stating (2), we meant to deny that our relation to our surroundings is always mediated by some "internal," "mental" representation. We summarized this view as follows: "At the heart of embodied realism is our physical engagement with an environment in an ongoing series of interactions. There is a level of physical interaction in the world at which we have evolved to function very successfully, and an important part of our conceptual system is attuned to such functioning. The existence of such "basic-level concepts"—characterized in terms of gestalt perception, mental imagery, and motor interaction—is one of the central discoveries of embodied cognitive science" (Lakoff and Johnson 1999, 90). Embodied realism reveals our ongoing coupling with our world through our bodily (sensory and motor) interactions with the energy patterns of our environments. But, as we have seen, the embodied, basic-level concepts that emerge at this level can become the basis for perceptual and motor inferences, for event and action frames, and for conceptual metaphors and metonymies, all of which play a crucial role in extending our knowledge beyond physical perception and object manipulation to more abstract domains.

If this is roughly correct, then Rorty's treatment of metaphor (and language generally) is incorrect. We can now understand why Rorty utterly rejected Dewey's emphasis on experience as the basis of all meaning and thought. Rorty mistakenly thought that any account of the character of experience would necessarily end up being foundationalist and wedded to an objectivist metaphysics. The parts of Dewey's view that Rorty could not abide—his reference to experience and the qualitative unity of a situation—are the very parts that make it possible to understand how our metaphors actually work.

In his article "Qualitative Thought" (1930), Dewey claimed that all meaning and thought must begin from a grasp of the pervasive unifying quality of the particular situation one is thinking about: "By the term situation in this connection is signified the fact that the subject-matter ultimately referred to in existential propositions is a complex existence that is held together in spite of its internal complexity by the fact that it is dominated and characterized throughout by a single quality" ([1930] 1988, 246). If our thinking is to be relevant to a given situation, it must arise through our discernment of the pervasive unifying quality that marks out *that* specific situation with all its relevant characteristics: "The underlying unity of qualitativeness regulates pertinence and relevancy and force of every distinction and relation; it guides selection and rejection and the manner of utilization of all explicit terms" (ibid., 247–48). Understanding and appreciating the significance of a situation involves discerning what is relevant and important in what is afforded you in that situation, and Dewey argued that relevance depends on how you circumscribe the situation—that is, how you mark it off as a meaningful unified whole. Moreover, this process of demarcating a situation and grasping its meaning is not accomplished only through language, but through the embodied structures of understanding of the sort discussed in the preceding chapters.

One of the key points I have been arguing for in this book is that it is precisely such body-based image schemas and conceptual metaphors that mark out for beings like us what is relevant to our inquiries and also constrain what we are able to count as knowledge and truth. To a large extent, it is these image schemas and metaphors that constitute the affordances we experience as relevant in a given context. It is these image schemas and metaphors that mark the boundaries of a particular situation, thereby shaping what appears meaningful to us, how we understand it, and how we are able reason intelligently about it. We are not necessarily "forced" to accept any particular metaphor, but the range of metaphors appropriate to a given situation will be marked out by the ways our bodies shape the affordances available to us at a particular point in time. So, Rorty was mistaken in thinking that as knowers we exist only within the cocoon of encapsulated vocabularies. To the contrary, we are always in and of our world, which we inhabit as bodily and social animals.

Applied to causal metaphor and truth, what this means is that our metaphors for causation are anything but arbitrary or random. They are not merely historically contingent linguistically defined terms. Rather, they are highly motivated and constrained by the nature of our bodies and the affordances of our environments. Therefore, if we ever hope to understand our concepts of causation, we must understand the semantics, logic, and inference patterns of each of the causal metaphors. Moreover, we must understand where our image schemas come from and how our conceptual metaphors are experientially grounded. Only *then* will we get even a partial grasp of how we make sense of causal relations at many levels and in different contexts. Only *then* will we understand what constitutes an appropriate truth claim, relative to a given metaphorical structuring of a situation. Our most basic metaphorical concepts are therefore neither absolute objective truths, nor irrational, blind ruptures in our present language game that institute some new vocabulary. Rather, image schemas and metaphors constitute the relevant structure of the situations we are inquiring into, and they constrain what can count as "true" relative to the type of inquiry we are engaged in. And, since success in inquiry (in pursuit of truth) can be judged only relative to our values concerning the purpose of inquiry, we must always ask, *successful with respect to which values and purposes*? It follows that there are always values implied in truth claims. There can be no value-neutral truth. Just like acts of knowing, truth is an intrinsically normative assessment of the degree of success relative to our ability to be at home in our world. That is at least part of what James meant when he said that truth is "the name of whatever proves itself to be good in the way of belief, and good, too, for definite, assignable reasons" ([1909] 1975, 42).

What a Theory of Truth Is

I end by drawing some summary conclusions about what an adequate view of truth would look like, some of which are supported by considerations of the sort I have been discussing in this essay, while others are and must remain, at this point in time, more speculative.

1. The classical correspondence theory of truth is hopeless. It is hopeless for many reasons. First, we have no neutral, universal perspective on a mind-independent reality against which we could test our truth claims. Second, our understanding, concepts, and reasoning are grounded in our bodily experience, and therefore truth claims will remain relative to some embodied perspective. Third, our understanding of virtually all our abstract concepts is defined by clusters of often inconsistent metaphors. Therefore, no disembodied or literalist view of truth as correspondence can even get off the ground.
2. Any understanding of the nature of truth must be compatible with our best and most stable empirical understanding of how the mind works. We must therefore examine the role of various bodily structures (such as images, image schemas, conceptual prototypes, basic-level categories, and conceptual metaphors) in what makes something true or false.
3. A key part of any adequate theory of truth will thus be an account of truths dependent on metaphors. In other words, some things will be "true" only relative to metaphorically defined concepts and metaphorically understood situations. For example, Lakoff and Núñez (2000) examined part of the vast metaphorical foundations of mathematics, showing in detail for case after case — ranging from our conception of addition all the way up to the mathematics of differential equations and infinitesimals — that our most fundamental mathematical truths depend on image schemas, cross-domain mappings (metaphors), and metonymies. This fact does not make those mathe-

matical truths any less true or any less impressive, but it does relativize them to embodied and imaginative understanding.

4. An empirical approach to truth is not merely about empirical studies of language and thought. It must ultimately be based in an account of the processes of our embodied understanding, which goes far beyond our linguistic capacities and speech acts. It must reach down into the depths of our embodied cognition, even probing the neural bases of meaning, thought, value, and action. There is currently extensive neural modeling, based on new knowledge about neural architecture, that attempts to explain how neural beings like us can perform the marvelous cognitive operations we do (Feldman 2006; Tucker and Luu 2012). Neural models of image schemas, prototypes, radical categories, metaphors, and other imaginative structures are being developed to help explain how meaning and thought are grounded in our embodiment and why metaphor plays such an important role in what and how we think (Lakoff and Narayanan 2017). When this research turns to questions about truth, it will ask such questions as: What is the neural basis for categorization? How are image schemas realized in our neural architectures? How does a neural activation for a sentence "fit" a neural activation for our understanding of a situation?

5. As cognitive neuroscience has progressed, there is now a very-well-developed "simulation theory of meaning," which uses numerous neural imagining studies to show that understanding a sentence activates a simulation process in which sensory, motor, affective, and action planning areas of the brain are activated that pertain to the scenes, events, and actions described in the sentence (Barsalou 1999; Feldman 2006; Bergen 2012; Lakoff and Narayanan 2017). This experimental research is giving massive support to embodied cognition views and shows what it means to say that the truth of a sentence is embodied.

6. Finally, a theory of truth will have to be grounded in an empirical account of how we have evolved and have developed our capacities for functioning within various environments. Truth is not merely about words fitting experiences. Truth is, more important, about which understandings allow us to function successfully. The structures of our embodied, imaginative understanding have emerged from massive numbers of constant, ongoing, second-by-second interactions and environmental feedback. This has given rise to an astounding number of constraints on our conceptual systems and the truths we

can know and state. An adequate theory of truth, therefore, must be based on an embodied pragmatist theory of understanding.

It is considerations like these that (1) leave me emphatically dissatisfied with any account of truth based on objectivist semantics and its connection to literalist and disembodied views of truth, and (2) leave me equally dissatisfied with Rorty's linguistic relativism regarding truth. This is also why I see the nature of truth as an empirical matter—a matter for empirical study from the perspective of linguistics, biology, cognitive psychology, developmental psychology, anthropology, and cognitive neuroscience. On this view, *a theory of truth is based on a theory of meaning and cognition, which in turn should be based on a theory of embodied understanding.* Since understanding is embodied and imaginative, any adequate account of truth must incorporate these dimensions into its generalizations and modes of explanation. An embodied theory of truth goes along with an embodied realism, which situates "reality" within the ongoing interactive process of our embodied experience. Truths are thus "tested" by our action as embodied living creatures acting within our ever-changing environments, and guided by strong motivational and normative processes. This is what is meant by a pragmatist theory of truth. Truth is not principally about whether any statements or propositions correspond to reality or to "the way things are" in any absolute sense, or for all time. Instead, truths are about understandings that allow us to function more or less successfully in our world, a world that is always evolving and therefore presents us with new challenges that require a plurality of modes of inquiry and that give rise to situated, embodied knowing and truth claims.

So, where does all this leave us with respect to Rorty's claim that we cannot have a philosophically deep theory of truth that would guarantee our knowledge claims, and we do not need such a theory? Rorty is right about this on both counts. The account of embodied understanding I have given explains why we cannot have a classical correspondence theory of truth, and why we should give up on literalist and objectivist views about truth. For Rorty, that's the end of it. But I have argued to the contrary: that a theory of embodied cognition and understanding can help us see why we have the particular body-based and metaphorically defined concepts (such as cause, force, event, purpose, action) in terms of which we put forward some of our most important knowledge and truth claims. Because Rorty had no deep theory of how meaning, concepts, and reason work, he concluded that there was nothing useful left to say, once we see that the classical theory is unworkable. In sharp contrast, the "more" that we get from embodied cognitive science is substantial and far reaching. It leads us to a theory of embodied meaning, understanding, valuing, knowing, and truth based on an embodied realism as is arises through our engagement with our surroundings and our earnest attempts to find ways to be at home in our world.

CHAPTER 9

Why the Body Matters

The essays collected here jointly make a case for the key role of the body in everything we experience, think, do, and say. My argument has not been merely that a living, functioning body is necessary for mind, meaning, and thought. Rather, I have been arguing the more signifi-cant claim that the nature of our bodies, as they interact with our struc-tured environments, shapes *what* things and events are meaningful to us and *how* we make sense of and reason about them. In other words, our embodiment is *constitutive* of the structure of our concepts and our reason. Our perceiving and moving bodies are not just conduits for sen-sory input that is allegedly then processed by innate mental structures that do not derive from the nature and activities of our bodies. Instead, our bodies are what make it possible for us to have any experience, to grasp any meaning, to think about ourselves and our world, and to share our understanding with others. That is why we need to investigate our body-based meaning processes as a starting point for any further philo-sophical reflection.

Taking our embodiment seriously unsettles many of our received opinions about mind, meaning, thought, and language. I want to pro-vide a brief summary of some of the more important implications that I have been arguing for, either explicitly or implicitly, in this book.

1. *"Body" and "mind" are not two separate things.* There is overwhelming scientific evidence that nothing we call "mind" can possibly exist separate from what we call "the body." Of course, no one can prove

that disembodied mind does not exist, but we now have more than a century of good neuroscience that is beginning to show us how various patterns of neural connectivity and emotional response underlie our capacities to perceive, feel, conceptualize, draw inferences, make evaluations, and act in the world. Add to that the mushrooming volume of cognitive science research from evolutionary psychology, developmental psychology, cognitive anthropology, linguistics, and the social sciences, and you have the foundation for an impressively comprehensive and interdisciplinary account of what makes us human and how cognition works. Consequently, there is no "mind-body problem" in the traditional sense, because everything we attribute to mind (or refer to as *mental*) is the result of at least a partially functioning brain, operating within an at least partially functioning body that is engaging its worldly surroundings in an ongoing fashion. Within and from these ongoing processes emerges all experience, meaning, and thought of which we are capable. *Mind* and *body*, as well as *mental* and *physical*, are therefore just terms we use to pick out certain aspects of the integrated processes of organism-engaging-its-world.

2. *Our embodiment shapes the very nature of meaning.* The embodiment of meaning hypothesis states that meaning begins in our most primitive bodily engagements with our surroundings and eventually develops, via recruitment of sensory, motor, and affective structures and processes, to constitute our "higher" cognitive operations that involve language and other forms of symbolic interaction. Our experience of meaning thus reaches far beyond language down into image schemas, force dynamic patterns, emotions, and value systems, and all this pre- or nonlinguistic activity provides the basis for our marvelous linguistic performances. In other words, linguistic meaning rests on a vast realm of embodied meaning structures and processes that far exceed our ability to use language. Meaning of this sort is evident in the plastic arts, music, dance, theater, athletic performance, spontaneous gesture, and ritual practices. However, even though there is more to meaning than linguistic meaning, it is clear that the development of natural language profoundly deepens, enriches, and expands our ability to experience meaning and to engage in creative thought. This justified appreciation of the many benefits that language acquisition bestows on our species does not support the mistaken claim that language is the condition for any meaning (and hence for any understanding and thought). Linguistic mean-

ing may be the crown-jewel, but it is itself dependent on other embodied meaning-making processes that reach down into the visceral
depths of our embodied experience.

3. *All thought is embodied.* Our impressive—and perhaps distinctive—
capacity for abstract conceptualization and reasoning is not the result of pure, body-independent form-giving capacities. Instead,
understanding, thinking, and reasoning grow from the patterns of
our sensory, motor, and affective encounters with our surroundings.
From an evolutionary perspective, this process is known as exaptation, which is the recruitment of previously evolved structures and
functional capacities to carry out new functions, especially "higher-
order" cognitive and linguistic activities. To say that thought is embodied means, minimally, that experience and thought cannot exist
without a living body; but I have been arguing that thought is embodied in the more radical sense—that what we are able to think
about, and how we think and reason about it, are the result of how
our bodies monitor our interactions with our environments and
how we act within those environments, both via accommodation
and adaptation. In short, the very nature of thinking and reasoning
is shaped by our embodiment.

4. *Logic is embodied.* Because meaning, understanding, and thought are
embodied, so, too, is logic. By this I mean that logical patterns and
principles do not drop down on us from some Platonic heaven of
eternal forms; instead, they rise up out of our embodied experience.
Against logical purists and absolutists, I am suggesting that logic and
mathematics emerge from the corporeal and spatial logics of our
bodily experience (Lakoff and Núñez 2000). The recognition that
logic is incarnate—that it is of and from our flesh—does not demean
the lofty status of logic. On the contrary, it explains to us why logic
(along with mathematics) can ever make any sense to creatures like
us, and it reveals how logic can actually apply meaningfully to our
daily lives, since it is grounded in those very acts of living and doing
(Dewey [1938] 1991).

5. *Knowledge is embodied, fallible, and perspectival.* Like everything else
human beings do, knowing is situated, value laden, and action oriented. The constraints on what we can know and how we know it
come from the body-based processes of perception, bodily movement, and emotional response that make us who and what we are.
Knowing is thus an activity—an activity in which experience is
transformed by inquiry—and it is judged by how well it allows us

to move forward in our lives, to integrate complex situations, to act within them to enhance meaning, to free up energies for new undertakings, to solve problems, and to harmonize conflicting values and ends. *Knowing is about learning the meaning of things and realizing this meaning in our attitudes and actions. Cognition is learning carried on over the course of our lives, and so our understanding and self-identity are always subject to reconstruction as we experience new things and situations.* To mistakenly conceive of knowledge as ever being fixed or complete is to miss the ever-changing character of experience, which never ceases to call for reconsideration, critical analysis, and imaginative planning for action.

6. *Truth is embodied and plural.* The truths we state are dependent on how we understand sentences, objects, people, situations, and events. All understanding is embodied—that is, grounded in and shaped by the ways our bodies can interact with their environments—so all truth is embodied. However, there are multiple levels of embodiment, by which I mean multiple levels of complexity of organism-environment interactions, and this means that different truths may issue from these different levels of embodied understanding. That is why there is no single way to specify what is true absolutely, and for all time, of a given situation. We need to think of truth relative to our evolving understanding of newly arising situations in which we find ourselves. The metaphor of truth as fixed correspondences between propositions and mind-independent states of affairs in the world is therefore misleading. A better metaphor might be one based on neuronal staining techniques, in which a section of tissue (typically from some brain region) is stained to reveal selected internal structures (such as a very small portion of the many neuronal connections in that stained section). Such stainings capture certain structures in the sample, but they leave out many other crucial structures, and they cannot capture the temporal development and living growth of the organ from which the tissue is taken. In a similar fashion, the statements we call "true" are just abstractions that we select from the complex, temporally developing knowing practices within our ongoing experience. So, individual truths are only as good as the knowing processes they are embedded in, and we can never escape the fact that they are but value-laden selections taken from some historically situated experiential process.

7. *Philosophy is not some pure expression of absolute reason.* Alasdair Mac-Intyre recognized the historical situatedness of all knowing and phi-

losophizing when he wrote: "Moral philosophies, however they may aspire to achieve more than this, always do articulate the morality of some particular social and cultural standpoint" (1984, 268). What MacIntyre says of moral philosophy is true of any philosophical system; namely, *every* philosophy is a philosophy expressing some historically contingent worldview. Philosophies (and scientific theories, for that matter) make sense to us only when they draw on the culturally shared resources of embodied meaning, understanding, and reasoning through which we make sense of selected aspects of our world. Consequently, philosophy has no special epistemic privilege that is not shared by other forms of analysis, criticism, and creative synthesis. This humble self-understanding of its limits and fallibility does not rob philosophy of the dignity it achieves in our lives by providing frameworks through which we understand, criticize, and reconstruct our most comprehensive grasp of how our world—and everything in it—works. We are all, every one of us, philosophers; but most of us are not very good philosophers, because we have little or no critical awareness of the beliefs, values, and practices that define our lives.

8. *Philosophy and science should co-evolve through ongoing dialogue.* Patricia Churchland (1986) paved the way for an empirically responsible philosophical perspective when she emphasized the need for a "co-evolution" between philosophy and the most well-supported bodies of scientific research available today. According to this view, the sciences grow and develop hand in hand with philosophical reflection, ideally in a dialogue that promotes mutual reconsideration and reconstruction. The sciences provide experimental research on a host of topics dear to philosophers, such as the nature of mind, body, concepts, reason, emotion, feeling, values, moral psychology, physics, language, meaning, and much more. But the sciences alone are not enough. We need philosophy—first, to inform us of the assumptions and limitations of various scientific methods and practices, and, second, to help us see the larger picture, that is, to fit certain scientific perspectives into a more comprehensive philosophical framework that goes beyond the confines of any given science and shows the relevance of the scientific research for our lives.

9. *The philosophy of mind and philosophy of language need to be reconceived.* The field that came to be known in the 1950s as "philosophy of mind" has come a long way from the early days when it was ob-

sessed with knowledge and therefore tended to think that knowing was the fundamental cognitive act. This led philosophers of mind to focus primarily, or even exclusively, on "intellectual" and "cognitive" processes as definitive of the mental, thereby leaving aside the crucial role of emotions, feelings, and various types of bodily perception and movement. With the advent of the cognitive sciences and neurosciences, this narrowness of focus, with its concomitant neglect of embodiment, is slowly being replaced with cognitive science research that reveals how our bodily makeup shapes who we are, how we think, and what we do. This is a promising start, but we still have a long way to go before we have a satisfactory scientifically grounded philosophy of mind.

Unfortunately, the field known as philosophy of language—which was born in the 1930s from logical empiricist investigations into how language can be about the world—has not grown nearly as much as philosophy of mind. Philosophy of language has remained too much an armchair enterprise motivated primarily by the desire to show how knowledge is possible by showing how language can map onto the world and express truth claims. Mainstream philosophy of language cannot seem to get over its fascination with a very limited range of knowledge-related topics like propositions, definite descriptions, reference, truth, ambiguity, indexicals, and speech acts. As a result of this impoverished conception of language, philosophy of language has still not come to understand the central importance of embodiment for all meaning, thought, and language. It has still not recognized the key role of image schemas, conceptual metaphor, semantic frames, and conceptual blending. It has still not fully appreciated how meaning extends beyond language into all sorts of bodily acts and expressions of the sort mentioned above (e.g., spontaneous gesture, dance, architecture, painting, sculpture, music, and ritual). Consequently, it has still not recognized the necessity of the cognitive sciences and neurosciences as resources for an adequate account of meaning, thought, language, and communicative interaction. By contrast, the "embodied meaning" hypothesis presented in these pages combines all these key dimensions that are required for an empirically adequate theory of language, even as it acknowledges that we are not anywhere near a comprehensive theory at present.

10. *Philosophy starts with meaning.* Before philosophy can help us criti-

cize our unreflective assumptions, before it can give us an expansive vision of the world, before it can guide us toward well-being and flourishing, it first has to help us grasp the meaning of the situations in which we find ourselves. *Everything starts with how things and events can be meaningful; understanding what something means requires a deep understanding of how we humans experience and make meaning through our embodied, visceral engagement with our world.* The meaning of some thing or event is what it affords us by way of experience, either past, present, or future (as possibilities). Therefore, the deepest and most significant grasp of what anything means requires an appreciation of the many and complex webs of relations that thing is embedded in. The more you understand about the multitude of relations obtaining among parts of your world, the less likely you are to have a very partial and limited grasp of your situation. The very possibility of intelligent reflection and deliberation rests on how deeply and broadly you grasp what some object or event means. Thus, before it is anything else, and before it can help us live well, philosophy is about revealing the meaning of our situation in the fullest, deepest, most comprehensive sense. I am suggesting that the view of embodied meaning and understanding developed in these pages should be an important part of any philosophy that speaks to our human condition.

All the other important things philosophy does for us are dependent on its ability to reveal what things mean to us. Dewey thought of philosophy, rightly, as "criticism of criticisms"(Dewey 1925 [1981], 298), by which he meant that philosophy gives us a reflective and appropriately self-critical understanding of human values and processes of valuing so that we can intelligently inquire into the adequacy of our basic beliefs and values. He understood that such a critical perspective was contingent on our ability to understand the deep and extensive connections between aspects of our experience, without which we have a narrow, uncritical conception of our world.

11. *Moral understanding is an embodied imaginative process.* I have not, in this book, addressed issues concerning the nature of morality and moral cognition. However, I think it should be clear that what I have argued here should have significant implications for how we think about morality. In *Moral Imagination: Implications of Cognitive Science for Ethics* (1993) and more deeply and extensively in *Morality for Humans: Ethical Understanding from the Perspective of Cognitive Science* (2014), I

have explored some of the ways in which appreciating the embodiment of mind, meaning, thought, and value requires an overhaul of
several of our inherited notions about morality. Our moral values—
which are many and diverse—emerge from our embodied, interpersonal, and cultural experience, without needing to be grounded in
some allegedly transcendent source of norms. From the embodied
cognition perspective, it all works its way from the bottom up, starting with our animal needs and capacities and developing into the
complex social relations of humans. Another key implication is that
our moral thinking and reasoning are embodied and tied to emotions, through and through. Like most of our cognition, our moral
appraisals go on automatically and beneath our conscious awareness,
and they are fueled by our motivational systems and our emotions.
Rather than being foes of good reasoning, our emotions and feelings are crucial to good moral thinking. But moral deliberation can
go beyond nonconscious valuations, insofar as we are able to imagine how various values would play out in experience, and therefore
to work out imaginatively what various situations and acts mean for
our lives. Moral deliberation is thus a form of embodied, embedded,
enactive problem solving that requires a capacity to explore imaginatively how possible courses of action might enrich meanings, resolve tensions, and expand the scope of our understanding to enhance the flourishing of the human and more-than-human world
(M. Johnson 1993; Fesmire 2003; M Johnson 2014b).

12. *All experience is shaped by its aesthetic dimensions.* Although I have not
made this a theme of the present book, I suggest that the structures
and processes of embodied meaning-making that I have examined
here are the sorts of things that have traditionally been treated in
aesthetic theory. Aesthetics, then, pertains not just to art, beauty, and
so-called aesthetic experience and judgment, but also to all the pervasive structures and processes by which we humans experience and
make meaning, such as images, image schemas, qualities, emotions,
and feelings. Dewey ([1934] 1987) thus argued that the arts are just
exemplary acts of meaning-making that reveal possibilities for how
our world can be meaningful to us. Embodied cognition theory becomes an aesthetics of meaning and understanding, and it lies at the
very core of any philosophy that can be relevant to our lives and can
help us work through the problems we encounter in our day-to-day
existence. Richard Shusterman (2000), Thomas Alexander (2013),

and I (M. Johnson 2007) have explored the implications for human life and well-being of this central role for aesthetics in every aspect of our experience, thought, valuing, and action.

These are some of the more significant implications of the account of embodied mind, meaning, and thought developed in this volume. Taking our embodiment seriously is a fairly radical existential act. It situates us firmly in our world and emphasizes our relations with other animals who share some of our capacities and actions, and who lack others. It shows us how who and what we are arises from our ongoing engagement with our environments (material, interpersonal, and cultural). It reveals how intimately and viscerally we are in touch with our surroundings, and this contrasts profoundly with traditional skeptical arguments that we are alienated from our world and cannot bridge the gap between mind and world. Finally, it explains how many of our most marvelous acts of imagination and creativity—in morality, the arts, politics, religion, science, and philosophy—are possible for embodied creatures like us. Studying our embodiment, and all its implications for who and what we are, helps us learn how to be at home in our world.

ACKNOWLEDGMENTS

I wish to express my profound appreciation for the highly detailed, insightful, and supportive editorial work done by Johanna Rosenbohm. She was a most worthy interlocutor who helped me clarify the developing argument of this book. Her abundant patience and precision in formatting all the metaphors, image schemas, and linguistic examples was exemplary. I am also grateful to others at the Press, especially Yvonne Zipter, who saw this project through to publication. I am exceedingly thankful for the excellent work of Devin Fitzpatrick in preparing the index.

Much of the work on this book was supported by a research leave at the Oregon Humanities Center, where I was the Provost's Senior Humanist Fellow during winter 2016.

Several chapters of this book are based on articles and book chapters previously published elsewhere, by permission of the publishers of each:

Some of the introduction is taken, with extensive revisions and addition of new material, from my article "The Embodiment of Language," in *The Oxford Handbook of 4E Cognition*, ed. Albert Newen, Leon de Bruin, and Shaun Gallagher (Oxford: Oxford University Press, forthcoming).

Chapter 1 is a slightly revised version of "Cognitive Science and Dewey's Theory of Mind, Thought, and Language," in *The Cambridge Companion to Dewey*, ed. M. Cochran (Cambridge: Cambridge University Press, 2010), 123–44.

Chapter 2 is taken from "Cowboy Bill Rides Herd on the Range of Consciousness," *Journal of Speculative Philosophy* 16, no. 4 (2002): 256–63.

Chapter 3 (coauthored with Tim Rohrer) is a version of Mark Johnson and Tim Rohrer, "We Are Live Creatures: Embodiment, American Pragmatism, and the Cognitive Organism," in *Embodiment*, vol. 1 of *Body, Language, and Mind*, ed. T. Ziemke, J. Zlatev, and R. Franck (Berlin: Mouton de Gruyter, 2007), 17–54. Tim Rohrer and I would like to acknowledge the many insightful comments on this chapter by the reviewers and the editors of this volume. Tim Rohrer would like to acknowledge the stimulating intellectual environment of the Sereno and Kutas cognitive neuroscience laboratories at the University of California–San Diego as he conducted the fMRI research outlined here, as well as the generous research support of a fellowship from the National Institutes of Health.

Chapter 4 is a revision of "The Meaning of the Body," in *Developmental Perspectives on Embodiment and Consciousness*, ed. W. Overton, U. Mueller, and J. Newman (New York: Lawrence Erlbaum Associates, 2008), 19–43.

Chapter 5 is taken from "The Philosophical Significance of Image Schemas," in *From Perception to Meaning: Image Schemas in Cognitive Linguistics*, ed. Beate Hampe (Berlin: Mouton de Gruyter, 2005), 15–33.

Chapter 6 is a slightly revised version of "Action, Embodied Meaning, and Thought," in *Action, Perception, and the Brain*, ed. J. Schulkin (New York: Palgrave Macmillan, 2012), 92–116.

Chapter 7 is a substantially revised version of "Knowing through the Body," *Philosophical Psychology* 4, no. 1 (1991): 3–18. A shortened version of chapter 7 was first presented at the Special Symposium in Cognitive Science, Knowing through the Body, Southern Society for Philosophy and Psychology, New Orleans, March 24, 1989. I am grateful to Lynn Stephens for his comments on this paper and to Ulric Neisser for his extended discussion of issues raised in the symposium concerning common themes in our presentations. I am indebted to Steven Winter not only for his criticisms, suggestions for development, and extensive editorial work on this essay, but especially for his ongoing discussion of the issues taken up here.

The analysis in chapter 8 of causation is a very partial selection, with some revisions, from the much longer and more detailed treatment of the many metaphors for events and causes that is presented in chapter 11 of George Lakoff and Mark Johnson, *Philosophy in the Flesh: The Embodied Mind and Its Challenge to Western Thought* (New York: Basic Books, 1999).

NOTES

Introduction

1. It was not until the last quarter of the century that books like Patricia Church-land's *Neurophilosophy: Toward a Unified Theory of the Mind-Brain* (1986) and George Lakoff's *Women, Fire, and Dangerous Things: What Categories Reveal about the Mind* (1987) revealed some of the possibilities for a productive co-evolution of philosophy and that cognitive science became evident.

2. I am not accusing Rorty of holding the ridiculous claim that our bodies are lin-guistic entities. Of course, he regarded bodies as material objects living and moving in space. What he objected to was the privileging of any one vocabulary of the body, as if it captured the essence of embodiment.

3. My first encounter with Dewey was actually a graduate course in phenome-nology and science taught by David Kolb at the University of Chicago. Kolb lit the spark of interest in me for Dewey, but at the time, I could not yet see the radical im-plications of Dewey's perspective that subsequently came into focus under Tom Alex-ander's tutelage.

4. Over the years, various Husserlians have politely informed me that many (or all!) of the insights I have described in my work on embodied cognition are anticipated in Husserl. My knowledge of Husserl is not sufficient to verify those claims, but I wel-come any Husserlians into the Church of the Embodied Mind, if only they are pre-pared to renounce any allegiance to a transcendent ego.

Chapter One

1. The following description of a possible neural basis for the experience of a per-vasive quality is taken, with minor revisions, from my book *The Meaning of the Body: Aesthetics of Human Understanding* (M. Johnson 2007), chap. 4.

Chapter Two

1. By "mental images" Damasio does not mean internal visual pictures. Rather, he uses this term for any of a wide variety of so-called representations or patterns of interaction that come to a person both through sensory perception or from changes in our internal states.

2. Damasio (1994, 1999) presents examples of patients who have suffered brain lesions and who experience their own present moment, but who have no coherent sense of themselves extending over time, since they have no extended memory.

Chapter Four

1. The following account of image schema composition is taken directly, in an abbreviated form, from Lakoff and Núñez 2000, 39.

2. See Lakoff and Núñez 2000, 44, for a complete mapping that shows how the abstract inference patterns are based on the spatial logic of containers.

3. This list is a selection from a longer list found in Lakoff and Johnson 1999, 50–54, which, in turn, is a slightly revised analysis of a subset of the primary metaphors listed in Grady 1997.

Chapter Five

1. Although the term itself was new, the basic idea had been partially anticipated, at least in the works of Immanuel Kant, William James, John Dewey, and Maurice Merleau-Ponty.

2. A Gibsonian "affordance" is a pattern of potential engagement and interaction with parts of our environment. A chair "affords" sit-on-ability for human beings, but not for elephants. A cup affords grasp-ability for a human being, but not for a sea slug. An affordance is thus relative to the makeup of the organism, and yet it is an objective feature of the environment *for that organism with its particular embodiment and perceptual and motor capacities*.

3. Husserl (1970) proposed a method of "suspending" one's practical engagement with everyday experience in order to supposedly allow the fundamental structures of experience to reveal themselves. I do not think such a process is even possible, let alone desirable or useful.

4. I am not claiming that an image schema analysis is sufficient to tell the whole story of human reasoning. A complete account would include the role of emotions, qualities, social interaction, speech-act conditions, and patterns of inquiry. However, the structural aspects of concepts and inferences would appear to be primarily a matter of image schema logic.

Chapter Six

1. The "::" notation indicates the content of a phase.

Chapter Seven

1. Representative examples of the cognitivist and experientialist approach to meaning are elaborated in Lakoff 1987; Sweetser 1990; Lakoff and Johnson 1999; Kovecses 2010; and Dancygier and Sweetser 2014.

2. Both Patricia Churchland (1986) and Paul Churchland (1979) have pointed out that sentential knowledge cannot be the whole picture, in light of the fact that both prelinguistic children and our prelinguistic ancestors must clearly be regarded as possessing knowledge of their world, and there is no way to show that their mode of knowing is fundamentally different in kind from that of a contemporary adult. Paul Churchland concludes that "linguistic activity, whether overt or covert, is just one of a great many tricks our basic machinery learns to perform" (135) and that "the idea that the fundamental parameters of cognitive development and intellectual virtue should find themselves displayed in the structure of human language is as parochial as it is optimistic" (137).

3. For an excellent accounts of much of this work, see Lakoff 1987; Hampe 2005; Gibbs 2006; and Feldman 2006.

4. This analysis is based on one worked out with George Lakoff, which appears both in Lakoff 1987 and M. Johnson 1987 (5).

5. For treatments of the metaphorical structuring of our conceptions of time, see Gould 1986; Lakoff and Johnson 1999; Casasanto and Boroditsky 2008; Boroditsky 2011; and Dancygier and Sweetser 2014.

6. I have dealt with most of these schemas in chapters 1 through 5 of *The Body in the Mind: The Bodily Basis of Meaning, Imagination, and Reason* (M. Johnson 1987), and there is now a substantial literature covering the operations of a broad range of image schemas (see especially Hampe 2005).

7. Although I believe that all logical forms and patterns are indeed imaginative structures rather than pure abstract forms, I have suggested elsewhere only a sketch of such an analysis for a few basic logical forms and relations. See the last sections of chapters 2, 3, and 4 in M. Johnson 1987; see also also Lakoff 1987; Lakoff and Núñez 2000.

8. I have cited relevant evidence for this view of semantic change in M. Johnson 1987. The case for this view of metaphor and semantic change is made most extensively in Sweetser 1990.

9. Still, we will be able to preserve a workable notion of truth-as-correspondence, so long as we remember that there is no simple univocal concept of correspondence. "Correspondence" will turn out to be a complex radial (see Lakoff 1987) category that will include certain prototypical cases that fit our crude sense of statements corresponding to states of affairs. However, such cases are those that are so commonplace, and those where the context is so stable and recurring that we can safely disregard its role in what we focus on as relevant significant structure, both in our experience of a situation and our understanding of a descriptive sentence.

Alexander, Thomas. 2013. *The Human Eros: Eco-Ontology and the Aesthetics of Existence.* New York: Fordham University Press.

Anderson, M. 2003. "Embodied Cognition: A Field Guide." *Artificial Intelligence* 149: 91–130.

Bailey, D. 1997. "A Computational Model of Embodiment in the Acquisition of Action Verbs." PhD diss., Computer Science Division, EECS Department, University of California, Berkeley.

Barsalou, L. 1999. "Perceptual Symbol Systems." *Behavioral and Brain Sciences* 22:577–660.

———. 2003. "Situated Simulation in the Human Conceptual System." *Language and Cognitive Processes* 18 (5–6): 513–62.

Bechtel, W. 2008. *Mental Mechanisms: Philosophical Perspectives on Cognitive Neuroscience.* New York: Psychology Press.

Bergen, B. 2012. *Louder Than Words: The New Science of How the Mind Makes Meaning.* New York: Basic Books.

Bergmann, G. 1967. "Logical Positivism, Language, and Metaphysics." In *The Linguistic Turn: Recent Essays in Philosophical Method*, edited by Richard Rorty, 63–71. Chicago: University of Chicago Press.

Bjerre, C. 2005. "Mental Capacity as Metaphor." *International Journal for the Semiotics of Law* 18:101–40.

Boroditsky, L. 2011. "How Languages Construct Time." In *Space, Time, and Number in the Brain: Searching for the Foundations of Mathematical Thought*, edited by S. Dehaene and E. Brannon, 333–41. London: Elsevier.

Boroditsky, L., and Ramscar, M. 2002. "The Roles of Body and Mind in Abstract Thought." *Psychological Science* 13 (2): 185–89.

Brandom, R. 2011. *Perspectives on Pragmatism: Classical, Recent, and Contemporary.* Cambridge, MA: Harvard University Press.

Brefczynski, J. A., and E. A. DeYoe. 1999. "A Physiological Correlate of the 'Spotlight' of Visual Attention." *Nature Neuroscience* 2:370–74.

Brooks, R. A. 1991. "Intelligence without Representation." *Artificial Intelligence Journal* 47:139–59.

Brooks, R. A., and A. M. Flynn. 1989. "Fast, Cheap and Out of Control: A Robot Invasion of the Solar System." *Journal of the British Interplanetary Society* 42:478–85.

Brooks, R. A., and L. A. Stein. 1994. "Building Brains for Bodies." *Autonomous Robots* 1 (1): 7–25.

Brugman, C. 1983. "The Use of Body-Part Terms as Locatives in Chalcatongo Mixtec." In *Studies in Mesoamerican Linguistics*, edited by Alice Schlichter, Wallace L. Chafe, and Leanne Hinton, 235–90. Survey of California and Other Indian Languages, no. 4. [Berkeley]: [Department of Linguistics, University of California].

Buccino, G., F. Binkofski, G. R. Fink, L. Fadiga, L. Fogassi, V. Gallese, R. J. Seitz, K. Zilles, G. Rizzolatti, and H. J. Freund. 2001. "Action Observation Activates Premotor and Parietal Areas in a Somatotopic Manner: An fMRI Study." *European Journal of Neuroscience* (2): 400–404.

Buonomano, D. V., and M. M. Merzenich. 1998. "Cortical and Plasticity: From Synapses to Maps." *Annual Review of Neuroscience* 21:149–86.

Carpenter, P., and P. Eisenberg. 1978. "Mental Rotation and the Frame of Reference in Blind and Sighted Individuals." *Perception and Psychophysics* 23:117–24.

Casasanto, D. and Boroditsky, L. 2008. "Time in the Mind: Using Space to Think about Time." *Cognition* 106:579–93.

Chomsky, N. 1965. *Aspects of a Theory of Syntax*. Cambridge, MA: MIT Press.

Churchland, Patricia. 1986. *Neurophilosophy: Toward a Unified Science of the Mind-Brain*. Cambridge, MA: MIT Press.

———. 2002. *Brain-Wise: Studies in Neurophilosophy*. Cambridge, MA: MIT Press.

Churchland, Paul. 1979. *Scientific Realism and the Plasticity of Mind*. Cambridge: Cambridge University Press.

Cienki, A. 1997. "Some Properties and Groupings of Image Schemas." In *Lexical and Syntactical Constructions and the Construction of Meaning*, edited by M. Verspoor, K. D. Lee, and E. Sweetser, 3–15. Amsterdam: John Benjamins.

———. 1998. "Metaphoric Gestures and Some of Their Relations to Verbal Metaphoric Expressions." In *Discourse and Cognition: Bridging the Gap*, edited by J. P. Koenig, 189–204. Stanford, CA: CSLI Publications.

Clark, A. 1998. *Being There: Putting Brain, Body and World Together Again*. Cambridge, MA: MIT Press.

Corbetta, M., J. M. Kincade, J. M. Ollinger, M. P. McAvoy, and G. L. Shulman. 2000. "Voluntary Attention Is Dissociated from Target Detection in the Human Posterior Parietal Cortex." *Nature Neuroscience* 3:292–97.

Coslett, H. B., E. M. Saffran, and J. Schwoebel. 2002. "Knowledge of the Human Body: A Distinct Semantic Domain." *Neurology* 59:357–63.

Craig, D., N. Nersessian, and R. Catrambone. 2002. "Perceptual Simulation in Analogical Problem Solving." In *Model-Based Reasoning: Science, Technology, Values*, edited by Lorenzo Magnani and Nancy Nersessian, 167–90. New York: Kluwer.

Damasio, A. 1994. *Descartes' Error: Emotion, Reason, and the Human Brain.* New York: G. P. Putnam's Sons.

———. 1999. *The Feeling of What Happens: Body and Emotion in the Making of Consciousness.* New York: Harcourt, Brace.

———. 2003. *Looking for Spinoza: Joy, Sorrow, and the Feeling Brain.* New York: Basic Books.

———. 2010. *Self Comes to Mind: Constructing the Conscious Brain.* New York: Pantheon Books.

Dancygier, B., and E. Sweetser. 2014. *Figurative Language.* Cambridge: Cambridge University Press.

Davidson, D. 1978. "What Metaphors Mean," *Critical Inquiry* 5:31–47.

DeBello, W. M., D. E. Feldman, and E. I. Knudsen. 2001. "Adaptive Axonal Remodeling in the Midbrain Auditory Space Map." *Journal of Theoretical Biology* 105:259–71.

Deneubourg, J., J. Pasteels, and J. Verhaeghe. 1983. "Probabilistic Behavior in Ants: A Strategy of Errors." *Journal of Theoretical Biology* 105:259–71.

Dewey, J. 1896. "The Reflex Arc Concept in Psychology." *Psychological Review* 3:357–70.

———. (1905) 1998. "The Postulate of Immediate Empiricism." In *The Essential Dewey*, edited by L. Hickman and T. Alexander, 1:115–20. Bloomington: Indiana University Press.

———. (1908) 1973. "The Practical Character of Reality." In *The Philosophy of John Dewey*, edited by J. McDermott, 207–22. Chicago: University of Chicago Press.

———. (1922) 1988. *Human Nature and Conduct.* Vol. 14 of *The Middle Works, 1899–1924.* Edited by Jo Ann Boydston. Carbondale: Southern Illinois University Press.

———. (1925) 1981. *Experience and Nature.* Vol. 1 of *The Later Works, 1925-1953.* Edited by Jo Ann Boydston. Carbondale: Southern Illinois University Press.

———. (1929) 1984. *The Quest for Certainty.* Vol. 4 of *The Later Works, 1925-1953.* Edited by Jo Ann Boydston. Carbondale: Southern Illinois University Press.

———. (1930) 1988. "Qualitative Thought." In *The Later Works: 1925-1953*, edited by Jo Ann Boydston, 5:243–62. Carbondale: Southern Illinois University Press.

———. (1934) 1987. *Art as Experience.* Vol. 10 of *The Later Works, 1925-1953.* Edited by Jo Ann Boydston. Carbondale: Southern Illinois University Press.

———. (1938) 1991. *Logic: The Theory of Inquiry.* Vol. 12 of *The Later Works, 1925-1953.* Edited by Jo Ann Boydston. Carbondale: Southern Illinois University Press.

Di Pellegrino, G., L. Fadiga, L. Fogassi, V. Gallese, and G. Rizzolatti. 1992. "Understanding Motor Events." *Experimental Brain Research* 91:176–80.

Dodge, E., and G. Lakoff. 2005. "Image Schemas: From Linguistic Analysis to Neural Grounding." In *From Perception to Meaning: Image Schemas and Cognitive Linguistics*, edited by Beate Hampe, 57–91. Berlin: Mouton de Gruyter.

Edelman, G. 1987. *Neural Darwinism.* New York: Basic Books.

———. 1992. *Bright Air, Brilliant Fire: On the Matter of Mind.* New York: Basic Books.

Edelman, G., and Tononi, G. 2000. *A Universe of Consciousness: How Matter Becomes Imagination.* New York: Basic Books.

Ellis, R. 1995. *Questioning Consciousness: The Interplay of Imagery, Cognition, and Emotion in the Human Brain.* Amsterdam: John Benjamins.

Fauconnier, G. 1985. *Mental Spaces: Aspects of Meaning Construction in Natural Language.* Cambridge, MA: MIT Press.

Fauconnier, G., and M. Turner. 2002. *The Way We Think: Conceptual Blending and the Mind's Hidden Complexities.* New York: Basic Books.

Feldman, J. 2006. *From Molecule to Metaphor: A Neural Theory of Language.* Cambridge, MA: MIT Press.

Feldman, J., and S. Narayanan. 2004. "Embodied Meaning in a Neural Theory of Language." *Brain and Language* 89 (2): 385–92.

Fernandez-Duque, D., and M. Johnson. 1999. "Attention Metaphors: How Metaphors Guide the Cognitive Psychology of Attention." *Cognitive Science* 23 (1): 83–116.

———. 2002. "Cause and Effect Theories of Attention: The Role of Conceptual Metaphor." *Review of General Psychology* 6 (2): 153–65.

Fesmire, S. 2003. *John Dewey and Moral Imagination: Pragmatism in Ethics.* Bloomington: Indiana University Press.

Fillmore, C. 1982. "Frame Semantics." In *Linguistics in the Morning Calm*, edited by the Linguistic Society of Korea, 111–37. Seoul: Hanshin Publishing.

Fodor, J. 1975. *The Language of Thought.* New York: Thomas Y. Crowell.

———. 1987. *Psychosemantics: The Problem of Meaning in the Philosophy of Mind.* Cambridge, MA: MIT Press.

———. 2000. *The Mind Doesn't Work That Way: The Scope and Limits of Computational Psychology.* Cambridge, MA: MIT Press.

Fogassi, L., V. Gallese, G. Buccino, L. Craighero, L. Fadiga and G. Rizzolatti. 2001. "Cortical Mechanism for the Visual Guidance of Hand Grasping Movements in the Monkey: A Reversible Inactivation Study. *Brain* 124 (3): 571–86.

Forceville, C. 1996. *Pictorial Metaphor in Advertising.* London: Routledge.

Forceville, C., and E. Urios-Aparisi, eds. 2009. *Multimodal Metaphor.* Berlin: Mouton de Gruyter.

Fouts, R. S., M. L. A. Jensvold, and D. H. Fouts. 2002. "Chimpanzee Signing: Darwinian Realities and Cartesian Delusions." In *The Cognitive Animal: Empirical and Theoretical Perspective in Animal Cognition*, edited by Marc Bekoff, Colin Allen, and Gordon M. Burghardt, 285–91. Cambridge, MA: MIT Press.

Fraser, S. E. 1985. "Cell Interaction Involved in Neural Patterning: An Experimental and Theoretical Approach." In *Molecular Bases of Neural Development*, edited by G. Edelman, W. E. Gall, and W. M. Cowan, 581–607. New York: Wiley.

Frege, G. (1892) 1966. "On Sense and Reference." In *Translations from the Philosophical Writings of Gottlob Frege*, edited by P. Geach and M. Black, 56–78. Oxford: Basil Blackwell.

Freyd, J., and R. Finke. 1984. "Representational Momentum." *Journal of Experimental Psychology: Learning, Memory, and Cognition* 10:126–32.

Gallese, V. 2003. "A Neuroscientific Grasp of Concepts: From Control to Representation." *Philosophical Transactions of the Royal Society of London* 358:1231–40.

———. 2007. "Before and Below Theory of Mind: Embodied Simulation and the Neural Correlates of Social Cognition. *Philosophical Transactions of the Royal Society B* 358 (1480): 659–69.

————. 2008. "Mirror Neurons and the Social Nature of Language: The Neural Exploitation Hypothesis." *Social Neuroscience* 3:317–33.

Gallese, V., and V. Cuccio. 2015. "The Paradigmatic Body: Embodied Simulation, Intersubjectivity, the Bodily Self, and Language." In *Open Mind*, edited by T. Metzinger and J. M. Windt, 1–23. Frankfurt: MIND Group.

Gallese, V., and A. Goldman. 1998. "Mirror Neurons and the Simulation Theory of Mind-Reading." *Trends in Cognitive Science* 12:493–501.

Gallese, V., and G. Lakoff. 2005. "The Brain's Concepts: The Role of the Sensory-Motor System in Conceptual Knowledge." *Cognitive Neuropsychology* 22:455–79.

Gaze, R. M., and S. C. Sharma. 1970. "Axial Differences in the Reenervation of the Goldfish Optic Tectum by Regenerating Optic Nerve Fibers." *Experimental Brain Research* 10:171–81.

Gendlin, E. 1997. "How Philosophy Cannot Appeal to Experience, and How It Can." In *Language beyond Postmodernism: Saying and Thinking in Gendlin's Philosophy*, edited by David M. Levin, 3–41. Evanston, IL: Northwestern University Press.

Gibbs, R. 1994. *The Poetics of Mind: Figurative Thought, Language, and Understanding*. Cambridge: Cambridge University Press.

————. 2003. "Embodied Experience and Linguistic Meaning." *Brain and Language* 84 (1): 1–15.

————. 2006. *Embodiment and Cognitive Science*. Cambridge: Cambridge University Press.

————. 2008. *The Cambridge Handbook of Metaphor and Thought*. Cambridge: Cambridge University Press.

Gibbs, R., and E. Berg. 2002. "Mental Imagery and Embodied Activity." *Journal of Mental Imagery* 26:1–30.

Gibbs, R. W., Jr., and H. Colston. 1995. "The Psychological Reality of Image Schemas and Their Transformations." *Cognitive Linguistics* 6 (4): 347–78.

Gibbs, R., P. Lima, and E. Francuzo. 2004. "Metaphor in Thought and Language Is Grounded in Embodied Experience." *Journal of Pragmatics* 36:1189–210.

Gibson, J. J. 1979. *The Ecological Approach to Visual Perception*. Boston: Houghton-Mifflin.

Glenberg, A. M., and V. Gallese. 2012. "Action-Based Language: A Theory of Language Acquisition, Comprehension, and Production." *Cortex* 48 (7): 905–22.

Goldberg, A. 2003. "Constructions: A New Theoretical Approach to Language." *Trends in Cognitive Science* 7 (5): 219–24.

Goldman, A., and F. de Vignemont. 2009. "Is Social Cognition Embodied?" *Trends in Cognitive Science* 13 (4): 154–59.

Gould, S. J. 1986. *Time's Arrow, Time's Cycle*. Cambridge, MA: Harvard University Press.

Grady, J. 1997. "Foundations of Meaning: Primary Metaphors and Primary Scenes." PhD diss., Department of Linguistics, University of California, Berkeley.

Guo, Y., and S. B. Udin. 2000. "The Development of Abnormal Axon Trajectories after Rotation of One Eye in Xenopus." *Journal of Neuroscience* 20 (11): 4189–97.

Hampe, B., ed., with cooperation from Joseph E. Grady. 2005. *From Perception to Meaning: Image Schemas in Cognitive Linguistics*. Berlin: Mouton de Gruyter.

Hauk, O., I. Johnsrude, and F. Pulvermuller. 2004. "Somatotopic Representation of Action Words in Human Motor and Premotor Cortex." *Neuron* 41 (2): 301–7.

Hodges, A. 1983. *Alan Turing: The Enigma*. New York: Walker.

Hopfinger, J. B., M. H. Buonocore, and G. R. Mangun. 2000. "The Neural Mechanisms of Top-Down Attentional Control." *Nature Neuroscience* 3:284–91.

Horst, S. 2016. *Cognitive Pluralism*. Cambridge, MA: MIT Press.

Husserl, E. 1970. *The Crisis of European Sciences and Transcendental Phenomenology*. Translated by David Carr. Evanston, IL: Northwestern University Press.

Hutchins, E. 1995. *Cognition in the Wild*. Cambridge, MA: MIT Press.

Ichikawa, Jonathan Jenkins, and Matthias Steup. 2012. "The Analysis of Knowledge." *Stanford Encyclopedia of Philosophy* (Spring 2014). Article substantively revised November 15. http://plato.stanford.edu/archives/spr2014/entries/knowledge-analysis/.

Jackson, F. 1986. "What Mary Didn't Know." *Journal of Philosophy* 83:291–95.

James, W. (1890) 1950. *The Principles of Psychology*. 2 vols. New York: Dover.

———. 1900. *Psychology*. American Science Series, Briefer Course. New York: Henry Holt.

———. 1904. "A World of Pure Experience." Reprinted in *The Writings of William James: A Comprehensive Edition*, edited by J. McDermott, 194–214. Chicago: University of Chicago Press.

———. (1909) 1975. *The Meaning of Truth*. In *Pragmatism and the Meaning of Truth*, 167–352. Cambridge, MA: Harvard University Press.

———. 1911. "Percept and Concept." In *Some Problems of Philosophy*, 21–60. Cambridge, MA: Harvard University Press.

Johnson, C. 1997. "Metaphor vs. Conflation in the Acquisition of Polysemy: The Case of SEE." In *Cultural, Typological and Psychological Issues in Cognitive Linguistics*, edited by M. K. Hiraga, C. Sinha, and S. Wilcox, 155–70. Current Issues in Linguistic Theory 152. Amsterdam: John Benjamins.

Johnson, M. 1987. *The Body in the Mind: The Bodily Basis of Meaning, Imagination, and Reason*. Chicago: University of Chicago Press.

———1988. "Good Rorty/Bad Rorty: Toward a Richer Conception of Philosophical Inquiry." Unpublished manuscript.

———1993. *Moral Imagination: Implications of Cognitive Science for Ethics*. Chicago: University of Chicago Press.

———2007. *The Meaning of the Body: Aesthetics of Human Understanding*. Chicago: University of Chicago Press.

———2008. "Philosophy's Debt to Metaphor." In *The Cambridge Handbook of Metaphor and Thought*, edited by Raymond Gibbs, 39–52. Cambridge: Cambridge University Press.

———2014a. "Experiencing Language: What's Missing in Lingusitic Pragmatism?" *European Journal of Pragmatism and American Philosophy* 2:14–27.

———2014b. *Morality for Humans: Ethical Understanding from the Perspective of Cognitive Science*. Chicago: University of Chicago Press.

Johnson, M., and G. Lakoff. 2002. "Why Cognitive Linguistics Requires Embodied Realism" *Cognitive Linguistics* 13 (3): 245–63.

Kant, I. (1781) 1968. *Critique of Pure Reason*. Translated by Norman Kemp Smith. Reprint, New York: St. Martin's Press. Original edition, *Critik der reinen Vernunft*. Riga: Hartknoch, 1781.

Kawamura, S. 1959. "The Process of Subculture Propagation among Japanese Macaques." *Primates* 2:43–60.

Kelly, M, and J. Freyd. 1987. "Explorations of Representational Momentum." *Cognitive Psychology* 19:369–401.

Knudsen, E. I. 1998. "Capacity for Plasticity in the Adult Owl Auditory System Expanded by Juvenile Experience." *Science* 279 (5356): 1531–33.

———. 2002. "Instructed Learning in the Auditory Localization Pathway of the Barn Owl." *Nature* 417 (6886): 322–28.

Kovecses, Z. 2000. *Metaphor and Emotion: Language, Culture, and Body in Human Feeling*. Cambridge: Cambridge University Press.

———. 2010. *Metaphor: A Practical Introduction*. Oxford: Oxford University Press.

Lakoff, G. 1987. *Women, Fire, and Dangerous Things: What Categories Reveal about the Mind*. Chicago: University of Chicago Press.

———. 1996. *Moral Politics: What Conservatives Know That Liberals Don't*. Chicago: University of Chicago Press.

———. 2006. *Whose Freedom? The Battle over America's Most Important Idea*. New York: Farrar, Straus and Giroux.

———. 2008. "The Neural Theory of Metaphor." In *The Cambridge Handbook of Metaphor and Thought*, edited by Raymond Gibbs, 17–38. Cambridge: Cambridge University Press.

Lakoff, G., and M. Johnson. 1980. *Metaphors We Live By*. Chicago: University of Chicago Press.

———. 1999. *Philosophy in the Flesh: The Embodied Mind and Its Challenge to Western Thought*. New York: Basic Books.

———. 2008. *The Political Mind: Why You Can't Understand 21st-Century American Politics with an 18th-Century Brain*. New York: Viking.

Lakoff, G., and S. Narayanan. 2017. "The Neural Mind: What You Need to Know about Thought and Language." Unpublished manuscript, last modified 2017. PDF.

Lakoff, G., and R. Núñez. 2000. *Where Mathematics Comes From: How the Embodied Mind Brings Mathematics into Being*. New York: Basic Books.

Lakoff, G., and M. Turner. 1989. *More Than Cool Reason: A Field Guide to Poetic Metaphor*. Chicago: University of Chicago Press.

Langacker, R. 1987–91. *Foundations of Cognitive Grammar*. 2 vols. Stanford: Stanford University Press.

Lewkowicz, D. J., and G. Turkewitz. 1981. "Intersensory Interaction in Newborns: Modification of Visual Preferences Following Exposure to Sound." *Child Development* 52 (3): 827–32.

Luu, P., and D. Tucker. 2003. "Self-Regulation by the Medial Frontal Cortex: Limbic Representation of Motive Set-Points." In *Consciousness, Emotional Self-Regulation and the Brain*, edited by M. Beauregard, 123–61. Amsterdam: John Benjamins.

MacIntyre, A. 1984. *After Virtue*. Notre Dame, IN: University of Notre Dame Press.

Magnani, L., and N. Nersessian, eds. 2002. *Model-Based Reasoning: Science, Technology, Values*. New York: Kluwer Academic/Plenum.

Marmor, G., and L. Zaback. 1976. "Mental Rotation by the Blind: Does Mental Rotation Depend on Visual Imagery?" *Journal of Experimental Psychology: Human Perception and Performance* 2:515–21.

Maturana, H. R., and F. J. Varela. 1998. *The Tree of Knowledge: The Biological Roots of Human Understanding.* Rev. ed. Boston: Shambhala Press. First published as *Arbol del concimiento*, translated by Robert Paolucci, 1987.

McConachie, B. 2015. *Evolution, Cognition, and Performance.* Cambridge: Cambridge University Press.

McGrew, W. C. 1998. "Culture in Nonhuman Primates?" *Annual Review of Anthropology* 27:301–28.

McNeill, D. 1992. *Hand and Mind: What Gestures Reveal about Thought.* Chicago: University of Chicago Press.

———. 2005. *Gesture and Thought.* Chicago: University of Chicago Press.

Meltzoff, A. N., and R. W. Borton. 1979. "Intermodal Matching by Human Neonates." *Nature* 282 (5737): 403–4.

Merleau-Ponty, Maurice. 1962. *Phenomenology of Perception.* Translated by Colin Smith. London: Routledge.

Merzenich, M. M., R. J. Nelson, J. H. Kaas, M. P. Stryker, W. M. Jenkins, J. M. Zook, M. S. Cynader, and A. Schoppmann. 1987. "Variability in Hand Surface Representations in Areas 3b and 1 in Adult Owl and Squirrel Monkeys." *Journal Comparative Neurology* 258 (2): 281–96.

Müller, M. M., W. Teder-Sälejärvi, and S. A. Hillyard. 1998. "The Time Course of Cortical Facilitation during Cued Shifts of Spatial Attention." *Nature Neuroscience* 1:631–34.

Narayanan, S. 1997. "KARMA: Knowledge-based Active Representations for Metaphor and Aspect." PhD diss., Department of Computer Science, University of California, Berkeley.

———. 1997. "Embodiment in Language Understanding: Sensory-Motor Representations for Metaphoric Reasoning about Event Descriptions." PhD diss., Department of Computer Science, University of California, Berkeley.

Newell, A., and H. Simon. 1976. "Computer Science as Empirical Inquiry: Symbols and Search." *Communications of the ACM* 19:113–26.

Noë, A. 2009. *Out of Our Heads: Why You Are Not Your Brain, and Other Lessons from the Biology of Consciousness.* New York: Hill and Wang.

Ogden, C. K., and I. A. Richards. 1923. *The Meaning of Meaning: A Study of the Influence of Language upon Thought and of the Science of Symbolism.* New York: Harcourt, Brace, & World.

Putnam, H. 1981. "Brains in a Vat." In *Reason, Truth, and History*, 1–21. Cambridge: Cambridge University Press.

Quine, W. V. O. 1960. *Word and Object.* Cambridge, MA: MIT Press.

Ramachandran, V., and W. Hirstein. 1997. "Three Laws of Qualia: What Neurology Tells Us about the Biological Functions of Consciousness." *Journal of Consciousness Studies* 4:429–57.

Regier, T. 1996. *The Human Semantic Potential: Spatial Language and Constrained Connectionism.* Cambridge, MA: MIT Press.

Rizzolatti, G., and L. Craighero. 2004. "The Mirror-Neuron System." *Annual Review of Neuroscience* 27:169–92.

Rizzolatti, G., and L. Fadiga. 1998. "Grasping Objects and Grasping Action Meanings: The Dual Role of Monkey Rostroventral Premotor Cortex (Area F5)." *Novartis Foundation symposium* 218:81–103.

Rizzolatti, G., L. Fogassi, and V. Gallese. 2002. "Motor and Cognitive Functions of the Ventral Premotor Cortex." *Current Opinion in Neurobiology* 12 (2): 149–54.

Rohrer, T. 2001a. "Pragmatism Ideology and Embodiment: William James and the Philosophical Foundations of Cognitive Linguistics." In *Cognitive Theoretic Approaches*, edited by R. Dirven, B. Hawkins, and E. Sandikcioglu, 49–81, vol. 1 of *Language and Ideology*. Amsterdam: John Benjamins.

———. 2001b. "Understanding through the Body: fMRI and of ERP Studies of Metaphoric and Literal Language." Paper presented at the Seventh International Cognitive Linguistics Association Conference, July 2001.

———. 2005. "Image Schemata in the Brain." In *From Perception to Meaning: Image Schemas in Cognitive Linguistics*, edited by Beate Hampe, 165–96. Berlin: Mouton de Gruyter.

———. 2007. "The Body in Space: Dimensions of Embodiment." In *Embodiment*, vol. 1 of *Body, Language, and Mind*, edited by T. Ziemke, J. Zlatev, and R. Franck, 339–77. Berlin: Mouton de Gruyter.

———. Forthcoming. "Embodiment and Experientalism." In *Handbook of Cognitive Linguistics*, edited by Dirk Geeraerts and Hubert Cuyckens. New York: Oxford University Press.

Rorty, R., ed. 1967. *The Linguistic Turn: Recent Essays in Philosophical Method*. Chicago: University of Chicago Press.

———. 1979. *Philosophy and the Mirror of Nature*. Princeton, NJ, Princeton University Press.

———. 1982. *Consequences of Pragmatism*. Minneapolis: University of Minnesota Press.

———. 1989. *Contingency, Irony, and Solidarity*. Cambridge: Cambridge University Press.

Rosch, E. 1975. "Cognitive Representations of Semantic Categories." *Journal of Experimental Psychology: General* 104:192–233.

Sanders, J. 2016. *Theology in the Flesh: How Embodiment and Culture Shape the Way We Think about Truth, Morality, and God*. Minneapolis: Fortress Press.

Savage-Rumbaugh, S., R. A. Sevcik, and W. D. Hopkins. 1988. "Symbolic Cross-Modal Transfer in Two Species of Chimpanzees." *Child Development* 59 (3): 617–25.

Schank, R., and R. Abelson. 1977. *Scripts, Plans, Goals, and Understanding: An Inquiry into Human Knowledge Structures*. Hillsdale, NJ: Erlbaum.

Schulkin, J. 2011. *Adaptation and Well-Being: Social Allostasis*. Cambridge: Cambridge University Press.

Searle, J. 1979. *Expression and Meaning: Studies in the Theory of Speech Acts*. Cambridge: Cambridge University Press.

Shepard, R., and L. Cooper. 1982. *Mental Images and Their Transformations*. Cambridge, MA: MIT Press.

Shelton, J. R., E. Fouch, and A. Caramazza. 1998. "The Selective Sparing of Body Part Knowledge: A Case Study." *Neurocase* 4:339–51.

Shusterman, R. 2000. *Pragmatist Aesthetics: Living Beauty, Rethinking Art.* Lantham, MD: Rowman & Littlefield.

Sperber, D. 2000. "Metarepresentations in an Evolutionary Perspective." In *Metarepresentations: A Multidisciplinary Perspective*, edited by D. Sperber, 117–38. Vancouver Studies in Cognitive Science, vol. 10. Oxford: Oxford University Press.

Sperry, R. W. 1943. "Effect of a 180-Degree Rotation of the Retinal Field on Visuomotor Coordination." *Journal of Experimental Zoology* 92:263–79.

Spitzer, M. 2004. *Metaphor and Musical Thought.* Chicago: University of Chicago Press.

Stawarska, B. 2009. *Between You and I: Dialogical Phenomenology.* Athens: Ohio University Press.

Steen, G. 1992. "Metaphor in Literary Reception." PhD diss., Vrije Universiteit Amsterdam.

Stern, D. 1985. *The Interpersonal World of the Infant.* New York: Basic Books.

Suzuki, K., A. Yamadori, and T. Fuji. 1997. "Category-Specific Comprehension Deficit Restricted to Body Parts." *Neurocase* 3:193–200.

Sweetser, E. 1990. *From Etymology to Pragmatics: The Mind-as-Body Metaphor in Semantic Structure and Semantic Change.* Cambridge, Cambridge University Press.

Talmy, L. 1983. "How Language Structures Space." In *Spatial Orientation: Theory, Research, and Application*, edited by H. L. Pick Jr. and L. P. Acredolo, 225–82. New York: Plenum Press.

———. 2000. *Toward a Cognitive Semantics.* 2 vols. Cambridge, MA: MIT Press.

Tikka, P. 2008. *Enactive Cinema: Simulatorium Eisensteinense.* Jyvaskyla, Finland: University of Art and Design Helsinki.

Tomasello, M., S. Savage-Rumbaugh, and A. C. Kruger. 1993. "Imitative Learning of Actions on Objects by Children, Chimpanzees, and Enculturated Chimpanzees." *Child Development* 64 (6): 1688–705.

Tucker, D. 1992. "Developing Emotions and Cortical Networks." In *Developmental Behavioral Neuroscience*, edited by M. Gunnar and C. Nelson, 75–128. Minnesota Symposium on Child Psychology, vol. 24. Hillsdale, NJ: Erlbaum.

———. 2007. *Mind from Body: Experience from Neural Structure.* Oxford: Oxford University Press.

———. 2017. "Right Wing, Left Wing: The Dialectical Development of Human Intelligence." Unpublished manuscript, last modified 2017. PDF.

Tucker, D., and P. Luu. 2012. *Cognition and Neural Development.* Oxford: Oxford University Press.

Turing, A. M. 1937. "On Computable Numbers, with an Application to the Entscheidungsproblem." *Proceedings of the London Mathematical Society*, 2nd ser., 42:230–65.

———. 1950. "Computing Machinery and Intelligence." *Mind* 59 (236): 433–60.

Turner, M. 1991. *Reading Minds: The Study of English in the Age of Cognitive Science.* Princeton, NJ: Princeton University Press.

Van Gelder, T. 1995. "What Might Cognition Be, If Not Computation?" *Journal of Philosophy* 92 (7): 345–81.

Varela, F., E. Thompson, and E. Rosch. 1991. *The Embodied Mind*. Cambridge, MA: MIT Press.

Warrington, E. K., and T. Shallice. 1984. "Category Specific Semantic Impairments." *Brain* 107: 829–54.

Wexler, M., S. Kosslyn, and A. Berthoz. 1998. "Motor Processes in Mental Rotation." *Cognition* 68: 77–94.

Winter, S. 2001. *A Clearing in the Forest: Law, Life, and Mind*. Chicago: University of Chicago Press.

Woodman, G. F., and S. J. Luck. 1999. "Electrophysiological Measurement of Rapid Shifts of Attention during Visual Search." *Nature* 400: 867–69.

Zbikowski, L. 2002. *Conceptualizing Music: Cognitive Structure, Theory, and Analysis*. Oxford: Oxford University Press.

———. 2008. "Metaphor and Music." In *The Cambridge Handbook of Metaphor and Thought*, edited by R. Gibbs, 502–24. Cambridge: Cambridge University Press.

Ziemke, T. 2003. "What's That Thing Called Embodiment?" *Proceedings of the 25th Annual Meeting of the Cognitive Science Society*, 1305–10. Lawrence Erlbaum.

INDEX

CPSIA information can be obtained
at www.ICGtesting.com
Printed in the USA
LVHW041358030122
707723LV00020B/439